who knew?

3

who knew?

3

Household Heroes
Money-Saving Miracles
& Astonishing Uses
for Everyday Items

Bruce Lubin &
Jeanne Bossolina Lubin

CASTLE POINT
PUBLISHING

Cover design: Richard Pasquarelli

Interior design: Christine Heun

Composed by Quadrum Solutions Pvt. Ltd.

Castle Point Publishing

58 Ninth Street

Hoboken, NJ 07030

ISBN: 978-0-9820667-5-1

Printed and bound in the United States of America

10 9 8 7 6 5 4 3 2 1

Please note: While this compilation of hints and tips will solve many of your household problems, total success cannot be guaranteed. The authors have compiled the information contained herein from a variety of sources, and neither the authors, publisher, manufacturer, nor distributor can assume responsibility for the effectiveness of the suggestions. Caution is urged when using any of the solutions, recipes, or tips in this book. At press time, all internet addresses and offers were valid and in working order; however, Castle Point Publishing is not responsible for the content of these sites, and no warranty or representation is made by Castle Point Publishing in regards to them or the outcome of any of the solicitations, solutions, recipes, or tips herein. Castle Point Publishing shall have no liability for damages (whether direct, indirect, consequential or otherwise) arising from the use, attempted use, misuse, or application of any of the solutions, recipes, or tips described in this book.

Dedication

For Jack, Terrence, and Aidan, as always

Acknowledgments

We're grateful to our families and friends for putting up with us while we wrote this book, and offering help and suggestions that were greatly appreciated. Thanks to Brian Scevola, who first suggested we start writing down all of our household know-how, and to Joy Mangano, whose support we will be forever grateful for. Thank you to Karen Matsu Greenberg for her energy and unsurpassed production wisdom, Jennifer Boudinot for performing miracles and not minding the PATH train, Richard Pasquarelli for his talent and generosity, and Christine Heun for her beautiful designs. Also thanks to Joanie Rudolph and Andrea Cajuste, who showed us around the frightening world of logistics and shipping; Beth Blackburn and Maureen Lordon, for keeping our engines running; and Rizwan Burji, Jatin Mehta, and everyone at Quadrum Solutions for doing a remarkable job, even though our manuscript is always late. Finally, a big thank you to all of our friends and fans who have given us tips through email and our website, WhoKnewTips.com. We couldn't do it without you!

Contents

Part Three: Making Your Money Go Further   328

PART ONE

Who Knew?
Heroes

As we searched near and far for the best household tips, we began to notice something: We were constantly running to the kitchen for vinegar, baking soda, salt, lemon, and cooking oil. To this essential tool kit we soon added aluminum foil, and after looking around the house at many of our "repairs," we decided duct tape was an absolute necessity as well. Take a look through this section and you'll be astounded at all you can do with these *Who Knew?* heroes and a little know-how. Soon, your family won't be surprised when you reach for the vinegar at practically every turn.

CHAPTER 1

Vinegar

Label Remover

If you're having trouble peeling off a label or sticker without leaving a gooey mess behind, trying applying white vinegar until it's saturated. It will peel right off!

Vanquish Smells with Vinegar

If you've burnt dinner, welcome to the club. To get rid of the smoky scent in your kitchen, simply boil a cup of vinegar in 2 cups water. In 15 minutes, the smell should be gone.

Power Shower Spray

Save at least one fight in the morning by keeping this daily shower spray within easy reach of all family members. Mix one part vinegar with 10 parts water in an empty spray bottle and you're ready to go. Bonus: You don't have to worry about a toxic cleaner hitting the baby's bath toys.

Who Knew?

The first cookbook ever printed was in 1375. It listed a number of recipes using vinegar, including one in which bread was soaked in a mixture of vinegar and herbs.

Help for Sunburned Skin

You had a great day on the beach, but now your back is burned to a crisp. To help ease the pain of a sunburn, rub vinegar on the affected area with a cotton ball or soft cloth. You may smell a bit like salad dressing, but your skin will immediately feel cooler.

Get Rid of Swimmer's Ear

If your children are prone to swimmer's ear, a bacterial infection of the ear canal, take this precaution when they've been in the pool: Dab a solution of one part vinegar and five parts warm water into each ear three times a day. The vinegar will ward off bacteria and keep your kids' ears pain-free.

Ease Wasp Stings

Stung by a wasp? Apply apple cider vinegar to the area with a cotton ball and the sting will subside.

Make Pots Like New

Remove the stains in clay and plastic flowerpots with vinegar. Just fill the kitchen sink with two-thirds water and one-third vinegar, and soak the pots. In an hour, they'll be good as new! Make sure to wash with soap and water before re-using.

Clean Knives

We used to throw knives in the dishwasher with everything else. Problem was, "gunk" (scientific word for stuck-on food left from chopping onions, raw meat, and tomatoes) would still be on the sides. Luckily, there's a neat trick for cleaning knives without dulling their edges—a cork. Simply dip one in vinegar and use it to rub off the gunk, then wash by hand with a soft cloth. No scrubbing necessary!

Dishwasher Done!

Soap film coating your dishwasher? Run it on an empty cycle using vinegar instead of detergent. It will be sparkling clean, and your next load of dishes will be too.

Get Rid of Greasy Hair

Vinegar is not just for the kitchen; it's also an effective degreaser for oily hair! Simply shampoo your hair as usual, rinse, then pour ¼ cup vinegar over it and rinse again.

Corn Removal

To get rid of corns, soak a Band-Aid in apple cider vinegar, and apply it to the corn for a day or two. You can also try soaking your feet in a shallow pan of warm water with half a cup of vinegar. Either way, finish by rubbing the corn with a clean pumice stone.

● Who Knew? CLASSIC TIP

Adding 5–10 fluid ounces of white vinegar to the rinse cycle of your washing machine has many benefits, the best of which is the reduction of lint in your clothing. Using vinegar in the wash cycle is also great for dissolving the alkalinity in detergents and getting out stubborn odors from clothes like smoke, gasoline, and bleach.

Vinegar as a Fabric Softener

Never buy fabric softener again! Instead, simply use white vinegar. Use the same proportions as you would for a liquid fabric softener—you'll never notice the difference.

Diapers Love Vinegar

If you use cloth diapers, soak them before you wash them in a mixture of 1 cup white vinegar for every 9 quarts water. It will balance out the pH, neutralizing urine and keeping the diapers from staining. Vinegar is also said to help prevent diaper rash.

Virtually Free Freshener

Vinegar is so perfect for neutralizing odors and cutting back on dust, that we like to keep a little in a small jar near heating vents. Our favorite *Who Knew?* hero will leave your room smelling cleaner than it ever did with air fresheners—just make sure to replace it once a week.

Blanket Fluffer

Before using your woolen or cotton blankets when the weather turns cold, wash them in the gentle cycle with 2½ cups white vinegar. It will leave them fluffy and soft as new.

—*Laura Jean Mucha, Cranford, NJ*

Tar Stain Removal

Tar stains are tough to remove, but vinegar can help. If you've stained cloth with tar, try pouring a few drops of white vinegar on the stain and washing as usual. We've also had luck removing grass, coffee, soda, and fruit stains with vinegar.

Who Knew?

You might think this chapter has an awful lot of uses for vinegar, but in earlier times, there might have been even more. In the Middle Ages, vinegar was thought to cure fever, snake bites, leprosy, and the plague.

Brighten Cloudy Glass

If your glasses are beginning to develop a fine film due to too many trips through the dishwasher, soak them in a bath of warm vinegar for an hour. They'll emerge sparkling clean.

Suede Cleaner

Got a grease spot on suede? Vinegar to the rescue! Simply dip an old toothbrush in white vinegar and gently brush over the grease.

The New Jeans Cure

Every time we get a new pair of jeans, we wash them in white vinegar mixed with water. Why? It will remove their stiffness and make sure they stay color-fast. Just throw them in the wash with 10 fluid ounces of vinegar and your usual amount of soap. Add feel free to add other clothes, too! Vinegar is great for your wash.

Underarm Stains

When dealing with stains left by sweat and deodorant, we always turn to vinegar. Soak underarm areas in vinegar for 10 minutes before washing, and the yellow stain (and the smell) will be gone by the rinse cycle. If this doesn't work, you can also try rubbing a paste of baking soda and vinegar into the stains before washing in the usual way.

White Marks Got You Down?

When you let down hems on clothes such as skirts, dresses, and pants, there is often a white mark where the fabric was turned up. Vinegar can be used to get rid of this pesky stain. First warm up your iron, and then scrub the mark with an old toothbrush dipped in white vinegar that has been diluted with small amount of water. Then press with the iron. The mark will usually come right out, but if it doesn't repeat the process until it does. If not, then repeat.

Stuck Gum

To remove gum stuck on fabrics, warm a cup of vinegar in the microwave. Dip an old toothbrush in the gum and brush the gum until it comes out. It saved my husband's shorts!

—Paulette Culpepper, Hermitage, TN

Prolong the Life of Your Propane Lantern

If you have a propane lantern, soak the wick in vinegar for several hours before you use it. This will prolong the life of your wick, helping you get more for your money.

The Marinade Secret

Vinegar helps tenderize the tough protein fibers in meats, so using it in marinades and braising liquids helps make your dishes even more succulent. Simply add some garlic and your favorite spices to balsamic or wine vinegar and you've got a marvelous marinade!

Diet Dressings

To cut calories, make vinaigrette salad dressings from milder vinegars like balsamic, champagne, fruit, or rice wine vinegar. They're less pungent, so you can use a higher ratio of vinegar to oil.

Hard-Boiled Eggs

It's easier to peel hard-boiled eggs if you add a teaspoon of vinegar and a tablespoon of salt to the water they cook in. The vinegar will also keep them from cracking.

For a Fluffier Meringue

When making a meringue, add ¼ teaspoon white vinegar for every three egg whites to watch it really fluff up.

Poaching Eggs

If you are poaching eggs in an ordinary saucepan, add a teaspoon of white or cider vinegar to the water in which you are poaching them. The whites will stay better formed, making it easier to cook more than one at a time.

⬤ Who Knew?

Vinegar can reduce bitterness and balance flavors in a dish. Try experimenting with it in your cooking and see what it can do!

Keep Cheese Fresher!

To keep cheese fresh and moist, wrap it in a cloth dampened in white vinegar and put it in an airtight container.

A Buttermilk Substitute

Next time you need buttermilk in a recipe, don't buy a whole carton that you'll later throw away half-full. Instead, make an easy buttermilk substitute by adding a tablespoon of vinegar to a cup of milk and letting it stand for five minutes to thicken.

Removing Fish Scales

If you're gutsy enough to scale your own fish, make it easier by rubbing it with vinegar five minutes before scaling.

Firmer Gelatin

Add a teaspoon of white vinegar to any gelatin recipe in hot summer months to keep Jell-O salads and desserts firm.

Making Pasta and Rice Less Starchy

Preparing pasta? If you put a few drops of vinegar into the water as it boils, the starch will be reduced, making the pasta less sticky. This also works with rice: For every cup of uncooked rice add a splash of vinegar.

Preserving Sour Cream

To make sour cream last longer, add white vinegar right after you open it (1 teaspoon for a small container and 2 tablespoons for a large container). You won't notice the taste, and the sour cream won't go bad as quickly.

Fluffier Rice

If you've prepared rice and it just won't fluff, add a few drops of vinegar before running through with a fork.

Mold-Free Melons

To keep melons from molding, rub them with a teaspoonful of undiluted vinegar every few days as they begin to ripen.

Get Rid of Weeds

Use white vinegar straight from the bottle to pour on the weeds and grass that come up through the cracks in your sidewalk or patio. After a couple of days, the weeds will die and won't reappear for several months.

Vinegar: Your Iron's Best Friend

When ironing, mix one part white vinegar and one part water in a spray bottle. Use it on your garment to help remove iron-made creases (or make creases where you want them). This vinegar and water solution can also help remove shiny areas on the fabric that can be caused by hot irons. When you're done ironing, spritz the solution on collars and underarm areas to prevent yellow marks. Then sprtiz on the ironing board itself and iron while it's still damp to keep the board fresh. A paste of vinegar and baking soda can also clean the base (sole plate) of your iron.

Keep Away Cats

One of the worst things you can discover in the backyard is that your cat has (once again) used your kids' sandbox as his litter box! Pour vinegar around the sandbox to keep cats away. Reapply about every two months just to be sure.

⬤ Who Knew? CLASSIC TIP

To get rid of calcium or lime buildup on your shower head, soak it in vinegar overnight. This is easily accomplished by pouring vinegar into a plastic bag, then securing the bag around the shower head with tape or a rubber band.

Increase Soil Acidity

If you live in a hard water area, add 1 cup vinegar to 4 liters water, then use it to water plants that love acidic soil, such as rhododendrons, heather, and azaleas. The vinegar will release iron into the soil for the plants to use.

Neutralize Garden Lime

Rinse your hands liberally with vinegar after working with garden lime to avoid rough and flaky skin.

Keep Flies Away from Your Pool

There's nothing more irritating than having flies and other bugs swarm around you while you're trying to take a dip in the pool. We've had some luck keeping bugs away by applying a liberal amount of vinegar around the perimeter of the pool with a sponge.

Drain Volcano

Most people know the old science fair project of mixing vinegar and baking soda to cause a chemical reaction worthy of a model volcano, but not many know that this powerful combination is also a great drain cleaner. Baking soda and vinegar break down fatty acids from grease, food, and soap buildup into simpler substances that can be more easily flushed down the drain. Here's how to do it: Pour 2 ounces baking soda and 5 fluid ounces vinegar into your drain. Cover with a towel or dishrag while the solution fizzes. Wait 5–10 minutes, then flush the drain with very hot water.

Rust Removal

To remove rust from nuts, bolts, screws, nails, hinges, or any other metal you might have in your toolbox, place them in a container and cover with vinegar. Seal the container, shake it, and let it stand overnight. Dry the objects to prevent corrosion.

Get Paint Off Glass

Accidentally paint the edge of your windowpane while doing some remodeling? Hot vinegar can be used to remove paint from glass.

Just microwave a cup of vinegar in the microwave until hot (about 1–2 minutes), then dip a cloth in it and wipe the offending paint away.

Vinegar for Your Car

If you have to leave your car outside overnight in the winter, mix three parts vinegar to one part water and coat the windows with this solution. This vinegar and water combination will keep windshields ice- and frost-free. A rag soaked in vinegar is also a great way to get rid of lime buildup on windshield wipers and other parts of the car.

Chrome Polish

Need a chrome polish? It's as simple as vinegar. Apply directly on chrome with a rag for a quick, simple shine.

Concrete Stains

Unsightly marks on sidewalks and patios are often caused by tar, gum, and pet urine. These can usually be removed with vinegar, so if you're having trouble removing a stain from concrete, try dousing it with vinegar and letting it sit for a day.

Get Rid of Salt Stains

If your shoes or boots are stained with salt from trudging through winter streets, simply dip a cloth or an old T-shirt into white vinegar and wipe away the stain. It's that easy!

Been out with smoky friends all night? To remove the smoke smell from your clothes, hang them on your shower-curtain rod and fill the bath with warm water. Add a cup of vinegar to the bath water and the smell will be gone from your clothes by the morning.

A Fish's Friend

If your fish tank is marked with hard-to-remove deposits, just rub the tank with a cloth dipped in vinegar, and rinse well. The spots should disappear.

Flower Food

To prolong the life of cut flowers without using commercial plant food, add 2 tablespoons vinegar and 1 teaspoon sugar to the water.

—*Kim Brickman*

CHAPTER 2

Baking Soda

Dishwashing Delight

If hard water in your home causes spots and stains on items that have been run through the dishwasher, add a spoonful of baking soda to your next load. Your dishes will come out spot-free.

> ### ● Who Knew?
>
> To be effectively used in cooking, baking soda must be combined with an acid to start a chemical reaction. Some ingredients that are often used to start this reaction are sugar, fruit, honey, and yogurt.

Cleaning Grout

Is there anything more satisfying than nice, clean grout? A simple paste of three parts baking soda and one part water is all you need. Make a new batch each time you plan to attack the space between your tiles.

Too Much Hair Product?

If your hair is starting to feel filmy, blend ¼ teaspoon baking soda into your normal amount of shampoo, then wash as usual. The baking soda will remove the filmy feeling from your hair.

—*Marcia Lubin, Edina, MN*

Great Breath Fast

You don't need expensive mouth washes to get better breath. Simply gargle with a mixture of 1 cup water, ½ teaspoon baking soda, and ½ teaspoon salt. This combo will knock out any germs that are causing your bad breath.

Jewelry Cleaner

Baking soda is safe and effective when it comes to cleaning gold and silver jewelry. For best results, use a paste of baking soda and hydrogen peroxide, and rub gently on your jewelry. It gets rid of dirt, grime, and body oils, and leaves your gold and silver sparkling.

Clean an Icky Brush

To make brushes and combs fresh again, soak them in a mixture of 1 quart hot water and 2 tablespoons baking soda for an hour. Rinse and enjoy your like-new brushes!

Protecting Your Plants from Mildew

Here's an old treatment to prevent plants from suffering from mildew or black spots. Mix together ½ tablespoon baking soda with a drop of vegetable oil and 2 cups soapy water. Spray on both sides of the leaves of plants that are normally affected. Complete this treatment in the evening and never in full sunlight, otherwise the leaves may scorch. While the soap helps to spread the mixture and the vegetable oil causes it to stick, the baking soda makes the surfaces of the leaves alkaline, which will inhibit the fungal spores. The biggest advantage of this is that there will be no adverse environmental impact, thanks to the all-natural ingredients.

Smelly Suitcases

Is your suitcase is a bit musty? The night before packing, pour a cup of baking soda in it, close it and shake. In the morning, vacuum up the baking soda and the smell should be gone.

Doormats

Your porch's doormat can be cleaned with a sprinkling of baking soda. Brush vigorously and then sweep away the dirt. The next time it rains, the job will be complete.

Baking Soda for Baby Mamas

Baking soda is a gift to anyone who is feeding an infant. Keep some on hand, and if (and when) your baby spits up, sprinkle baking soda on the spot to neutralize odors and absorb the spill before it sets.

Get Rid of Stains Before They Start

If you're cooking over the stove and grease splatters onto your clothes, think fast. Grab some baking soda from the cupboard and rub it into the spot to absorb as much grease as possible. This will make it harder for the stain to set, and soak up as much grease as possible before it works its way into the fibers of your clothes.

Clean Greens

To wash spinach, Swiss chard, or any other leafy vegetable, fill a large bowl with cold water and add a teaspoon of baking soda. Move the vegetables around in the water, soaking them for three minutes, then rinse. All the dirt will fall to the bottom of the bowl and you'll have clean greens.

Substitute with Soda

If you don't like harsh chemicals, use baking soda instead of scouring powder. Baking soda is slightly abrasive, but still gentle, so it's perfect for getting stains out of countertops, tile, and kitchen appliances.

—Julie St. John, Brentwood, CA

Scuff Remover

To remove scuff marks left on your floor by dark-soled shoes, rub some baking soda into the spot with a wet rag. They'll virtually disappear.

Shiny Leaves

Want your houseplant leaves to shine the way they did in the nursery where you bought them? It's easy, even if you don't have time to spray them every day with a light mist. Instead, mix ¼ cup baking soda with ½ gallon cold water and use to clean each leaf with a soft rag. (Fuzzy leaves are better left *au natural.*)

Tobacco Killer

Get rid of stubborn odors and stains from cigarettes by adding a half a cup of baking soda to the wash cycle when doing your laundry.

Cleaning Paint

What's the easiest way to remove crayon, pencil, ink, and furniture scuffs from painted surfaces? Just sprinkle baking soda on a damp sponge, rub clean, and rinse.

> ### ● Who Knew? CLASSIC TIP
>
> Your child's favorite teddy bear is covered in grease and grime, but you're afraid it won't be recognizable after you get it out of the washing machine. Try removing some of the dirt by placing the stuffed animal in a bag and adding ½ cup baking soda. Shake the bag vigorously, then brush or vacuum off the baking soda for a cleaner companion for your child.

Not Even a Mouse

As cute as they are, you don't want a mouse in the house, and certainly not around the kitchen. Shake baking soda around their hiding spots, and they'll stay away. It's safe for pets and kids, and easy to clean up with a broom or vacuum.

Milk Protector

To keep milk from curdling, stir in a pinch of baking soda before you heat it.

Stainless Steel Wonder

To get the cleanest bathroom fixtures you've ever seen, apply a paste of vinegar and baking soda to stainless steel faucets, knobs, and towel bars. Lay old towels or rags on top and wait one hour, then buff off. Rinse the fixtures and then let them dry for sparkling fixtures without a hint of water marks.

Regulating Your Pool's pH

When alkalinity needs to be increased in your swimming pool or hot tub, baking soda can be added to restore a balance if there is too much chlorine.

> ### ● Who Knew?
>
> The chemical symbol for baking soda is NaHCO3—it's made up of sodium (Na), hydrogen (H), carbon (C), and oxygen (O). More than 100,000 tons of baking soda is created each year through a chemical reaction involving ammonia, sodium chloride, and carbon dioxide.

Cleaning Battery Leaks

If battery acid leaks inside the compartments of your appliances, there's no need to throw them away. Simply take few spoonfuls of baking soda and add water until it's the consistency of toothpaste. Spread it on your battery terminals, let it sit 15 minutes, and wipe clean. The acid should come off easily.

Crystal-Clean Crystal

To clean your cut crystal, mix a teaspoon of baking soda with warm water, then dab it onto the crystal with a soft rag. Rinse with water, then buff with a dry, soft cloth.

Brighten Yellowed Sheets

Make yellow sheets white again by soaking them in a tub with warm water along with a cup of salt and a cup of baking soda. Rinse well and dry.

—Anna Zaia, Baltimore, MD

Cleaning Makeup Brushes

If you're having trouble getting your makeup brushes and sponges clean, make a simple cleaning solvent. Combine ½ cup baking soda with 2 tablespoons water and mix together. Then add the resulting paste to one more cup of water and half a cup of fabric cleanser. Dip your brushes and sponges in the final solution, rinse clean, and reshape before allowing to air dry.

Who Knew? CLASSIC TIP

Prevent flaking and cracking when making cake frosting by adding a pinch of baking soda when mixing it together.

Make Better Coffee

Combine ¼ cup baking soda with 1 quart water and run it through your coffee maker as if you were making a cup of coffee. The baking soda will get rid of any mineral deposits that have built up inside. After your baking-soda cycle, run a pot full of plain water through. Now you're ready to make some of the best-tasting brew to ever come out of your old coffee maker!

Cleaner Plastic

An inexpensive way to clean your plastic storage containers when they start to smell is to wash them with hot water and 2 tablespoons baking soda.

Dispose of Properly

Instead of throwing baking soda away when it's fulfilled its 30-day stint in your fridge, dump it down the garbage disposal with running water. Baking soda will keep your disposal fresh, too!

Restore Shoes

Are your white shoes suffering from scuff marks? Rub a little baking soda into the offending areas and all the marks will practically disappear.

Freshen Your Car

If you don't smoke, there's an even better use for your car's ashtrays. Fill them with baking soda and they'll keep your car fresh without those annoying pine tree–shaped air fresheners. Replace the baking soda every two or three months.

Removing Newsprint from Surfaces

If you've ever left a newspaper on a damp surface, you know that the ink stains that are left behind can be a real pain to get rid of. But with baking soda, it's easy. Make a paste with baking soda and a little water and rub gently until the stain disappears.

Cleaning Blenders and Food Processors

If you haven't had time to do the dishes and dried-on food gets stuck in the blades of your blender or food processor, baking soda can help. Add 1 tablespoon baking soda along with 1 cup warm water to the bowl, put the lid on, and let it blend for 10–15 seconds. Then wash as usual.

Less Yuck

If you have kids, it's happened—you've had to clean up vomit. Use baking soda to make the job a little less gross by sprinkling some on top as soon as possible. It will soak up some of the mess and make the smell easier to deal with when you have to go at it with the paper towels.

Get Gloves on More Easily

Sprinkle a little baking soda into each of your latex kitchen gloves and they'll stick less when you're putting them on and taking them off.

● Who Knew?

Baking soda has been a valuable substance for centuries. In fact, the Egyptians used it to keep their mummies fresher—no joke!

Fire Prevention

Because baking soda creates carbon dioxide, it's a useful substance to have around where there are flammable chemicals or grease. Keep a package handy and throw on a fire in case of emergency. The soda will prevent oxygen from feeding the flames.

Perk Up a Room

Guests are arriving and you finally enter the guest room that's been closed off for months, only to find that the mattress smells musty even though it's perfectly dry. To solve this problem, turn the mattress and sprinkle a little baking soda on it before you make up the bed with fresh bedding. You can also sprinkle baking soda into pillow cases to freshen up pillows.

Air Freshener for Carpets

A mixture of equal parts baking soda and cornstarch can be sprinkled on a smelly carpet or rug to freshen it up. Sprinkle it on at night, then vacuum up the powder in the morning and the smell should be gone.

—La'Dasha J., Thomasville, AL

Vacuum Cleaner Treat

Sprinkle some baking soda into the bag of your vacuum cleaner to keep it smelling fresh.

Midas Touch

We tend to think that because gold is valuable it must be hard to clean, but the truth is it's simple. Solicit the kids' help for this one if you'd like. All they need to do is make a paste from ½ cup water and 2 teaspoons baking soda and use a soft rag to rub whatever gold piece you want clean. Then rinse with water.

● Who Knew? CLASSIC TIP

You can use baking soda to get rid of oil spots on your driveway. Sprinkle baking soda on the stains, then scrub with a wet brush and hot water. Baking soda breaks apart oil particles, so with a little elbow grease you can have your driveway clean in no time.

CHAPTER 3

Lemon

Worry-Free Carving

To quickly and easily sanitize a cutting board, rub salt into it with a wedge of lemon.

Weightless Cakes

We all know homemade cakes should not double as free weights, but what is the secret to keeping them light? A dash or two of lemon juice added to the butter and sugar mixture. That's it!

Who Knew? CLASSIC TIP

Sprinkle lemon juice on guacamole, apple slices, and other foods that brown quickly to keep them from oxidizing, which causes the brown color.

Shower Curtain Saver

If your shower curtain has become more disgusting than you'd like to admit thanks to mildew, first wash it in hot, soapy water. Then rub a wedge of lemon on the stains and leave the curtain out in the sun. By the time it dries the stains will be gone.

Odor Eliminator

To remove the fragrance of bleach (and other cleaning materials) from your hands, pour lemon juice over them and rinse. Bleach is alkaline and lemon is acidic. Together they cancel each other out and balance out the pH of your skin.

Say Goodbye to Mineral Deposits

If mineral deposits have built up in your faucet, cut a lemon into quarters, then shove one quarter up into the faucet until it sticks. Leave for about 10 minutes, then twist the wedge out. Repeat with remaining lemon quarters until the deposits are gone.

> ### ◖ Who Knew? CLASSIC TIP
>
> To easily extract juice from a lemon, first roll it on the counter under your hand. Heat it in the microwave for 10 seconds, then insert a toothpick. You'll be surprised at how easily the juice dribbles out.

Freshen Your Humidifier

Humidifier smelling musty? Simply add 2 tablespoons lemon juice and it will never smell fresher!

Removing Ink Stains

Ink stains on the carpet? Make a paste of cream of tartar and lemon juice, and dab at the stain. Let it sit for five minutes or so, then clean with a damp cloth.

Solve Your Silverfish Problem

Our boys are pretty tolerant of (read: obsessed with) creepy crawlies, but the delicately named silverfish are too gross even for them. Sliced up lemons are effective in keeping them at bay. Put lemon slices down where they like to appear, and replace with fresh lemons every few days.

Buffing Aluminum and Brass

Lemon is an effective cleaning agent for aluminum and brass. Sprinkle cream of tartar on a wedge of lemon and rub it into the surface. Let sit for 10 minutes, then rinse and buff dry. If you don't have any cream of tartar, you can also try this trick with baking soda.

Fluff Up Your Rice

When cooking rice, add lemon juice to make it fluffier. Simply add 1 teaspoon lemon juice for every quart of water.

—*Mary Terlecky, Sandusky, OH*

Who Knew? CLASSIC TIP

To get rid of stubborn stains and odors in the microwave, place a bowl of water and lemon slices inside. Heat on high for six minutes. Let stand for a few minutes and then remove. Wipe the inside with a soft cloth and the stains will lift easily.

Refresh Your Lettuce

You've left the lettuce in the crisper for a few days, and now it's too wilted to use for a salad. Perk it right up by submerging it in a bowl of cold water and 1 tablespoon lemon juice. Let sit for 5–10 minutes and it will be as good as fresh.

Cutting Board Stains

Remove stains on cutting boards by pouring lemon juice on the stain and letting it sit for 20 minutes. Then rinse with water.

Easily Clean Graters

Clean soft cheese, garlic, or any other food from your grater by cutting a lemon in half and rubbing the pulpy side against the grater. For extra abrasion, add a little salt.

Soothing a Sore Throat

Relieve your sore throat with a time-tested home remedy. Slice one-third of a lemon off, then take the two-thirds-sized piece and place it on a shish kebab skewer or barbecue fork. Set your gas stove to high and roast the lemon over the open flame until the peel acquires a golden brown color. (This works on electric stoves too, although not quite as well.) Let the lemon cool off for a moment, then squeeze the juice into the smallest cup you have. Add one teaspoon of honey, mix well, and swallow.

Cleaner Glass

Lemon juice makes an excellent glass cleaner, and will even give it an extra shine. Pour it directly onto glass and rub with a soft cloth to dry. Rub newspaper over the area to get rid of any streaks.

Lemon Peels for Kindling

The best thing to use as kindling in your fireplace isn't newspaper (or printed-out emails from your ex). It's lemon peels! Lemon (and orange) peels smell delicious when they burn, and they contain oils that not only make them burn longer, but help ignite the wood around them. Finally, they produce less creosote than paper, which will help keep your chimney clean.

Soothe Stings

If you're stung by a wasp, hornet, or bee, reach for a lemon. Make sure the stinger is gone and quickly rub the area with some lemon juice. It will neutralize the venom.

Ease a Scratchy Throat

Sore throat? Here's another lemon remedy: Gargle with one part lemon juice and one part warm water. Lemon helps fight bacteria and soothes your throat.

Repel Dandruff

To keep your scalp naturally dandruff free, use a little bit of lemon juice. Mix 2 tablespoons lemon juice with 2 cups warm water and pour over your head after you rinse out your conditioner. Let it dry in your hair and it will not only keep dandruff away, it will smell wonderful.

Who Knew? CLASSIC TIP

Brown spots on your skin are usually caused by dead skin cells. Slough off dead skin and brighten what's underneath by rubbing lemon juice on the spot. Let it dry, then rub vigorously with a washcloth.

Great for Fingernails

Rub a wedge of lemon on your fingernails to whiten the enamel. A perfect activity during downtime while baking!

Go Blonde

If you have brown or dark blonde hair, you can add highlights without chemicals and with hardly any cost. Cut a lemon into quarters or eighths, then cut a slit in the middle, as if you were going to put the wedge on the rim of a glass. Wash your hair as usual, and while it's still wet, place a strand of your hair in the slit, beginning at your scalp and running the wedge down to the tips of your hair. Sit outside in direct sunlight until your hair dries, and you'll have lovely blonde streaks. Repeat in one week to make the streaks even brighter.

Lemon Juice as Toner

There's no need to spend money on facial toners and astringents. Just dab lemon juice on your face with a cotton ball and it will tighten your pores and prevent blemishes. Use it in the morning and the smell will also help wake you up.

A Little Lemon in Your Bath

You've finally found a few secret minutes to have a relaxing bath! But as you're drawing the water you realize you're out of bath salts. It won't be as nice, but to add a bit of scent to your bath, squeeze a lemon into it. Lemon juice is also great for loosening dry skin, so bring a sponge or washcloth with you.

● Who Knew?

Most of our nation's lemons come from California. Why? California gold rushers planted an abundance of lemon trees in 1849 because they valued the fruits as a natural remedy for scurvy.

CHAPTER 4

Salt

Clean Vegetables More Easily

If you're having a hard time trying to get the last pieces of grit off of a vegetable or herb, give it a bath in salt water. It works especially well with leafy greens like spinach.

Easy Egg Clean-up

Salting your eggs may not be good for your health—unless the egg is on the floor. Dumping a pile of salt on top of a cracked egg will make it easier to clean.

Protect Yourself from Grease Splatters

Add salt to the pan when you're cooking greasy foods like bacon, and the grease will be less likely to pop out of the pan and burn your hand.

Who Knew? CLASSIC TIP

To revitalize artificial flowers, forget about using expensive cleaners. Just pour salt into a large paper bag, place the flowers inside petal-side down, and shake vigorously. The dirt will be transferred to the salt.

Frost Fix

If your windows are frosting over, dissolve 1 tablespoon salt in 1 gallon hot water and rub on the panes with a soft cloth. Then wipe away with a dry cloth. This will keep your windows frost-free.

Wicker That Won't Age

To keep wicker from yellowing in the sun, bathe it in salt water with a wet rag when it's new.

Sticky Iron?

Get rid of unwanted residue on the bottom of your iron by sprinkling salt on a piece of printer paper and ironing on a low level with no steam.

Hassle-Free Spill Clean-Up

Oops, that pot in your oven boiled over, and there's a sticky mess on the bottom of your oven! To easily clean any oven spill, sprinkle salt on top immediately after noticing it. After a little while in a hot oven, the spill will turn to ash and it can easily be cleaned.

Chill Drinks Faster

Because salt lowers the freezing point of water, your beverages will cool more quickly if you use salt in your cooler. Simply layer ice with salt, throw in the bottles and cans, and wait for them to chill.

Safety Salt

Water should never, ever be thrown on a grease fire, because it will only spread. If there's a fire caused by grease or oil in your kitchen, throw salt on it until it is extinguished. The salt will absorb the liquid that is causing the flames.

● Who Knew?

There are a few stains that salt will actually help set. Never sprinkle salt on red wine, coffee, tea, or cola spills!

Fried Fish's Friend

To keep fish to keep from sticking to your skillet while you're frying it, toss a handful of salt in the pan before the fish.

Keep Milk Fresh

Keep your milk lasting longer by adding a pinch of salt to it after you open it.

For Beet-Stained Hands

If your skin has become stained from beets, sprinkle the affected area with salt, then add a drop of dishwashing liquid and rub.

Lipstick on Your Glass? Use Some Salt

Who knew salt was the best way to remove lipstick from a glass? Rub a little over the stain to remove a pretty imprint on the side of the glass, then wash as usual. Sticking glasses with lipstick on them in the dishwasher hardly ever does the trick, because lipstick is made to resist water. Use this salt pretreatment and you'll get them sparkling.

⬤ Who Knew?

The largest salt flat in the world is the Salar de Uyuni in Bolivia, which has an area of 4,086 square miles. It is so reflective (and the air around it so clean) that it is often used to calibrate satellites that are in orbit over Earth.

Clean Up a Doughy Counter

You've just made a delicious loaf of bread and placed it in the oven, now what do you do about all that dough and flour stuck to the counter? Make your cleaning job easy by first sprinkling salt on the counter. Its abrasive action will help you easily scrub off any sticky spots.

Cleaning Burned Milk

If you've ever scorched milk in a pan, you know it's almost impossible to remove the stain. However, salt can help. Dampen the pan, then sprinkle salt all over the bottom. Wait 10 minutes and scrub away the stain. The odor will be gone, too!

—Maureen Delepine, Italy

Perk Up Your Coffee

It's 3 p.m., and with the day you've had, you're headed back for a second (or third) cup of coffee. Unfortunately, once you heat up some cold joe that's been sitting in the pot, it tastes thick and a little bitter. Make your coffee taste like it's just been brewed by adding a pinch of salt and a dollop of fresh water to your cup. Heat it up in the microwave and you're ready to power through the rest of your workday.

Make Colors Last

Brighten rugs that have faded by rubbing them down with a rag that has been soaked in salt water (then wrung out). You can also submerge throw rugs and drapes in a solution of salt water, then wash as usual.

Yellowed Counter?

If the enamel on your counter or tub has turned yellow, add a handful of salt to turpentine and rub onto the enamel, then wash as usual. Make sure to test on a small area of the counter to ensure it doesn't harm it.

Drip-Free Candles

To keep candles from dripping, soak them in a strong salt-water solution after purchasing. To make sure your salt water is as strong as possible, heat up some water and add salt until it won't dissolve anymore—then you'll know the water is completely saturated. Leave your candles in this solution for two hours, then remove and dry.

Make Sponges Like New

Whether it's your kitchen sponge or the head of your mop, porous cleaning materials can be revived with a little salt. Fill a bucket with a mixture of ¼ cup salt and 1 quart warm water. Then soak your mops and sponges for 8–10 hours and their grunge will be gone.

Loosening Soot

If you throw some salt in your fireplace every now and then, soot will be easier to clean from your chimney. It will also make your fire burn a cool yellow color!

Put Out a Fire

You're ready to go to bed, but the fire you started a few hours ago is still awake, glowing with its last few embers. Instead of making a mess with water, throw some salt over anything that's still burning. It will snuff out the flame and you'll end up with less soot than if you let it smolder.

Freshen Shoes

Get rid of nasty shoe odors by sprinkling salt in them and leaving overnight. The salt will absorb moisture and odors.

> ### ● Who Knew?
>
> The United States produces about 48 million tons of salt per year, making it the saltiest country in the world.

Drain Renewal

Pour a half a cup of salt down the drain of your kitchen sink with warm running water. The salt will freshen your drain and keep it from getting bogged down with grease.

Removing Cooking Odors from Hands

A quick way to remove the smell of garlic or onion from your hands is to rub them with a bit of table salt. It will absorb the oil and smell in a matter of seconds.

Make a Broom Last Longer

There are all kinds of new products available to get your floor clean, but sometimes a simple straw broom is your best bet. Soak your straw broom's bristles in a bucket of warm salt water for a half an hour and then let dry. It will keep your broom lasting longer.

—*Crystal Garito*

Make a Room Smell Wonderful

Who hasn't had a beautiful bouquet of flowers that they wish they could make last longer? Give your flower petals a second life by layering them with non-iodized salt in a small jar—this works best with flowers that have pulpy petals and woody stems, like roses, lavender, and honeysuckle. The salt will bring out their natural scent and help freshen your entire room. Keep a lid on the jar when you're not around to make the scent last even longer.

Dandruff Problem?

If you're afflicted with dandruff, try this homegrown fix. Rub 2 tablespoons of salt into your scalp before shampooing and watch those flakes become a thing of the past.

Fix Puffy Eyes

Soak cotton pads in a solution of ½ teaspoon salt and 1 cup hot water, then apply them to your eyes and relax. Your eyes will be less puffy in 15 minutes or less.

⬤ Who Knew? CLASSIC TIP

If you're having trouble sleeping, try this salty tip: At bedtime, drink a glass of water, then let a pinch of salt dissolve on your tongue, making sure it doesn't touch the roof of your mouth. Studies have shown that the combination of salt and water can induce a deep sleep.

Poison Ivy?

To help relieve the itching of a rash caused by poison ivy, soak the affected area in a strong salt bath. Make sure the water is warm to fully get the itch out.

Repel Pantyhose Runs

If your nylons seem prone to getting runs, try soaking them in salty water before you wash and wear them. Use a half a cup of salt for each quart of water, and let them soak for 30 minutes. Then launder as usual.

Displaying Fake Flowers

Make a holding place for your fake flowers using salt. Fill your vase with salt and add just enough cold water to get the salt wet, but not submerge it. Then stick the stems of your artificial flowers inside. The salt and water mixture will turn hard, keeping your flowers exactly where you want them. When you're ready to take the flowers out, fill the vase with warm water until the salt starts to dissolve.

Make Copper and Brass Shine

To clean and polish brass and copper, make a paste of one part salt, one part flour, and one part vinegar. Rub this paste into the item using a soft cloth, then rinse with warm water and buff with a dry cloth for a glistening

CHAPTER 5

Vegetable and Olive Oil

Duct Tape Residue

If you've been using the last chapter of this section (Duct Tape) a lot, you may need this tip: To get rid of duct tape residue, simply rub with oil. Let it sit for 5–10 minutes, then wipe up. The residue should now be much easier to scrape off with the rough side of a kitchen sponge and some warm water.

Untangling Necklaces

For annoying tangles in thin chains, place on a glass surface. Add a drop of oil and use a pin to tease out the knots. Then rinse in warm water.

Who Knew?

Olive oil does not get better with age—it's best to use as close to its production date as possible. Store in a dark place that isn't too airy to preserve it as long as possible.

Better Than Hand Soap Alone

To remove oil-based paint from your hands, simply rub them with a drop of oil, then wash off with soap and water.

Quick Candle Clean-Up

Rub a bit of oil on candlesticks before inserting candles and they'll be easy to remove. Any dripped wax will also peel off with ease.

Olive Oil and Eggs

If your recipe requires eggs but you don't want the calories of egg yolk, use the egg white mixed with a teaspoon of olive oil instead. This gives a better consistency than using the whites on their own, which can make the mixture too light, plus you'll reap extra health benefits.

—*Cheryl Dunn, New York, NY*

The Trick for Sticky Pasta

If your pasta came out too sticky, let it cool, then sauté it with enough olive oil to lightly coat each noodle. Make sure to stir or toss while reheating.

Silence Squeaky Hinges

Who needs WD-40 when you have vegetable oil? Simply rub oil on squeaky hinges with a cloth, letting the oil run down the sides of each hinge.

● Who Knew?

Vegetable oil has a higher smoking point than olive oil, which means that it's better for cooking foods on high heat, like pan-seared fish and fried chicken.

Unstick a Zipper

Zipper won't budge? Try adding a tiny bit of vegetable or olive oil to the stuck teeth with a Q-tip, being careful not to get any on the fabric. This will lubricate your zipper and allow it to move more easily.

Wood Cleaner

Out of Pine Sol? Use vegetable or olive oil to dust your wooden furniture.

Keep Bugs Away from a Birds' Bath

Just a few drops of canola or vegetable oil will keep mosquitoes from laying eggs in the water in your birdbath and won't hurt the intended residents.

For the (Humming)birds

Are ants overrunning your hummingbird feeder? Rub a bit of olive oil on the tip of the feeding tube, and they'll stay away. The ants can't get through the oil, but hummingbirds can.

Say Goodbye to Moles

Use olive oil in the yard to keep moles away: just soak an old rag and stuff it into a mole hole. They hate the smell and will stay away.

Greasing the Racks

After you've cleaned your oven racks, coat the sides with a bit of vegetable oil. They'll slide in and out of the oven with ease.

—*Claire Beevers, Essex, UK*

Unstick Stuck Glasses

You reach to get a glass out of a stack of glasses, only to realize they're stuck together. Reach into the cabinet again to get some vegetable oil, then pour a bit down the side of the glass to unstick them without the risk of breaking the glass.

Scratch Eraser

For tiny scratches in your wooden table or floor, rub vegetable or canola oil into the surface. The oil will darken the area and help it blend in.

Quick, Cheap Makeup Remover

A wonderful, inexpensive way to remove eye makeup is to dab a little olive oil under your eyes and rinse off with a washcloth. You can also use hair conditioner!

Who Knew?

In ancient Greece, women used olive oil to make eye shadow by mixing it with charcoal.

Cuticle Cure

Using a Q-tip, dab a bit of oil on your cuticles to keep your nail bed moisturized. You'll be less likely to get hangnails!

Soften Rough Feet

For the softest feet you've ever experienced, try this before-bed routine: Rub down your feet with vegetable oil, then put on some old socks. When you wake up, the oil will be gone and your feet will be supersoft.

Is This How Popeye Shaves?

Shaving cream feels great, no doubt, but did you know it's actually not the most efficient way to get a good shave? Next time, try shaving with olive oil instead—you'll get a closer, smoother shave.

Paint Be Gone

If your kids love to paint like our sons do, they'll inevitably get some paint in their hair—or in the dog's! Don't fret, though—acrylic paint is easily removed from hair by using a cotton ball soaked in olive oil.

Fur-tastic Olive Oil

Add up to ¼ teaspoon olive oil to your cat's moist food to stave off hairballs and make his coat extra shiny.

Help with a Splinter

Got a splinter you can't get out? Try soaking the area in vegetable oil for several minutes. It should soften your skin enough to allow you to ease the splinter out.

CHAPTER 6

Aluminum Foil

Fix Your Flooring

If your vinyl flooring is coming up, put it back where it belongs! Lay a sheet of foil on top (shiny side down), then run a hot iron over it several times until you feel the glue on the bottom of the tile remelting. Place something heavy, like a stack of books, on top and leave it overnight to set.

Broken Toy?

If you have an electronic toy whose batteries are loose due to a missing spring, don't throw it away or pay to get it fixed. Simply ball up a small amount of aluminum foil and put it in the spring's place. The aluminum will conduct electricity in lieu of the spring.

Protection While Painting

Before you begin that big painting project, cover doorknobs, drawer pulls, and any other small object you're worried about catching spills with aluminum foil. The foil easily molds to any shape and comes off when you're done.

Who Knew? CLASSIC TIP

Covering your ironing board with foil before you iron your clothes will get them wrinkle-free twice as fast, saving you time and energy!

Silverware Saver

To keep your silver from becoming tarnished, store it on top of a piece of aluminum foil. You can also wrap clean silverware in plastic wrap, then in foil, for tarnish-free long-term storage.

Polish Your Silver

You can also polish silver with aluminum foil, but not in the way you think. Line a pan with aluminum foil, add a tablespoon of salt, and fill with cold water. Then add your silverware to the mix and let it sit for a few minutes before removing and rinsing. The aluminum acts as a catalyst for ion exchange, a process that will make the tarnish transfer from your silver to the salt bath.

Make Your Grill Super Hot

To get your grill even hotter (making sure the bar marks on your steak are extra impressive), cover it with a large sheet of foil for 10 minutes before cooking. This will keep the heat from escaping.

Pie Crust Saver

Keep your pie crusts from getting too brown by covering the edges of your pie in strips of aluminum foil.

Cool Pan Handles

The handles on pots and pans can get very hot, hence the invention of potholders. If you have hollow handles, however, you can place some aluminum foil inside to keep them cool. It seems counterintuitive, but the foil blocks heat from traveling up from the burner. Don't tell anyone how you did it. Use your bare hands. Impress your friends!

Easy Oven Clean-Up

Cooking something messy in the oven? Cover the rack below the one you are using with aluminum foil. It will make it easy to wipe up any drips, and is safer than lining the bottom of the oven.

Fuzzy TV Signal?

If the picture on your television isn't crystal clear, it may be caused by interference. Place a sheet of aluminum foil between any electronics (like your DVD player, cable box, or TV) that are stacked on top of each other and those wavy lines will be history.

Soften Brown Sugar

If you find that everything in your brown sugar box is one giant lump, place it in a ball of foil and bake in a 350° oven for five minutes. It will be back to its old self in no time.

Perk Up Houseplants

If your houseplants aren't getting enough sun, maximize the amount of light they *are* getting by placing them on top of a table covered in foil (shiny side up). The foil will reflect the light, and your plants will thank you.

Keep Bugs Away

Protect your soft drinks from bees and other bugs when you're enjoying a beverage outside. Cover the top of the cup or can with foil, then poke a straw through. Now you can sip in peace!

Deter Hair Dye

When dyeing clients' hair, I use this tip when they want to catch up on *Cosmopolitan* but can't read without their glasses! Just cover the arms of the glasses in foil and you'll make sure none of the strong hair dye gets on them.

—*Shelia H., Carlisle, PA*

A Giant Vessel

When you started preparing the recipe, you didn't realize its contents would double in size! If you run out of space in your bowl and you're in a pinch, simply line your entire kitchen sink with foil and throw your ingredients in there. Then serve in smaller containers.

Who Knew? CLASSIC TIP

When you're done grilling, place a large piece of aluminum foil over the entire top of your grill, then put the top back on and let it sit for 10–15 minutes. The caked-on mess from the burgers and hot dogs will turn to ash.

Keep Away Wetness

Whether you're on a big camping trip or your kids are just sleeping in the backyard for fun, place a long sheet of aluminum foil underneath sleeping bags to keep moisture from sinking into the fabric.

Deter Pests in Your Garden

If you've ever bitten into a shred of foil that was stuck to a piece of candy, you know how unpleasant the sensation is. Rodents hate the feeling of foil between their teeth, too, so placing strips of foil in your garden mulch will help deter rodents and some bugs. If rodents are eating the bark of your tree, you can also wrap the trunk in foil.

Funnels of Foil

If you have aluminum foil in your kitchen, you don't need a funnel. Simply fold a sheet of foil in half width-wise and roll into a funnel shape. You can make a funnel of any size and to fit any hole!

Fireplace Quick Clean

Cleaning out a fireplace is easy when you line the bottom with aluminum foil. Just wait for the ashes to cool, fold up the foil, and lay a fresh layer out.

Makeshift Platter

If you're looking for a platter for deviled eggs, brownies, or other picnic items, simply cover a piece of corrugated cardboard with aluminum foil (dull side up), then throw it away when you're finished!

Mattress Protector

If you need to accident-proof your child's mattress and you don't have a waterproof mattress cover, just lay overlapping sheets of foil on top of your mattress, then cover with a couple of old towels and the rest of your sheets. Now onto the harder task: Coming up with a potty-training strategy!

Fresher Paint

Keep paint in half-used cans from developing a film on top. Before you close the can for storage, place the lid of the can on top of aluminum foil and trace around it. Cut out the circle, then drop it gently into the can so it covers the paint. When you open the container later, just take out the foil and you won't have any messy dried paint bits to worry about.

Toasty Toes

This trick is an old family favorite. Wrap rocks in foil and place them in your campfire. When it's time for bed, place them at the bottom of your sleeping bag and they'll be comfortingly warm.

—*Greg Schoenfeld, Dawson, MN*

Replace Steel Wool

You have a pot that's in need of a good scrubbing, but you're out of steel wool. Simply reach for the aluminum foil! Roll it into a ball and use it (with some dishwashing liquid) to scrub off caked-on grease. This is also a great way to reuse foil before you recycle it.

Brighten a Backyard

You're hosting a backyard barbecue that's turned into an evening affair. Unfortunately, your outdoor accent lights aren't bright enough, but you don't want to have to turn on the glaring light by your door. Instead, fold pieces of aluminum foil in half (shiny side out) and wrap like a bowl around the bottom of the light, then attach with a few pieces of electrical tape. The foil will reflect the light in a nice, shimmering pattern.

⬤ Who Knew? CLASSIC TIP

Brrr, it's cold in here! Wrap a very large piece of corrugated cardboard in aluminum foil (shiny side out), and place it behind your free-standing radiator. The foil will reflect the heat, and you won't have to keep telling your landlord to turn up the boiler.

Fisherman's Friend

If you're caught without a lure and have a fishing trip ahead, use aluminum foil instead. Cover your hook with foil, then rip it away in small sections so that it will dance in the water. Fish will be attracted to the movement and reflected light.

Arty Aluminum

Art project? Make paint-mixing easy by using a piece of cardboard covered in aluminum foil as your artist's palette. Kids will especially love it if you cut the cardboard in the shape of a palette first.

Clean an Iron

If you've been ironing too many clothes with starch and your iron is starting to get sticky, run it over a piece of aluminum foil to clean it.

Who Knew?

Have you ever wondered why aluminum foil has one shiny side and one dull side? The shininess is produced during the foil's final press at the factory. However, foil is so thin that it's virtually impossible to create a press that can press something that thin. Therefore, two sheets are pressed at the same time. The sides of the foil that are on the inside (touching each other) end up dull.

Leaking Gutter?

If your steel gutter is leaking, aluminum foil can help. First patch the hole with roofing cement, then cover the cement with foil and another layer of cement. For an even heavier-duty fix, add an additional cement-and-foil layer. This combination will plug the hole better than cement alone.

CHAPTER 7

Duct Tape

Quick Fix for Long Pants

You've bought a great pair of jeans, but they're too long and you don't have time to hem them before you need to wear them. Simply fold them up and tape with duct tape. The hem will last the whole night— and maybe even through a couple of washings. This is also a great tip if you're not sure exactly where you want to hem your pants. Have a "trial run" using the duct tape, and they're all ready to sew.

Out of Rope?

Duct tape is so sturdy, you can use it as a rope by twisting it around itself. Use as a backup for clotheslines, leashes, tying twine, or anything else you would normally use rope for.

Winterize Your Door

If you have a sliding glass door that's rarely used during the winter, seal the top, bottom, and sides with duct tape to keep cold air from coming in.

—Belinda Duchin, Portland, ME

Mend a Shingle

If one of your roof's shingles has fallen off, you can make a temporary replacement using duct tape. Cut a ¼-inch thick piece of plywood to match the same size as the missing shingle. Then wrap it in duct tape (you will need several strips) and wedge it in place.

Camper's Aid

Always, always pack duct tape when you're going camping. It's a must-have to repair rips or holes in tents and air mattresses, and can be used to string up food so it's out of bears' reach.

Reinforce Folders

For a pocket folder you know is going to take a beating—like the one we keep near our tool kit that holds instructions—reinforce it on the sides and pockets with duct tape. It will last forever!

⬤ Who Knew?

Duck Products, a manufacturer of duct tape, sponsors an annual competition that offers a college scholarship to the person who creates the most stylish prom dress made from duct tape.

Picnic Pleaser

When going on a picnic, bring a roll of duct tape. Use the tape to tape the sides of the tablecloth to the picnic table, and you won't have to worry about it blowing away.

Reinforce Hockey Sticks

Make your hockey sticks last longer by covering the bottom with a layer of duct tape and replacing it when it gets nicked and worn.

Make Hanging Holes

If tubes of glue, caulk, and other home-repair necessities are cluttering up your work bench, hang them from the wall with nails. Create holes that the tubes can hang from by wrapping a piece of duct tape from front to back on the bottom (non-dispensing end) of the tube. Leave an extra ½-inch flap of tape at the end that doesn't touch the tube and just folds onto itself. Then poke a hole through this part and you'll have a handy hanging hole. Wrap another piece of tape around the tube the other way to reinforce the tape you've already applied.

Secret Key

Duct tape a spare key to the undercarriage of your car or in a wheel well and you'll never get locked out again. Make sure to do it in a location other than near the drivers' side door, where thieves may check.

> ### ● Who Knew? CLASSIC TIP
>
> Duct tape may be the best aid for a last-minute Halloween costume. Make a robot or the Tin Man using a brown paper bag or box as a mask. Cover it, as well as a shirt and an old pair of jeans, with duct tape, then send your kid out for some much-deserved candy.

Goodbye Flies

Each summer we travel to our cabin, and when we arrive there are always droves of flying insects inside. We tape five to ten pieces of duct tape to themselves (making a ring with the sticky side out), then hang them from the rafters near the overhead lights. The bugs become stuck, we throw out the tape, and our problem is solved!

—*Frank R., Michigan City, IN*

Keep Kids' Hands Warm

If your child refuses to wear gloves or mittens, don't give him the opportunity to take them off once he goes outside to play. Duct tape the cuffs of the gloves to the cuffs of his coat!

Perfect for Boots

Make your winter boots a little warmer—and make sure they're completely waterproof—by lining the bottom of the insides with duct tape. The tape will create a waterproof seal, and the shiny silver will reflect your body heat back onto your feet.

Vacuum Fix

If your vacuum hose has developed a crack and is leaking air, simply cover the crack with duct tape and keep on cleaning.

Leaky Shower Arms

If you have a shower that has a detachable shower head, use duct tape to repair any holes when the connecting arm inevitably begins to leak.

Customize Tools

If the screwdriver, hammer, or other tool that you're using is hard to grip, wrap duct tape around the handle until it more easily fits your hand.

● Who Knew?

Even given its name, duct tape is not actually safe to use on heating ducts. This is because the adhesive can be ineffective at high heat.

Vacuum Bag Fix-Up

If your disposable vacuum cleaner bag is full and you don't have replacement on hand, it's duct tape to the rescue! Remove the bag and cut a slit straight down the middle. Empty it into the garbage, then pinch the sides together at the slit and fold over. Tape the fold with a liberal amount of duct tape. The bag will hold a little less, but you'll be ready to vacuum again without having to run to the store.

Splinter Removal

If you get a splinter, a little duct tape does the trick to get it out. Cut off a piece and gently press it to the affected area.

Big Hat (or Small Head)?

Make your ball cap tighter by cutting a piece of duct tape lengthwise and wrapping a few layers around the sweat band.

Pool Liners

When pool liners tear, it can be very costly to repair them. But duct tape can do the job. Simply cover the tear, and keep and eye on it to make sure it doesn't start to peel off. Believe it or not, a single piece of duct tape can usually last underwater for an entire summer.

A Hiking Must-Have!

Before you start out on your hiking trip, tape your pant legs to your boots with duct tape. This will ensure you'll get no bites from ticks, flies, and mosquitoes.

Protect Your Grill

Make sure squirrels, mice, and other critters don't chew through the rubber pipeline that connects your propane tank to your grill—reinforce the entire thing with duct tape. This is a good idea for anything else in your yard made out of rubber, as this is a favorite chew toy of rodents!

Keep Wood From Splitting

When cutting plywood, first reinforce where you plan on cutting with a strip of duct tape. The tape will keep the wood from splitting as you saw, and then you can peel the tape right off.

Trash Can Tip

If your curbside trash can has a crack, the easiest way to repair it is to just slap some duct tape over it on both sides. Duct tape can withstand the rigors of the outdoors, and it's not like you're worried about your can looking nice, anyway.

Who Knew?

The television show *MythBusters* may have discovered some of the most fun uses for duct tape. In their duct tape–centric episode, they lifted a car with it, constructed a boat out of it, and created a cannon made entirely out of the beloved tape.

Goodbye, Hose Thieves!

Our hose hookup is on the side of our house, and unfortunately, we had our hose stolen twice! We were forced to keep rolling it up and putting it in our garage until a neighbor mentioned why she thought her hose had been spared—it was full of holes that had been repaired by duct tape. We slapped some duct tape on our hole-free hose, and it hasn't been stolen since.

—*Janice K. Smith, AZ*

Quick Seal

If the seal around the window in your car is leaking air and making an annoying sound as you drive, patch it up with duct tape until you have the time (and money) to take it to the shop.

Make Your Slippers Even Better

To make your slippers waterproof and therefore safe to wear on a quick trip outdoors, simply cover the bottoms with—you guessed it—overlapping layers of duct tape.

Basket Mending

If you have a plastic laundry basket that has cracked or has a handle partially torn off, cover the rip with duct tape on both sides. It may not be pretty, but it works just as well as a new basket.

Cleaning Velcro

It's hard to get bits of lint and hair out of Velcro...unless you have some duct tape. Firmly press it into each side of the Velcro several times to easily clean it.

Let's Twist Again!

If you're having trouble getting a dead light bulb out of its socket due to arthritis or a particularly tricky bulb (we always have trouble with those enormous floodlight bulbs with the long, flat fronts), use some duct tape to help you. Pull off a strip of tape that is about two feet long, then fold about six inches of the middle portion back on itself, sticky side to sticky side. You'll now have a six-inch "tab" of duct tape with two sticky ends. Tape these ends to either side of the bulb, then twist the tab to get some leverage. Replace the bulb and thank duct tape for another job well done!

A Better Way to Take-In Pants

If you have a child who is super-skinny (despite his grandmother's best efforts to fatten him up), you've probably taken in your fair share of sweatpants using a safety pin. However, using duct tape will allow you to take in the pants without worrying about the pin being uncomfortable. Simply fold the elastic band of the pants onto itself, then tape the fold with duct tape.

Protect an Injury Quickly

If you receive a cut or gash while hiking in the woods, working at a jobsite, or somewhere else where medical care isn't readily available, duct tape can help. Use a bit of tape to cover cuts and hold your skin together if they're deep. This isn't a permanent solution, of course, but the tape will keep germs out while you go to get help.

Duct Tape for Warts

It's long been stated as fact—then disputed—that duct tape can help cure warts. It may seem strange, but medical studies have concluded that when patients cover their warts with duct tape every day for a month, 85 percent of them will see a reduction in the wart. That's compared to only a 60 percent reduction in patients who used cryotherapy (having the wart frozen off by a dermatologist). It's hard to believe, but many people swear by the treatment! Our opinion? Especially if you don't have health insurance, it's worth a shot!

● Who Knew?

Enough duct tape is sold each year to make a duct tape rope that extends all the way to the moon.

PART TWO

Household Help

Want to know the easiest way to carry drinks at a party? The best recipe for a homemade foot bath? How to keep your car battery from corroding? What to do when you spill paint on the rug? Our Household Help section will tell you all this and more, but it's not just about knowing that corn syrup will remove grass stains or that an old toothbrush holder makes a great vase. It's about making your day easier and (hopefully) stress-free by giving you simple solutions to simple problems. So the next time you oversalt the soup, bees overrun your party, or you over-perfume your wrists, don't fret. Just reach for *Who Knew? 3* and open to the Household Help section.

CHAPTER 8

Cleaning Wonders

Cleaner Windows

Do you feel like you can never get a window completely clean? Here's an easy tip that will help you to tell which side of the pane those godforsaken streaks are on. Simply wash your windows from top to bottom on the inside, then switch to washing side-to-side on the outside.

Homemade All-Purpose Cleaner

A good all-purpose cleaner is essential to any well-run home. Keep this one on hand at all times (but out of reach of the kiddos). Start with ¼ gallon water and mix in ½ cup rubbing alcohol, a squirt of dishwashing liquid, and ¼ tablespoon ammonia (non-sudsy). Fill a spray bottle and you're ready to go.

Rings Around the Table

If you've got kids, you probably have watermarks on your finished wood table. Since they may never listen to your pleas to use a coaster, use a little petroleum jelly to remove the white stains. Just rub the area with the jelly and let sit for several hours (or even overnight). Then rub again with a soft cloth and the stain should disappear.

How to Easily Clean a Dirty Radiator

Dreading cleaning your radiator? Here's a simple way to get the job done. Hang a damp cloth or damp newspapers on the wall behind it. Then use your hair dryer to blow the dust off it. The dust will stick to the wet surface behind it, and then you can simply throw it away.

Polish Marble

Polish marble surfaces by first pulverizing a piece of chalk using a mortar and pestle or a hammer. Sprinkle the chalk dust on the marble, then rub in with a soft, damp cloth. Buff with a clean cloth for a brilliant shine.

Restore Robust Rugs

To get the color back in your carpet or rug, take a small bucket and pour 2 cups white vinegar, 2 gallons hot water, and 2 teaspoons ammonia into it. Mix well, dip a washcloth into it, and scrub away on the carpet. Soak up any excess with a dry towel.

—*Carla Renaudo*

Cast Iron Cookware Cleaner

To remove charred food from your cast iron cookware, boil a mixture of salt and vinegar in it and let simmer for 10–20 minutes. Rinse your pan thoroughly and then re-season it with vegetable oil before storing it.

Sparkling Can Opener

When even your can opener is super clean, you know you have mastered the art of home maintenance. Putting it in the dishwasher can lead to rust so just churn a folded paper towel through it after each use to remove the residue, then quickly wash and rinse.

Clean Fiberglass

This is, unfortunately, an adults-only chore. Using plastic gloves in a well-ventilated room, mix together 1 cup vinegar, ½ cup baking soda, ½ cup clear ammonia, and 1 gallon warm water. Designate a sponge just for this purpose (or use a rag) and make sure not to let the solution touch your skin as you rub it onto any fiberglass that needs cleaning.

Who Knew? CLASSIC TIP

Keep tarnish off your silver in storage by keeping a couple pieces of chalk wrapped in cheesecloth with them. The chalk absorbs moisture, keeping tarnish away.

Fireplace Finisher

If you've been burning a lot of fires this winter, get your brick fireplace nice and clean in the spring with a simple household solution. Take 3 cups vinegar, 3 cups ammonia, and 3 cups borax, mix the ingredients thoroughly, and scrub the bricks clean. This will work for any bricks inside or outside your home.

Paint Spills

If you've spilled paint on your carpet, stop cursing and head to the kitchen. Mix together 1 tablespoon vinegar, 1 tablespoon dishwashing liquid, and 1 quart warm water. Douse the area with this mixture and try rubbing it away. If that doesn't work, you may be out of luck. Wait for the paint to dry and snip off the area that has paint on it—your carpet's "haircut" will be less noticeable than a giant paint stain.

Paint on Windows

Were you a little sloppy when painting around your windows? To easily remove paint from glass, dab the area with nail polish remover, then wash off after 2–3 minutes.

Restore Shine to a Plant's Leaves

Easily dust your houseplant by rubbing the inside of a banana peel on each leaf. Not only will it remove dust, it will also leave the leaves even shinier than before.

Quick Carpet Cleanser

If you've got guests coming over and need a last-minute way to clean your dirty carpet, simply mix a cup of ammonia with a quart of water. Use a mop to rub this solution onto the carpet, and it'll help remove the grime. You might want to test this method beforehand on an unseen area of carpet—such as underneath a chair—and make sure to never use it on wool carpets.

The Black Bag Treatment

Make your oven racks easier to clean by coating them with cleanser, placing them in a black plastic trash bag, and setting them outside in the sun. After a few hours, they'll be ready to spray off with a hose.

—*Trish Mackay, Newark, DE*

Garbage Disposal

Cleaning your garbage disposal is as easy as throwing a few ice cubes down your drain. Run the disposal until you no longer hear grinding, and your job is done! The cold cubes will congeal any grease in the drain, allowing your disposal to break it up. Add a peel from any citrus fruit to give it a fresh scent!

One Great Beverage Deserves Another

Coffee stains can be frustrating, but did you know you can get them out of your carpet by pouring beer on them? That's right—just pour a couple of sips onto the stain and it should vanish. Dab up the extra beer with a paper towel, and if the coffee stain doesn't go away completely, repeat the task a couple more times. This works for tea stains, too.

Venetian Blinds

The easiest way to clean blinds is to wrap a kitchen spatula in an old cloth and secure it with a rubber band, then dip it in rubbing alcohol or your favorite cleaner, close the blinds, and go to it!

Pledge Allegiance to Your Sink

You already know Pledge has many household uses, but did you know that one of the best ones is keeping your sink clean? If you've got a stainless steel sink, wipe wood cleaner over it after you wash it out. If you do this at least once a month, the cleaner will keep your sink shiny by preventing water and food stains from taking hold.

Greasy Wallpaper

To eliminate grease on wallpaper without chemical cleaning products, first cover the area with a brown paper bag or craft paper. Apply a warm iron and the paper will absorb the grease.

Untarnished Silver

Here's an easy household solution we use to polish up our old heirloom silver. Combine 1 quart whole milk with 4 tablespoons lemon juice, and let your silver items soak in the solution overnight. The next day, just rinse it off with water and dry it.

A Great Future for Your Plastics

There aren't many cleaners made especially for plastics, but it's easy to make your own. Simply take a quart of water and mix it with three tablespoons of either lemon juice or white vinegar. Mix it together and put it in a spray bottle, and you've got some plastic cleaner.

Clean Grease Like Lightning

If you have kids, you're going to end up with a grease stain on your carpet sooner or later, guaranteed. The big thing to remember is to not touch the stain at all—don't sop it up, wipe it, or anything else. Instead, pour a large amount of cornstarch on top of the spot and gently stir it with your finger. Let it sit for a day, and make sure not to walk on it. The next day, use your vacuum cleaner's hose attachment (the plastic one, not the one with bristles) to suck away the cornstarch. The stain should have mostly disappeared, but if not, keep repeating this tip until it's completely disappeared. You can then use the brush attachment to clear away the last remnants of cornstarch.

Clean, Then Clean Your Dust Mop

The most efficient way to clean a dust mop without making a mess is to put a large paper bag over the head of the mop, secure it with a rubber band, and shake vigorously. The dust on the mop will fall into the bag, and then you can throw it away.

—Ceclia Oczkowski, Patterson, CA

Your Shower Likes Wine, Too

Rid shower doors of stains and lime scale by wiping them over with a bit of white wine—the cheapest you can find, of course.

Erase Vacuuming Mistakes

You can prevent marks on baseboards and walls when you vacuum by covering the edges of the vacuum head with masking tape. That way, you won't leave behind dark smudges from the metal when you inevitably bump the wall.

Cleaning a Crystal Chandelier

Our kids are getting better about pitching in with housework, but this is one chore we tend not to delegate to them. (We also don't tell anyone how easy it is!) First, make sure the light switch is off. Next, lay a blanket underneath the chandelier in case any pieces fall. Now mix ½ cup rubbing alcohol with 1½ cups water in a jar. The crystals clean themselves—all you have to do is bring the jar up to each one and dip it in, then let it air dry. You can use a little bit of the solution on a clean cotton rag to wipe areas that can't be dipped.

Another Way to Eradicate Crayon Marks

To remove crayon marks from wood, rub mayonnaise over the area and leave on for 10 minutes, then easily wipe off.

Who Knew?

If the hole in one of the burners of your gas-powered stove is clogged, never use a toothpick to clean it out, as toothpicks can easily break instead. Instead, use a straight pin or a pipe cleaner.

The Best Way to Deodorize Your Freezer

Add a shallow bowl of freshly ground coffee, uncovered, to your freezer. Leave for a few days and any funky freezer odors will disappear.

Getting Rid of an Iron Disaster

If you've ever had scorched, melted polyester or vinyl on your iron, you know what a mess it can be. Wait for your iron to cool, then rub the melted muck with a rag that has been dipped in nail polish remover. Scrape off the mess with a wooden spoon (or anything else made from wood—metal can scratch). Wipe with water before ironing again.

It's Not Easy Being Green

We admit we kind of like the look of that green coating (patina) over copper, and it was popular as a pigment in oil paintings in the Middle Ages. But the deposit signals damage and should be removed from jewelry, antiques, coins, nameplates, and the like. Using a soft cloth but lots of elbow grease, rub a mix of equal parts baking soda and deodorized kerosene into the affected item. If it's a utensil that can take the abrasion, use fine steel wool and/or a toothbrush to get in between tiny pieces.

Ceramic Tile

The easiest way to clean ceramic tile is with rubbing alcohol. Just pour it straight on, and mop until it dries.

● Who Knew? CLASSIC TIP

For a great glass cleaner, fill a 3-cup spray bottle with ½ teaspoon liquid dish detergent, 3 tablespoons white vinegar, and 2 cups water. For very dirty glass, use more detergent.

Get Rid of Food Odors

To remove odors from dishes, bottles, or plastic containers for good, add a teaspoon of mustard to hot water and let the item soak in it for five minutes. The mustard will get rid of the smell, and you can wash as usual.

Scrub, Baby, Scrub!

You love steel wool for its abrasive cleaning power, but hate the rust stains it sometimes leaves. One idea is to keep your steel wool pads in an ordinary soap or sponge dish, but an even better idea is to use the tray part of a terra-cotta plant pot. These are made to soak up water—so put them to work!

Wax Splatters

Nothing is more disheartening than discovering hot wax has just dripped on your sofa. But there may be a way to fix it. Place a brown paper bag on top of the wax, then iron the bag with an iron set on medium heat. The wax should transfer to the bag, and you can peel it right up.

Preventing Fingerprints

You just bought the coffee table of your dreams, but when it was sitting in the store you didn't realize it would attract fingerprints like bees to honey. To get rid of a persistent fingerprint problem, rub down the tabletop with cornstarch. The surface will absorb the cornstarch and it will repel prints.

Cornmeal Cure

Cornmeal absorbs grease stains on light-colored fabric or upholstery. Just pour enough on to cover the soiled area and let sit for 15–30 minutes, then vacuum. The stain will be gone!

Cleaning Leather

The best advice for clean leather furniture is to keep your children and pets away! But there are a few ways to clean it if it becomes dirty. Treated leather can be rubbed down with a damp cloth, and an occasional date with warm soapy water won't harm it. If you get a spot on your leather furniture, try removing it by rubbing it with artists' gum—a super-powerful eraser that can be found at art supply stores. If you accidentally get a liquid that badly stains on your leather, blot up as much as you can, then apply hydrogen peroxide with a cotton ball to wipe it up.

When to Clean Your Bathroom

The best time to clean your bathroom is right after you've taken a shower. The steam loosens dirt and grime and makes it easier to get that perfect shine.

Safe Septic Tank Cleaner

When buying your first new home, you probably thought about the backyard parties and a basement rec room. Cleaning the septic tank? Not so much. Still, the time will come when it needs to be done. Add 2 teaspoons baker's yeast and 2 cups brown sugar to 4 cups warm water. Flush the mix down the toilet and let sit overnight.

Refrigerator Drawers

If you never feel like contending with a filthy vegetable drawer again, line it for easy cleaning. Newspaper will keep veggies from getting too moist, while bubble wrap will make sure your food stays bruise-free. Either will make for an easy clean-up job: just remove and replace!

Glass Dishes

To remove baked-on stains from a glass casserole dish, fill it with warm water and add two tablets of Alka-Seltzer or denture cleaner. Leave for an hour and the stains will be gone.

—Sandy Martis, Sandpoint, ID

Stuck-On Food

If the bottom of your pot or pan is a burnt-on mess, stick it in the freezer for an hour or two. The stuck-on food will freeze and be easier to remove.

Stained China

Impossible-to-remove stains on your china? There may be hope yet. Apply a bit of nail polish remover to the spots with a soft cloth, then wash as usual. The spots should quickly fade.

Get Rid of Greasy Fingerprints

Believe or not, a good way to get greasy fingerprints off walls or wallpaper is to rub the area with a slice of white bread.

Cleaning Hard-to-Reach Places

Unless your arms are six feet long, dusting behind radiators or under appliances can be a real drag. Try making a dusting tool by slipping a heavy-duty sock on a yardstick and securing it with a rubber band. Spray it lightly with dusting spray (we like water and a little bit of fabric softener) and you're ready to finally grab all that dust you've been avoiding.

Who Knew? CLASSIC TIP

Removing candle wax from your wood floor is easy: First soften the wax with a blow dryer, then wipe with towel soaked in vinegar and water.

Microwave Window

To clean the smudged, greasy, food-flecked window of your microwave, use ashes from your fireplace. Rub them on the window with a wet rag, then rinse clean.

Removing Red Wine

What's the easiest way to remove red wine spills from your carpet? Try applying a bit of shaving cream (after checking that the carpet is colorfast) and letting it sit for a minute. Then wipe away. Shaving cream will also work on grease stains.

Easy Clean for a Dishwasher

To get rid of mineral deposits and iron stains in your dishwasher, run it through an empty wash cycle using powdered lemonade mix instead of detergent. The citric acid in the mix will eliminate your problem.

Cleaning a Melted Plastic Mess

It's happened to us tons of times, and it's probably happened to you, too—a bag of bread is in the wrong place at the wrong time while you're making breakfast, and you end up with melted plastic all over the toaster. To remove melted plastic from metal, glass, or other plastic, first make sure the surface is cool (that is, unplug the toaster!). Then rub the affected area with nail polish remover until the plastic scrapes off. Wipe down the surface with a damp sponge, let it dry, and you're back in business.

Forgotten, But Not Gone, Grime

It's time to do what you've been dreading: Clean the caked-on grime that's been accumulating on top of your refrigerator. But don't worry, the job's easier than you think. Simply mix 1 tablespoon ammonia with 1 cup hot water. Apply a generous amount to the top of your fridge with a sponge or rag and let set for 5 minutes. Then wipe away with ease.

Burning Hair Dryer Smell?

If it's beginning to smell like fire every time you blow dry your hair, your dryer's motor may be clogged with hair and lint. Use an old toothbrush to brush clean the back of the dryer, where it sucks in air. Now you can dry your hair without someone poking their head in the bathroom to make sure everything's okay!

For Caked-On Filth in Your Bathroom

If your porcelain sink or tub has rings that refuse to be removed, it's time to call in the big guns: oven cleaner. Oven cleaner can eat through a plastic shower curtain and bleach colored porcelain fixtures or tile, but if your sink and tub are white, this is the cleaner for you. Simply spray oven cleaner on the affected areas, wait about an hour, and rinse off. It's that easy!

Best Gum Remover

The best way to get gum out of carpet, clothes, or hair is with a chemical called methyl salicyclate. Luckily, you don't have to make any methyl salicyclate yourself. Just look for it in an analgesic heat rub like Bengay. Put it on the gum and then apply heat in the form of your hairdryer set on low. Then press a plastic sandwich bag on the gum and pull it away easily. Make sure to wash the area after you've removed the gum.

Caked-On Food, Go Away!

If you're cleaning your oven, make the job a bit easier with this solvent. Blend a quarter cup of ammonia with a box of baking soda to make a soft paste. Apply this paste to the stained, cooked-on spots inside your oven and let sit overnight. Rinse it well with regular water the next day, and your oven will look good as new.

Who Knew?

In a survey of British residents, people rated cleaning the oven as their most-hated chore.

Ceiling Clean

It seems cruel that, after spending so much of your time cleaning your home, dust still manages to get places you never thought to clean—like your ceiling. To vanquish this last bit of dirt, use a clean, dry paint roller with a long arm to quickly dust above your head.

Lampshade Lifter

Dust your lampshades using a fabric softener sheet and their static-fighting properties will keep the shades cleaner for longer.

Shiny Countertops

For a scratch-free cleaner that will make your countertops sparkle, apply club soda with a moist sponge.

Dirty Kitchen Sponges

To quickly kill the dangerous bacteria that makes its home in your kitchen sponge, simply wring them out, then microwave on high for 30–60 seconds.

Coffee-Stained Carpet

Your best bet for removing coffee stains from carpeting is to rub a beaten egg yolk into the spot, leave for five minutes, then rinse with warm water. This will also work for coffee stains on clothing!

Keeping Trash Bins Clean

When cleaning kitchens and bathrooms, sprinkle a little scouring powder like Comet (or better yet, a generic brand) at the bottom of trash cans. The powder will soak up any liquids if there is a leak in your bag, repel mildew, and keep your bin smelling fresh.

Get Rid of That Ring

If your shaving cream can is leaving rusty rings on the side of your tub or sink, perform this trick right after you purchase a new container: Coat the rim around the bottom of the can with clear nail polish, then let it dry. The nail polish will keep out water and prevent rust.

Remove Old Stickers and Labels

To remove the gummy remains of a label or sticker on glass or a mirror, cover it in mayonnaise and let it sit for 5–10 minutes, then gently scrape off with a putty knife.

Another Use for Alka-Seltzer

Effervescent tablets aren't just good for curing hangovers—dissolve a tablet in warm water at the base of a vase to remove stains and leave it shiny-new.

Easy Ashtray Emptying

To make ashes slide right out of your ashtray without leaving a mess behind, first clean it and then coat it with a fine layer of furniture polish.

Your Electric Dustpan

Forget the feather duster—the easiest way to get loose dust off your knick-knacks and anywhere else in your home is to blow it away with a hair dryer.

Get Ahead of Grime

Instead of spraying your shower down every time you use it, try this solution for keeping your shower mildew- and grime-free. Apply a thin layer of car wax to a completely clean shower, then buff with a dry cloth. Your cleaning job will be much easier, and you'll only have to reapply the wax once a year. You can also perform this trick in your refrigerator to keep food stains at bay.

Rusty Sink

As long as you're very careful, you can use lighter fluid to buff out rust stains on your sink! Just make sure to thoroughly wash your hands and the sink afterward.

● Who Knew?

Even if your carpet doesn't look dirty, you should still vacuum it regularly. Dust mites, which are invisible to the naked eye, love rugs and carpeting! Nearly 100,000 dust mites can live in one square yard of carpet. Ick!

Easy Toilet Bowl Cleaner

For a cheap and easy way to clean your toilet, use mouthwash. Just pour 1 capful into the bowl, leave for 10–15 minutes, and wipe clean with your toilet brush.

Shower Door Scum

Easily erase soap scum from shower doors by rubbing them with a fabric softener sheet.

Mildew-Fighting Booze

For an unusual mold and mildew fighter, try vodka! It works especially well on the caulking around your tub. Just spray on, leave for 10 minutes, and wipe clean.

Keep the Lid Up

This may go against years of training your boys, but in rarely used bathrooms the lid on the toilet should always be kept up. Keeping the lid up allows air to circulate in the bowl, which will prevent mold and mildew from forming. Also make sure to leave toilet lids up when you go on vacation!

—Jennifer Pilcher, Olathe, KS

Toothpaste Trick

Most optometrists will try to sell you an expensive cleaner when you buy your glasses. Instead of buying theirs, simply use a tiny dab of white toothpaste (not a gel) on both sides of the lenses to polish them and keep them from fogging up.

Impromptu Glasses Cleaner

The next time you're digging through your pockets looking for a cloth you can clean your glasses with, try a dollar bill. Press hard and it will do the job of a glasses cloth in a pinch.

Quick Drain Fix

Not only is drain cleaner expensive, it can weaken your pipes. Instead of using Drano to unclog a slow-moving drain, use a gel dishwasher detergent like Cascade. Pour the detergent into the drain and chase it with boiling water.

Cleaning Golf Clubs

By now you've probably realized that we have a substitution for just about every household cleaner. But what about when your prized golf clubs get dirty? Resist the urge to spend money on fancy cleaners. Instead, soak your clubs for one minute (no longer) in a bucket of water that you've dissolved one scoop of laundry detergent in. The detergent has the exact same ingredients as those expensive club cleaners.

Another Reason to Love Coca-Cola

When you buy a rust remover, what you're really paying for is phosphoric acid. However, phosphoric acid can also be found in something you probably have around the house—cola. Dip screws or anything else that needs de-rusting into cola and leave for several minutes. Then scrub away the black substance that remains and repeat if necessary.

Fireplace Cleaning Secret

Before cleaning the ashes from your fireplace, sprinkle some damp coffee grounds over them. They'll weigh the ashes down and keep dust to a minimum.

Easy Sponge Disinfection

Another way to make your kitchen sponges and brushes last longer is to wash them once a week in the utensil compartment of your dishwasher with a load of dishes.

Clean Ceiling Fans

To easily clean a ceiling fan, spray glass cleaner or a mixture of half vinegar and half water on the inside of a pillowcase. Put the pillow case over one arm of the fan, then pull the pillowcase off while applying gentle pressure toward the floor. The pillowcase will wipe the top of the blade clean.

Beautiful Brass

To clean brass, apply white, non-gel toothpaste on a soft cloth, and then rub firmly on the brass. Use a fresh cloth to wipe clean.

Good Fix for a Bad Sink

Your stainless steel sink has seen better days, but it might not be beyond repair yet. For a sink that's been scratched, stained, and treated with every harsh chemical in the book, it might be time for a facelift. Use chrome polish to buff it back to life.

Mirror Makeover

For a unique cleaner for the mirrors around your home, use aerosol air freshener. It will bring your mirrors to a glossy shine and will have people wondering where that flowery scent is coming from.

Spilled Hair Dye?

To remove hair dye from wooden furniture and cabinets, wipe with a cotton ball dipped in fresh hydrogen peroxide. This method is tried and true by hair salons.

—*Jennifer Pilcher, Olathe, KS*

Clean with a Coffee Filter

We always prefer to clean our windows with something reusable, like an old rag. But if you like to go the disposable route, try coffee filters instead of paper towels. They won't leave behind any lint or paper pieces.

Stained Containers?

If you have plastic containers that have been stained by tomato sauce or curry, the solution isn't ten rounds in the dishwasher or simply throwing them away. Instead, place the containers in direct sunlight for a day. The sun will bleach out the stain naturally and your plastic will be as good as new.

A Fix for a Pull-Cord Problem

There always seems to be one thing around your house you just haven't figured out how to clean easily. At our house, that thing used to be the pull cords on our Venetian blinds. They were grimy from years of use by greasy hands, but taking down the blinds always seemed like too much work. Finally, we found this solution: Get a step ladder or something else that you can rest a jar on top of that is the same height as the top of the blinds (where the pull cord begins). Then fill the jar with cold water and add a tablespoon of bleach, soak the cord for two to three hours, and rinse. Just make sure to pull your blinds up first, so the maximum amount of cord possible is exposed.

CHAPTER 9

Around the House

Mark Your Tape's End

Nothing's more irritating than trying to find the end of a roll of packaging tape. So after you tear off a piece, stick a toothpick to the tape at the end of the roll. It will make it easy to find and easy to lift.

Make Scouring Pads Last Twice as Long

When we use scouring pads, a lot of the surface tends to get wasted, so we cut them in half before using them. That way the box lasts twice as long—and it'll help sharpen your scissors, too.

For a Great-Smelling Home

To freshen your whole house fast when it's too cold to open the windows, place a couple of drops of vanilla extract on your furnace's filter. Your house's heating system will do the rest of the work for you.

Plants Like It Warm

When watering houseplants, always use lukewarm water. Cold water may chill their roots.

Easy Roach Repellent

To get rid of roaches, chop up cucumber skins and bay leaves, mix together, and spread around the areas that have been invaded. The hideous creatures will steer clear, meaning you don't have to do the dirty work of throwing the dead ones out as you do with traditional traps (one of our least-favorite chores).

A Solution for Mice

If you've got problems with mice getting into places they're not supposed to, fill in any openings or gaps with steel wool. This will kill the mice by causing internal bleeding after they eat it. If you'd rather not kill them, just put some caulk into the crevice, too, which will keep them out altogether.

—Tayshaun Boyd, Chanute, KS

Who Knew? CLASSIC TIP

Here's a trick that could save you hundreds: If your cell phone gets wet, first take the battery out and dry it with a paper towel. Then bury the phone and the battery in a bowl of uncooked rice for 24 hours. The rice will draw the rest of the water out of the phone, and hopefully it will be back in business again.

Picking Up After a Glass Accident

You've just shattered a vase or glass, and there are shards of glass everywhere. Don't panic. Put on some shoes, keep kids and pets away from the area, and then head for your newspaper bin. Wet several sheets of newsprint (usually an entire section will do) and use them to wipe up the mess. First pick up any big pieces, then wipe the newspaper on the floor. The small pieces will stick to the wet paper, making sure you get every last piece.

Light Candles Without Burning Your Fingers

To light hard-to-reach wicks at the bottom of jar candles, use an uncooked strand of spaghetti. Light the end of it, then use it like a fireplace match.

Eternal Flame

If you have a favorite candle you may wince each time you go to light it, knowing it will eventually be gone. Yet letting it sit unused on the shelf seems like bad feng shui. As a compromise, try this: Let your favorite candle be a candleholder. When there's a big enough hole worn down the middle, put another, smaller candle inside and light that one. Votive candles work well for this and can be easily replaced when they burn down.

Green Thumb Water Test

No matter how long you've been gardening, it's still hard to tell exactly how much water each plant needs. Our son loves performing this test to see when a plant has had enough to drink. (It's just like sticking a fork in a pan of brownies to see if they're done.) Poke a pencil into the dirt and pull it back out. Clean means it's time to water. Soil on the pencil means the plant is okay for now.

Plants Like Beer, Too

If you host a big party at your house, don't throw away all the beer from those half-empty bottles. Instead, pour it into a bucket, let it sit for a day or two until the beer gets flat, then pour it on your indoor or outdoor plants. The nutrients from the beer will give the plants an extra boost. Wait a minute, wasn't this in *Little Shop of Horrors*?

Neat Way to Dry Gloves

You've just come in from outside, and your snowy gloves have quickly turned into sopping wet ones. To dry them out in time for your next excursion into the winter air, pull them over the bottom of a jar, then place the jar upside down on top of a radiator or heating vent. The warm air will fill the jar and dry out your gloves in no time.

Get Rid of Telltale Creaks

Back when our kids were still tiny, this trick was a lifesaver. There's nothing worse than finally getting a grouchy baby to sleep and tip-toeing out of the room only to have the wooden floor in the hallway creak like the second coming. Shake talcum powder over the cracks and rub in with an old rag, and you can escape in silence!

Fun Fern Facts

If you have a fern that's seen better days, water it with lukewarm salt water and that'll help it recover. If your fern is plagued by worms, that problem is easily solved, too. Just stick half a dozen unlit matches into the soil, coated end facing down. The sulfur content in the matches will keep the worms away.

Select Your Pot Carefully

Although fancy pots may look pretty, the best kind of container to grow plants in is an unglazed clay pot. It's porous, which allows the soil to breathe, and the hole at the bottom makes it difficult to over-water. Be wary of both plastic pots and decorative glazed clay pots.

Tea Plants

If you have any doubt that tea really is a panacea, here's one more amazing use for it: nurturing your plants and keeping them moist. Place a lining of tea bags along the bottom of the plant container, then pot and water as usual.

No More Gnats

If you suspect that one of your plants has a gnat problem, here's how to find out for sure. Slice off one-third of an uncooked potato and place it face down (peel side up) on top of the soil. Leave it for a week to 10 days, and if the potato is still clean, there are no gnats to worry about. If gnats are present, however, there will be larvae on the underside of the potato slice. To rescue your plant, kill the gnats with vodka. (Yes, vodka.) Mix one part vodka to three parts water, pour it into a spray bottle, and spray away. Do this for a week and the pests will be long gone.

Who Knew? CLASSIC TIP

If you have a scratch in your wood floor or furniture, cut a pecan in half and rub the meat of the nut over the scratch. The dark color of the nut will blend right in.

A Must for Musty Areas

If a closet, garage, or rarely visited corner of your home is starting to get musty, use this trick to get rid of excess moisture. Fill a coffee can halfway with charcoal briquettes, then punch some holes in the lid and put it back on the can. Place one or two of these cans in the area and the mustiness will be a thing of the past.

Get Rid of Roaches

To repel roaches, make a "tea" with catnip by submerging the leaves in hot water and straining them. Then spray the solution in your kitchen, bathroom, and other areas where roaches like to stray. Repeat every time you mop or vacuum to permanently keep cockroaches away.

—Anna Boudinot, Los Angeles, CA

Easy Wasp Killer

If some wasps have found their way into your home, don't panic. Fill a wide-mouthed jar with 1 cup sugar and 1½ cups water. The wasps will be attracted to the sugar, and drown in the water trying to get to it.

Best Bait for Mice

If you've seen a lot of Disney movies, you probably think mice live for cheese. But when you're baiting a mousetrap, a better bet is peanut butter. Since it's sticky, you can be sure the mouse won't grab it and run, and some people say they love its sweet scent even more than your best piece of cheddar.

Tread on Traction

Those nonslip bath strips aren't just good for providing traction in the tub. They can provide traction for anything that slips you up, whether it's the stairs to your attic or a tiled floor, and are available at any hardware store.

Find a Lost Contact Lens

Nothing's worse than crawling around the floor trying to find a lost contact. If you've been looking, one-eyed, for too long, try this trick. Get an old nylon stocking and secure it over the end of your vacuum hose using a rubber band. Then run your vacuum where you think you lost the contact. The lens will stick to the stocking.

Waterproof with Wax

To waterproof something you've written with marker on your child's school supplies or on a package you're sending, rub over the writing with a white candle. The wax will repel water, but you'll still be able to see through it.

Repair a Braided Rug

If your braided rug is coming undone, it's not a goner yet. Try repairing it by using a hot glue gun. Just lay down some newspaper, then carefully apply a small amount of glue in between the braids. Press them back together again and hold for a few seconds for the glue to dry.

Fix Stuck Plugs

If an electric plug on an appliance fits too snugly and is difficult to pull out, rub its prongs with a soft lead pencil and it will move in and out more easily.

Potpourri Substitute

Instead of spending money on costly potpourri, give your house a delightful aroma much more inexpensively. Heat your oven, toss some ground cinnamon on a sheet of foil, and leave the oven door slightly ajar. The cinnamon will unleash its delicious aroma as it warms up, giving your home a delightful scent.

—*Evelyn Quigley*

The Only Way to Dry Wood

If a piece of your wood furniture or a wooden windowsill have gotten wet, resist the urge to dry it out with a space heater or hair dryer. Too much heat will make wood crack and warp. Instead, keep the area at room temperature and aim a fan at it.

Free-Flowing Electronics

Use a pencil eraser to wipe off the metal contacts on rechargeable items such as your cordless phone and drill and they'll get a better charge. You can also use this trick for your cell phone, iPod, or between batteries and their contacts in electronics.

Boost Your Alarm Clock's Power

If "brrrring!!" isn't enough to wake you up anymore, maybe it's time to make your alarm even louder. Place it on a cookie tin lid, metal tray, or ceramic tile. The material will amplify the sound, creating a "BRRRRING!!" you can't ignore.

Plant Revival

Give dying indoor plants a second chance with this odd little treatment. Let three empty eggshells sit overnight in a couple of cups of water. (Multiply the amounts as needed.) Then use the eggshell water the next day when it's time to water the plants.

Debug a Plant

To get rid of bugs that are harming your houseplant, place the entire plant (pot and all) in a clear, plastic dry-cleaning bag. Throw several mothballs in with it, and tie a knot at the top. The sun will still get through, but the bugs will die after a week in seclusion with the mothballs.

Hit the Right Switch

The switch for our garbage disposal is right next to the one for an overhead light, and I used to always flick the disposal switch when I just wanted more light in the room. It's bad for the disposal to run without any water running, not to mention the fact it would always startle me half to death! To get rid of this problem I finally found a very simple solution. I put a dot of red nail polish on the disposal switch. No more accidental grinding!

—*June Panella, Phoenix, AZ*

Repel Frost on Windows

To keep your windows or sliding glass door from frosting over on the coldest days of winter, wash them with a mixture of 1 quart warm water and ½ cup rubbing alcohol. Now you'll be able to see clearly, even if it's too cold to actually venture outside.

Protect Your Table

An easy way to protect your dining room table is to purchase table pads that go underneath your table cloth. But since they usually have to be custom-made, they can cost a bundle. For a large, rectangular table, use a twin-size mattress pad instead. It's not as nice, but it will do the job.

So Long, Static

You know, of course, that dryer sheets remove static cling from your laundry—but did you know they remove it from just about everything else, too? Just wipe down your computer screen, television—or even your hair!—with a sheet of Bounce, and the static cling will disappear.

If the tiny screws of your glasses keep coming loose, add a dab of clear nail polish to the threads of the screw before screwing back in. The polish will keep them from coming out again.

This Solution's a Corker

Avoid slamming kitchen cabinets by putting homemade silencers on them. Just save the cork from your next bottle of wine, slice it into skinny pieces, and glue them onto each inside corner of your cabinet. Problem solved!

Cheapo Paper "Shredder"

Worried about identity theft, but can't afford a proper paper shredder? Use your washing machine instead! Put the papers in a stocking, tie the end, and throw them in for a wash. By the time the cycle is over, the ink will be bleeding, the papers a shredded mess, and your secrets safe from anyone picking through the trash.

A Better Way to Hide Things

Instead of leaving your valuables where burglars can find them, hide them out in the open. For instance, wash out an old mayonnaise jar and paint the inside of it white. Let the paint dry and then place your money, jewelry, and other items inside. Store it in the back of your fridge and it'll still be there even if you're burglarized.

Stamp Removal Stamp of Approval

We don't recommend snooping, but if you need to unseal a letter, or get an unused stamp off an envelope, simply leave it in the freezer overnight. The next morning, the glue will be undone and you should be able to use a pair of tweezers to complete the job. Another way to get a stamp off an envelope is to leave it in a cup of water for a few hours. It'll float right off; then just let it dry and use paste to stick it onto the new envelope.

Makeup to the Rescue

To fix tiny furniture scratches, use an eyeliner in a matching color to fill in the hole.

—*Margie Parker, Tampa, FL*

A Shocking Solution

If you can't escape static electricity on your carpet, here's an easy fix. Mix 3 cups water with ½ cup liquid fabric softener, put it in a spray bottle, and apply to your carpet. Not only will the static electricity disappear, but the mixture will serve as a carpet deodorizer too.

Minty Magic Insect Repellent

Here's a great way to use the gum you regularly confiscate from unruly offspring—leave the mint-flavored variety in the pantry to keep away insects. A few slices (even wrapped) can do wonders.

Bees Begone

Swatting at bees is unnecessary (and never leads to anything good). Just turn out the light and open a window. The light from outside will attract them even more than your nice, juicy arm.

Silence a Squeaky Door

If your door won't stop squeaking and you're sick of constantly reapplying WD-40, try this trick. Take the door off its hinges, then rub them all over with a candle. The wax will stick and prevent the parts of the hinges from rubbing against each other, which causes that annoying sound.

Avoid Musty Books

If you're placing some old books in storage and don't want them to acquire a musty smell, here's the solution for you. Just place a new sheet of fabric softener inside the pages, and that old copy of *To Kill a Mockingbird* will stay nice and fresh until you need it again. If you fail to follow this tip or if you have books that are *already* musty, just place them in a paper grocery bag with an open box of baking soda. Fold over the bag, staple it shut, and let it sit for a week or two. Your books should smell considerably better when you take them out.

Freshen That Air

Here's an easy way to make your own eco-friendly air freshener with ingredients you have around the house. Mix 2 cups warm water with 2 tablespoons baking soda and ½ teaspoon orange or vanilla extract. If you prefer, you can use an essential oil for the scent: lemon, jasmine, rose, and lavender all smell wonderful. If you leave out the extract or oil, it's safe to spray around pets, kids, and most furniture (although you might want to spot-check first).

Quiet a Loud Washer

Does it sound like there's an earthquake in your laundry room every time you run the washer? If your washing machine's vibrations are driving you nuts, try placing a scrap of carpet underneath. The carpet should keep the machine from dancing around. For safety reasons, just make sure the carpet you choose is flame-resistant.

Stuck Photos

If your photographs are stuck to each other or to a glass frame, the solution is steam. Use a steamer, a steam iron set on its highest setting, or a pan of boiling water to get steam as close as you can between the photo and whatever it's stuck to (being careful not to burn yourself). As the photo gets warmer and wetter, it should become easy to peel away. Lay out to dry, then flatten with a fat book if it has curled.

How to Store Stamp Pads

Here's one for your home office: Always store stamp pads upside down. This will ensure that they don't dry out in between uses.

Easy Fix for Some Broken Umbrellas

Before you throw away an umbrella, see if you can fix it by sewing the fabric back onto the metal arm—easily accomplished with a simple sewing kit!

Another Way to Bring Back Old Books

Make your old, musty book smell like new with this simple trick. Sprinkle a half an inch of cat litter in the bottom of a container that has a lid, then seal the book inside for 12–24 hours. It will come out smelling like a book again.

—*Nina Harbert, Mt. Vernon, WA*

Keeping Utensils Safe

If your plastic lids, baby spoons, and other small items in the dishwasher keep falling through the rack, place them inside a zippered mesh bag that is usually used for washing delicates in the washing machine.

Never Buy Flypaper Again

To get rid of crickets or other critters, place packaging tape sticky-side up along the wall in your basement or wherever else you find them. This inexpensive flypaper will snag the insects so you can stomp them out and throw them away.

Carpet Cleaning Work-Around

Finally getting around to shampooing your carpet? You don't necessarily have to remove all your furniture from the room. Slip plastic bags over the feet of tables and chairs and secure them with rubber bands. You can clean underneath, then move the furniture a bit and wash where its legs were. The plastic will keep the furniture from getting wet.

Stuck Drawer?

If you've been fussing with a drawer that won't open, it's probably expanded due to humidity. Dry it out with a hair dryer, or place a work lamp with a 60-watt bulb inside and leave for 30 minutes. Once you can get the drawer out, rub its runners or anywhere else it seems to be sticking with a bar of soap or a candle. This should grease it up enough to get it moving again.

See It Quickly

It's often hard not to misplace your household scissors, cell phone, and remote control...and the list goes on! Find lost items more quickly by slapping on a piece of reflective tape. The shimmering surface will pop out at you, even from between couch cushions.

● Who Knew?

According to the American Time Use Survey, 52 percent of women and 20 percent of men do housework every day.

Broken Shoelace?

If you or your child's shoelace breaks, use a ribbon as a replacement. It often looks better than the original!

—Francie J. Shor

Halve Your Paper Towels

Many paper towels now offer rolls with "half sheets"—that is, the perforated lines are closer together. We were shocked at how much longer our paper towel roll lasted when we bought one of these brands! And if your favorite brand doesn't offer half sheets, you can simply tear them in half yourself, of course!

Avoid Falls

If you've ever accidentally skipped the last step of your basement stairs and fallen on your face, you'll take us up on this tip immediately. Paint the last step a bright white. Even if your basement is pitch black and your arms are full, you still won't miss it.

Houseplant Favorite

Forget expensive food for your houseplants. Just feed them flat club soda periodically and they should thrive. The minerals in club soda are beneficial to plants.

Replacing a Cracked Bulb

If a shattered light bulb needs replacing, don't try unscrewing it with your bare hands, since there are almost always shards of glass left behind. Instead, make sure the lamp is unplugged, then put on some dishwashing gloves and use a wadded-up piece of newspaper. If there is a substantial amount of the bulb left, you can also use a wedge of apple. Place the apple on top and force it down onto the shards until it sticks, then turn.

Roach Resolution

If you've tried every other solution and those pesky roaches still want to call your house home, it's time to make roach balls. Here's how: Combine 2 cups borax, ½ cup sugar, ½ cup chopped onion, 2 tablespoons cornstarch, and 2 tablespoons water in a bowl, then roll into small balls. Place three balls into an unsealed sandwich bag and place the bags wherever your roach problem exists. Remember, though, that the roach balls are poisonous; be sure to place them where kids and pets can't reach them.

CHAPTER 10

The Great Outdoors

Covered in sand after a day at the beach? Sprinkle baby powder on yourself to easily brush the sand off. This is also a great tip for when your kids have spent the afternoon in a sandbox.

Preparing a Garden

If you've never had a vegetable garden, now is the time to start! Here's how: In the fall, decide where you'd like your garden to be and mow away the grass. Then cover the area with several layers of newspaper. Add as much mulch and leaves as you can to the top (aim for five inches), then get the entire area wet with a hose. By the time spring rolls around, the area will be grass-free and primed for planting.

Gardening After Heavy Rain?

If it's too muddy for even your beater sneakers out in your garden, keep them clean by sticking plastic bags over them. Secure them with rubber bands and you're ready to go to work.

Starting Seedlings

Don't buy cardboard "seed starters" from your garden store. Instead, use a cardboard egg carton, or toilet paper and paper towel tubes. The tubes will need to be cut in halves or fourths, then placed on a tray, while the egg carton can be used as is. Put a little soil in each, place in a warm, moist area (it doesn't even need to get any light), and wait for your seeds to sprout with some regular watering.

Early Bird Gets the Water

Early morning is the best time to water your lawn or garden because you'll minimize evaporation. The absolute worst time to do it is during the bright sun of the afternoon.

A Must-Have for Growing Carrots

The best thing you can give your carrot seeds is also what keeps you going during the day—coffee! Mix carrot seeds with coffee grounds before you plant them. Having some extra bulk to plant will ensure they don't end up all lumped together, and the coffee will provide your growing plants with much-needed nutrients.

Food for Your Geraniums

Who knew geraniums love potatoes? They contain all the nutrients a growing geranium plant needs, and can also make it easier for you to transplant these beautiful flowers. Simply carve out a hole in a raw potato using the end of a vegetable peeler and insert the stem of a geranium, and then plant the entire thing in its new pot or in your garden.

Healthy Pepper Patch

This advice definitely sounds like an urban legend, but it's such an easy way to grow fantastic sweet peppers that you have to try it. A matchbook buried with each pepper plant will transmit sulfur, a great fertilizer for them. To give these nutrient-seeking plants the magnesium they also need, add 2 tablespoons Epsom salts to ½ gallon water and soak the plants with the mixture when you see the first blossoms of the year.

Daily News Keeps Weeds Away

The most inventive idea to keep weeds away we've heard of is this: Wet newspapers and layer them around the plants (then cover with dirt and mulch so your yard doesn't look like a trash heap).

Critter-Free Garden

Try this easy, natural recipe to keep cats and squirrels away from your property. First mix ⅓ cup flour, 2 tablespoons cayenne pepper, and 2 tablespoons powdered mustard. Then use the mixture to sprinkle around the perimeter of your yard. Or, mix it with 4 cups water and 4 cups vinegar to make a spray.

Keep Pests Out of Your Trash

To keep raccoons and other critters out of your garbage, regularly spray the side of your cans with a mixture of one part ammonia and one part water.

—Holly L., Wenham, MA

● Who Knew?

Half of all Americans only get outside to enjoy outdoor recreational activities once every other week.

Get Mosquitoes to Scram

It's a little-known fact that mosquitoes hate basil and tansy. Keep those plants in your yard and around your porch. If you're not familiar with it, tansy is a pretty yellow perennial, which has been harvested for its medicinal properties for several thousand years. In colonial times it was used to preserve meat and keep insects away. It's a low-maintenance flower, except for the odor, which irritates some people almost as much as the bugs.

From the Kitchen to the Garden (and Maybe Back Again)

Cut down on the trash your family generates and help your garden at the same time with these easy composting ideas.

✦ Mix dried banana peels in with the soil next time you plant something new; you'll give it the potassium and phosphorous it needs to grow beautifully.

✦ Coffee grinds can go straight into the garden as fertilizer to provide nitrogen to roses, azaleas, rhododendrons, sunflowers, and many other plants and trees.

✦ Finally, transfer fireplace ashes to your flowers in the spring. Keep wood ashes away, however, from potatoes, blueberries, rhododendrons, azaleas, and any plants that like acid. And be careful handling the ash: Use gloves and protection for your eyes and make sure you spread it out to prevent clumping and leaching.

Snow Shoveling Made Easy

Here's a tip that you northerners will appreciate. Before going out to shovel snow, coat the blade of your snow shovel with cooking spray. That way the snow and ice will slide right off the shovel instead of sticking to it. This works on both plastic and metal shovels.

An Alternative to Rock Salt

Icy sidewalk? Throw cat litter down instead of rock salt. It won't harm your grass, stain your clothes, or hurt the environment, but it will provide plenty of traction for safe walking and driving.

Make Your Birdbath Shine

If your birdbath is dirty, it could be spreading germs to birds who alight there. To safely and easily clean it, drain all the water, then spread newspapers that have been soaked in bleach on top. After 30 minutes, any algae should be history. Rinse the birdbath, then add some colorful marbles to attract neighborhood birds.

Brown Lawn?

If your grass turns brown after mowing, either you've cut it too short or the lawn mower's blades are dull. Dull blades tear up the grass instead of clipping it cleanly. It may be time for a new mower.

Bees, Spiders, Mosquitoes—Oh My!

Use this (almost) all-natural insect spray to make your yard and garden a little less all-natural. Chop 1 small onion and 1 head of garlic. Mix together with 4 cups water, 4 teaspoons cayenne pepper, and 1 tablespoon liquid dish soap. Spray around your deck and in places where your children play rather than on the children themselves. This mixture will last a week or so if stored in a jar with a tight-fitting lid and kept in a dark, cool place.

Cleaning Wicker

If your white wicker deck furniture has turned a grimy brown, you have some work to do. But take heart, it isn't hard! First, vacuum up the free-standing dirt on the seat and arms. Then cover the whole piece with a mixture of 1 gallon warm water and 3 tablespoons ammonia. Scrub it with a brush to get between the fibers, then let it sit in a shady area to dry.

Silence Squeaky Lawn Furniture

If your wicker seems to scream every time you sit in it, it's become too dry. Take off any cushions and spray the wicker with a hose. The water will give it enough moisture to silence the squeaks.

Vanquishing Anthills

Ants hate oranges, so blend orange peels with water and pour the concoction wherever the little guys are bothering you. Some people also swear by hot chili peppers. Use whichever smell you prefer to have permeating your living space!

Get a Leg Up on Centipedes

Borax works for repelling centipedes and millipedes. Sprinkle around areas where you've spotted them making a run for it. (It also works for the less offensive cricket.) Unfortunately, borax is not pet- or kid-safe, so sprinkle wisely.

Rusty Concrete

If you have rust stains on your concrete, pour on a little cola and let it sit. By the next time it rains, the stains will be gone.

—Jess Holman, Syracuse, NY

Coil Your Cord

Do you have a long extension cord you use with your electric mower, weed-whacker, or power washer? Keep it from getting tangled and running all over your garden's plants with a big bucket. Drill a hole in the bottom of the bucket and run the end of the cord through it. Then coil the rest of the cord inside. The cord will easily pull out and easily coil back up when you're finished.

Mosquito Secret

Mosquitoes are attracted to dark blue clothing. (It's true!) If you usually have trouble with mosquito bites, trying wearing light clothes when you're outdoors.

Remove Ticks with Ease

Oh no, you've got a tick! If you're having trouble prying the little bugger off, apply a large glob of petroleum jelly to the area. Wait about 20 minutes, and you should be able to wipe him off with ease.

● Who Knew?

While 68 percent of children aged 6–12 participate in outdoor activities such as camping, picnics, sporting events, hiking, and fishing, only 26 percent of adults over the age of 65 do.

Eco-Friendly Way to Water the Lawn

Unless you live in a desert (where technically, you should not have a lawn), you don't need a lot of water to keep the grass green and healthy. One inch a week is all you need. To find out how long you need to run the sprinkler, mark a jar with a piece of masking tape or permanent marker at one inch and place it on your lawn. Start the sprinkler and see how long it takes before the water reaches the mark. Next time, skip the jar and just set the timer.

Never Clean a Lawnmower Again

Before mowing your lawn, spray the blades of your lawnmower with nonstick cooking spray. They'll keep cut grass from sticking to its insides.

How to Kill Spider Mites

Do you have trees that are infested with spider mites? You can make a mixture to get rid of them using ingredients already in your kitchen. Take a pound of flour, five gallons of water, and a cup of buttermilk, mix it all together in a large bucket, and put it in a plastic spray bottle. Use it on your trees once a week, and that should keep the mite population under control.

A Spray a Day Keeps Pests Away

One way to keep unwanted pests out of your garden is to infuse it with a garlicky odor that will be unpleasant for insects. Take a ¼ cup garlic and mix it with 2 cups water in a blender, strain it with an old nylon stocking, and scrape the paste into a jar. Add 2 teaspoons mineral oil and several squirts of liquid dish detergent. Carefully replace the lid on the jar and shake well. Transfer the solution to a spray bottle and use it on your garden in the early morning hours.

Snail Solution

Did you know that snails and slugs like beer almost as much as people do? If you're tired of these pests invading your garden, leave a flat, shallow container—such as a pie tin—in your garden and fill it with a can of beer. Let it sit there for a couple of days, and you'll probably find it full of drowned slugs.

If you've gotten tree sap on your hands, try rubbing margarine or butter on the area before washing with soap and water. The sticky stuff will come right off.

So Long, Squirrels

If squirrels are making a nuisance of themselves around your home, keep them away with a homemade pepper spray. Take a cup of your favorite hot sauce, add a spoonful of cayenne pepper and a capful of Murphy's Oil Soap, and mix together. Spray the mixture in whatever areas you want the squirrels to steer clear of.

—*Megan Rye, Washington, DC*

Green Gardens

Make your garden work for you by filling it with plants that repel pests, add fertilizer to the soil, and more. Here are some super-powered flora to get you going.

✦ Plant savory and chamomile throughout your garden; they'll attract the "good" kinds of insects that will help pollinate your plants.

✦ Plant mint and nasturtiums, which will repel white flies and aphids.

✦ French marigolds are practical because they have a strong odor that helps bewilder insects in search of their preferred eating plant.

- ✦ Garlic planted everywhere will help keep away beetles and aphids.

- ✦ If you plant basil, it will add to the flavor of whatever other plants grow near it.

- ✦ Fertilize your garden for free by planting clover, which will help repair the soil while also providing a nice green carpeting.

Aphid Awareness

Are aphids invading your garden? Here's another easy, organic way to keep them out. Chop up an onion, place it in a cup of water, and puree it until it's liquid. Pour the concoction into a plastic spray bottle and use it to mist the plants aphids are attracted to. For best results, try it at dawn before the sun starts blazing.

Keep Your Plants Covered

If you have smaller outdoor plants, you don't necessarily need to bring them inside to keep them protected from frost. Simply cover them at night with small plastic garbage bags (the kind that have pull handles), and tie the handles snugly around the pots. Don't forget to remove the bags in the morning, though, so the plants can soak up the sun.

You Say Tomato, I Say Grow Faster!

If the end of growing season is nigh and you'd like your tomatoes to ripen on the vine more quickly, there are a few things you can try. Remove damaged, dead, or diseased leaves, and cut off all new flowers. Keep a daily eye on the tomatoes and pick them as soon as they're ripe, so the plant can devote its effort to developing new fruit.

Harvest the tomatoes when they're red, but still firm. Believe it or not, watering the plant less will ripen the tomatoes more quickly!

The Many Benefits of Epsom Salts

Did you know Epsom salts are one of the best natural lawn fertilizers around? They're composed of magnesium and sulfur, both of which are highly beneficial to grass. Magnesium kick-starts seed germination, and is also a player in manufacturing chlorophyll, the substance that plants manufacture from sunlight in order to feed themselves. Sulfur, meanwhile, also helps with chlorophyll, while also enhancing the effects of other fertilizer ingredients such as nitrogen, phosphorus, and potassium. It also deters certain pests such as ground worms. With all these benefits, it's no wonder that savvy lawn care specialists have been using Epsom salts for years. You can either sprinkle them on your lawn using a spreader, or make a liquid solution out of them by adding some water and putting it in a spray bottle.

The Egg and the Rose

Did you know that eggshells help rose bushes grow? The nutrients contained in the shells are a great benefit, especially if you crush up the eggshells and deposit them under the surface of the soil, near the bush's roots. The same applies to water that you've used to boil eggs in—when you're finished cooking, just dump the nutrient-enriched water on your rosebush.

Reviving Plants

This may sound like a cure from the Middle Ages, but garlic does a fine job of reviving diseased plants. Grate two cloves into four cups water and use as much as you need to quench the thirst of your struggling plant. Given the myriad health benefits garlic offers to humans, it's not surprising it can help the immobile organisms that share your home (and we don't mean your spouse and kids).

Keep Good Neighbors
(Protect Your Fence Posts)

When it comes to chores around the house and yard, we're not the handiest family on the block, so we like those one-time projects that last a lifetime. It's true the ingredients for this fence post protector sound like they're meant for a witches' brew, but it really does work like magic! Mix together pulverized charcoal and boiled linseed oil to get a paint-like consistency, then simply paint onto the bottom of each post.

Who Knew? CLASSIC TIP

Your garden hose will last twice as long if you store it coiled, rather than folding it, which can lead to crimps and cracks.

Get Rid of Plant Fungus

If your garden is infected with fungus, mix one piece of ground-up aspirin with a quart of water and use it to water your plants once a week. (Be careful, as too much aspirin can damage your plants.)

Keep Bees Away

For an easy way to keep away bees, put a sheet of fabric softener in your pocket. The yellow pests will buzz right by you!

—*Miahua Huang, Dale City, VA*

Deer Repellant

If deer are getting to your flower garden, throw a few mothballs on the ground. Deer hate the smell of mothballs. (Who doesn't?)

Reclaiming Your Yard from Raccoons

Have the raccoons grown rather bold around your backyard and trash cans? Try this equivalent of a phony "Beware of Dog" sign by distributing dog hair around your property. You can also try planting cucumbers, which both skunks and raccoons avoid like the plague.

Check for Compost Collection

You've just weeded your entire yard, put new edging along your flower beds, and trimmed your bushes. Now what do you do with all that garbage? Check with your town to see if they collect yard waste to turn into compost. Many municipalities will even come pick it up for you.

For Easy-to-Raise Plants

At PlantNative.org, you can find lists of flowers, shrubs, trees, vines, and grasses that are native to your area. This means they'll not only be less expensive to buy, but they'll also hold up well in your garden.

Woodpecker Problem?

If woodpeckers in the garden bother you, try hanging a metal pie plate to the tree where the pests reside. The reflection off the plate will scare the birds away.

Keeping Neighborhood Cats Away

If your neighbors' cats are causing havoc in your yard, don't even try to go talk to their owners—once the cats are let out there is really nothing they can do to keep them fenced in. Instead, sprinkle the edge of your yard with orange peels and coffee grounds. Cats don't like the smell, and they'll eventually create great compost for your lawn.

> ### ⬤ Who Knew? CLASSIC TIP
>
> To get rid of ants for good, sprinkle cornmeal near ant hills. They'll eat it, but they can't digest it, which will cause them to die out. Wait a couple of weeks and see if your ant problem improves.

Feeling a Bit Rusty?

Don't just toss your garden tools in a bin or bucket when you're done with them; they'll eventually rust. To prevent this, keep them in a bucket of sand instead, and just submerge the metal parts in the sand whenever the tools are not in use. (Better yet, add some mineral oil to the sand.) Make sure the sand is stored in a dry place where rainwater can't get into it, though. If you decide you don't want to store your tools in sand, then a good thing to do is toss a handful of tea leaves in whatever container you keep them in. For whatever reason, the leaves will help keep the metal nice, new, and rust-free.

Protect Roses from the Japanese Beetle Invasion

Keep your rosebush the pride of your garden by getting rid of those icky Japanese beetles. Pour a bowl of self-rising flour and go outside, sprinkling it over the whole bush like it's some kind of magic potion (which, in this case, it is).

Tough Love for Trees

Treating your fruit trees like they're bad will yield a good crop. A newspaper rolled up works well to smack the trunks and get the sap moving more efficiently through the branches, which, in turn, helps the tree produce more fruit. Think of it like a massage to increase blood flow. And be prepared for strange looks from passers-by.

Tree Sculpting

Pruning will be less of a chore if you keep your eye on the goal of a strong and healthy tree. If it's more of a motivator, though, remember you don't want to get sued if a weak branch falls on a neighbor. On pruning day follow a simple plan: First get rid of any branches that are clearly dead, dying, or infested. Then home in on the ones that are too long, criss-crossing each other, or growing weak. Step back and admire your work.

Protect a New Lawn

If a scarecrow doesn't work to keep birds from feasting on your grass seeds, try this modern-day equivalent before you resort to netting. Place stakes at the four corners of the area you want to protect. Now cut two pieces of string, long enough to reach diagonally in an X across the lawn. Every foot or two along the strings you'll want to tie one-inch strips of aluminum foil. The breeze will keep the aluminum pieces flapping about and scare off would-be invaders.

Ramp Up Your Mowing Game

Save yourself the boring task of poking holes in your soil to aerate it. Instead, multitask the easy way by wearing spiked golf shoes or soccer cleats to aerate while you mow your lawn.

A Second Life for Seafood Shells

You may not have time to build a compost bin (or the stomach for a bucket full of worms), but you can easily crush shells from last night's seafood dinner and scatter them over your lawn. The calcium helps the grass grow.

Who Knew? CLASSIC TIP

Never pay to have your gutters cleaned again! To easily keep falling leaves from clogging them up, place a Slinky (yes, the child's toy) in your gutters. Stretch it out, then fasten the ends to your gutters with binder clips. The coil will allow water to get through, but keep leaves out.

Inventive Weed Killer

If you had a hammer, you wouldn't have so many weeds. Kneel down, turn the hammer backward, and bang it onto the soil to catch the weed between the claw. Now just pull. Yes it *is* okay to hammer when you're in a bad mood. As long as you can check something off your to-do list while you are at it.

Get Rid of Poison Ivy

When it comes to poison ivy, an ounce of prevention really is worth a pound of cure. So if you've got a patch of this pernicious vine on your property, kill it. Mix ½ gallon soapy water with a 1½ pounds salt, spray the plant, and run in the other direction.

Plant Doctor

A broken stem doesn't have to mean the end of a flower. If you catch it in time, you can save the limb by making a little splint out of a toothpick and tape. It looks a little funny, but your kids will get a kick out of it and it makes a great lesson in resilience.

Ripen Tomatoes

There's a frost predicted for tonight, and you have several unripened tomatoes on the vine. Don't risk them getting bitten by frost. Instead, pick them now and bring them inside. Place them inside a paper bag or wrap them in newspaper, then place them in an airtight container and put them in a dark area like a cabinet or closet. Check back in a few days and they'll be just-off-the-vine ripe.

Make Your Own Bonemeal

As you may know, bonemeal is an excellent source of nutrients for your plants. But instead of spending $8–$10 on a bag at your local gardening store, make your own! Bonemeal is just bones, after all. Save bones from chicken, turkey, steaks, and stews, then dry them out by roasting them in a 425° oven for a half an hour or microwaving them on high for 1–6 minutes (depending on how many bones you have). Then place them in a plastic or paper bag and grind them up by hitting them with a hammer, then rolling them with a rolling pin. The resulting powder is a life-producing treat for your plants, and you didn't spend a cent.

Wise Way to Wash Your Hands

Sometimes running your hands under the hose isn't enough to clean off all the dirt and grime that comes with gardening. Meanwhile, even stepping into the house with those filthy hands usually means something's going to get smudged. Fix this problem by keeping a bit of soap near your outdoor spigot. Tie it up in the leg of an old pair of pantyhose or a mesh bag and hang it nearby.

Repel with Peels

Another ingenious way to keep mosquitoes from biting you? Rub any exposed skin with orange or lemon peels. Mosquitoes hate the smell and will find someone else to attack. Ants also don't like to smell of lemon and orange peels, so grind them in your blender with some water, then spread in areas you find ants to keep them away.

Looking for Worms?

If you're getting ready for a big fishing trip by looking for bait in your backyard, begin by soaking an entire newspaper with water, then spreading it out in one hunk in your garden or on your lawn. Lift it up in the early morning, and loads of worms will be underneath. To keep your worms alive until it's time to use them, store them in a can with soil and coffee grounds.

Gone Fishing

If you use a hollow plastic tub jig on your fishing line, slip a small piece of Alka-Seltzer or denture cleaner inside before tossing it into the water. It will release a string of bubbles that will attract fish.

Sweet Fish Bait

Did you know that fish have a sweet tooth? It's true! To make some scrumptious bait, mix 2 cups flour, 2 cups cornmeal, and 2 tablespoons molasses into a thick dough. Roll it into balls and boil in water for 20 minutes. Place the balls directly in an ice water bath after removing them from the boiling water, and now you're ready to catch some fish.

An Easy Way to Identify Your Campsite

When going camping, mark your campsite by tying brightly colored helium balloons to a few trees nearby. Your tents will be easy to find even from far away.

—John T., Murfreesboro, TN

Who Knew?

Almost 12 million Americans go camping each year.

Can't Start a Fire

Rain on a camping trip is enough of a bummer; it doesn't have to ruin your campfire as well. Melt paraffin (available from the supermarket) in a coffee can inside a pot of water on the stove. Remove the can and begin to mix in sawdust until you have about three parts sawdust to two parts paraffin. Pour into paper cups and let cool. Then all you need to do is pop them out of the cups and store them in a Ziploc bag. They'll light up easily when the time comes. Now all you need is a spark.

Another No-Fail Fire Starter

Before your camping trip, smear petroleum jelly on some cotton balls and keep them in a Ziploc bag. Even if you find yourself camping in the middle of a rainstorm, these bits of kindling will definitely get your fire roaring.

CHAPTER 11

Celebration Time! Tips for Holidays and Entertaining

Great Decorating Tip for Any Holiday

Fresh flowers and greenery make beautiful holiday decorations, but where do you put them? All you need are some empty wine or other bottles (like beer or juice bottles), old newspaper, and spray paint. Place the bottles outside on the newspaper, spray paint them gold, silver, or the holiday color of your choice, and let them dry. Voilà!—unique vases that will have your guests guessing as to where you purchased them.

Stock Up a Year Ahead of Time

We always hit up stores after each holiday to check out what kind of deals we can get on decorations or gifts for the following year. Also keep in mind that many stores start discounting holiday items a week before the holiday—so if you're willing to wait until the last minute, you can save big.

Holiday Flowers

Flora-lovers don't need fancy arrangements to celebrate every holiday with style. Start your own tradition of dyeing white carnations whatever color is fitting for the occasion. You can use various shades of red and pink for Valentine's Day, green for St. Patrick's Day, a combination of red, white, and blue for July Fourth, orange and black for Halloween, and so on. It's also fun to do favorite colors for birthdays. All you need to do is add a bit of food coloring to your flowers' vase with some warm water. Half the fun watching the flower take on the new color as it sucks up the water, so make sure the kids don't miss out.

"Oh Yeah, Those Other Holiday" Trees

Whoever had the idea for the first Christmas tree must have retired young. Why not spread the wealth and decorate an indoor tree you already have for other holidays? Our kids love to hang eggshell ornaments and tie pastel ribbons on the dracena in our kitchen at Easter. And when they were younger, we used to arrange their stuffed bunnies, ducks, and lambs on a blanket spread out on the floor underneath the tree. For Valentine's Day, a simple afternoon project of making and hanging paper hearts cut out of last year's Valentines (hole-punch the top and tie a ribbon) can become a family tradition.

● Who Knew? CLASSIC TIP

If you've just removed your candlesticks from the cupboard for a party and they're covered in wax, try this handy trick: Just stick them in the freezer for a couple of hours. The wax will harden and chip right off.

The Gift of Memory Lane

For the couple who has everything, why not show them how much they've already had? A tour of places they used to live (or went to school or worked) is a personal and moving way to celebrate a special day. For an anniversary, find out where they met, where they had their first date, and where they got married. You can start out narrating, but be prepared for the recipients to take over. They'll likely enjoy telling stories as much as anything else you can give them.

—*Marge Lenkel, Laguna Beach, CA*

Think of Your Guests During the Super Bowl

Having a Super Bowl party? Consider having two TVs—one of which is reserved for the hardcore fans only. A lot of people will come to the party just looking to socialize (and maybe watch the halftime show), so let them watch away from the football freaks, who will want to be able to catch every moment of pig-skinned glory.

Free Valentines

It's Valentine's Day and you haven't gotten a card! Instead of buying a valentine for your sweetie, trying making your own with magazine clippings or colored paper. If you're not the creative type, visit DLTK-Holidays.com/valentines/cards.htm, which has links to various websites that offer free valentines that you can print and send.

Early Morning Valentine

Instead of worrying all day about how to make the perfect romantic dinner for your valentine, try breakfast in bed and get a whole day's worth of credit for it. A flower, a chocolate, and a heart-shaped placemat are all you need to make eggs, toast, and a fruit bowl look especially festive.

Easy Easter Egg Dye

Never, ever pay for egg dye! Simply mix ½ cup boiling water with ½ teaspoon white vinegar, and add food coloring until you get a hue you like. For a striped egg even the Easter Bunny would be proud of, wrap tape around the egg before dipping. Once the egg dries, remove the tape, tape over the colored parts, and dip again in a different color. You can also use stickers in the shapes of hearts, stars, and letters.

Egg Dyeing for Toddlers

You might think only older kids can dye Easter eggs, but we started our boys off when they were still in diapers. Give your little helpers a plastic container filled with food coloring, water, and a little vinegar.

Let them drop the hard-boiled egg in, help them seal it closed, and tell them to "Shake, shake, shake." Pure magic.

O Say Can You...Be Careful With Those Sparklers?

It's Fourth of July and time to bust out the legal explosives. Kids love to hold sparklers, but make sure their hands are safe by sticking the sparkler in Play-Doh inside its container, which is the perfect size for the kids to wrap their patriotic hands around.

Add Halloween Atmosphere

Adding stretchy cobwebs to the door jambs and corners of your home is a great way to add Halloween flair to the entire house. Instead of buying the ones packaged as spider webs, though, simply go to a craft store and buy a bag of fiberfill. It's the exact same stuff, and a 16-ounce bag of fiberfill is less than half the cost. You can usually find bags of plastic spider rings for super-cheap at party supply stores or superstores—add them to the webs and on tables around your house for more atmosphere, and encourage your guests to take them home!

Looking for a Last-Minute Costume?

For ideas on how to make costumes out of clothes and materials you may have around the house (no sewing!) head over to CostumeIdeaZone.com. This is the perfect site for your pre-teens who want to dress up, but want to do it themselves and don't want a big fuss made over the whole thing.

Creepy Halloween Drinks

Getting dry ice to put at the bottom of the punch bowl is a bit difficult, so to make your punch seem haunted quickly and easily, freeze grapes to use as ice cubes. Once they're frozen, peel off the skin and they'll look like creepy eyeballs.

An Inexpensive Thanksgiving

If you're trying to save this Thanksgiving, don't be afraid to make it a potluck! Most guests love to bring a dish that shows of their culinary skills, and those who don't can bring the wine!

Fun Thanksgiving Activity

Give hyper kids something to do *and* decorate your table at the same time this Thanksgiving by sending them out into the yard to find the last remaining yellow, red, and orange leaves. Make sure they're not visibly dirty, then arrange them along the middle of the table in lieu of a runner. We love this activity because it's good for kids of any age, and the older ones can help the younger ones.

Hot Potatoes

Skip the last-minute panic on major holidays and mash the potatoes first thing in the morning. Transfer them to a slow cooker while you move onto the stuffing and string beans. Two hours before you're ready to serve the meal, turn on the slow cooker. You won't have to give the potatoes another thought until the guests are seated and it's time to serve the meal.

—Sue Pratt, Jasper, GA

Smells Like the Holidays

This little gem of a recipe will give your home an instant cozy and home-for-the-holidays feel. Mix whole cloves, crushed cinnamon sticks, bay leaves, juniper berries, orange peels, nutmeg, and allspice. (You can store the mixture in a jar until you are ready to use it.) To get the smell to disseminate, boil water in a saucepan and pour in some of your homemade potpourri. Simmer gently and your house is guaranteed to start smelling like Christmas.

Deck the Halls—and the Wreath

If you're getting tired of that old drab-looking Christmas wreath, don't get rid of it—just spruce it up a little. Use a glue gun to attach some pinecones from your yard onto it, or buy some cheap doo-dads at your local crafts store and do the same. You'll get a brand-new wreath for a fraction of the cost.

Do It With Ribbon

Used wisely, a little holiday ribbon can go a long way. Wrap it around just about anything—a vase, throw pillow, lamp shade, curtain, pillar candle, and the list goes on—to create a festive atmosphere at little or no cost.

Be the Color Police

If you want your home to look super-Christmassy, scan your living room for brightly colored objects that aren't red or green, and move them to invisible or inconspicuous locations for the season. Without the other colors to distract people's eyes, your red and green Christmas decorations will stand out even more.

Outdoor Christmas Decorations

When pruning your trees and bushes in the spring or summer, make sure to save some branches for later use. Then spray paint them red, white, silver, or gold and you have an instant Christmas decoration! Place them in planters of flowers that are dead for the winter, and add lights or ornaments for extra flair.

Long-Lasting Wreaths

We love the look of a pine wreaths and garlands, but hate it when needles get all over the floor. To keep the needles from falling, spritz your holiday greenery with hair spray right after you purchase it. The hair spray will keep the needles moist and where they belong.

Sappy Hands

The scent of evergreens is pure magic, but you could do without the sticky sap left on your hands after collecting branches for a wreath or making one. Bring out the Hellmann's (or whatever mayonnaise you have on hand). Rub a small spoonful on your hands like lotion and the sap will wash right off.

It's a Wrap! Tips for Wrapping Holiday and Other Presents

Keep gift-wrapping fun and inexpensive by coming up with different materials to decorate your presents. Here are some of our favorite ideas.

✦ Use pages from the past year's calendar (photo-side up, obviously) to wrap smaller gifts—two taped together are great for books or DVD sets.

✦ Copied sheet music makes for unique and festive wrapping paper. At your local library it should be easy enough to find books of whatever music suits your friend (classical, show tunes, rock music, etc.). Make a copy on colored paper if you can, and be sure the title of the piece shows when you fold it over the gift.

✦ Instead of doling out cash for fancy bows to decorate gifts, use your actual dollars to *make* the bows. Fold a dollar bill (or more, if you're a high roller) accordion-style and affix with a ribbon over a wrapped gift. As a variation, give a nod to Chinese New Year by putting two dollars inside a traditional red envelope and taping it to the top of a gift for good luck.

✦ Do you have collections of paper napkins that are "too pretty to use"? Then use them in a way that takes advantage of their design—as wrapping paper for little gifts or candy bars.

✦ Have your kids draw on some taped-together printer paper and use it to wrap gifts that are "from them."

✦ Quickest buzz kill when wrapping presents: trying to reuse tired out, wrinkled tissue paper and hoping the recipient won't take it personally. Turns out you can iron used tissue paper on low to get it to look "like new!" Amazing.

✦ After everyone's done opening their presents, don't forget to save bigger sheets of paper, bows, and pretty cards (to use for next year's gift tags). We keep our stash in one of those giant popcorn tins with a Christmas design from years ago!

Make Your Own Cards

Show your friends you care and save money by making your own cards to send for birthdays or other occasions. Look through old magazines for funny photos (or shots of your friend's celebrity crush) to use for the front. Or for something more complicated, visit Card-Making-World.com for ideas and free backgrounds and embellishments to download.

⬤ Who Knew?

Approximately 1.2 billion birthday cards are purchased every year. Time to buy stock in Hallmark!

Shipping Secret

When packing up those holiday presents, make sure nothing rattles in the box and the lid closes firmly (without being easily depressed into the box). This will ensure your presents arrive safely, even if heavier boxes are stacked on top (plus, the post office won't insure your package if it sounds like it contains loose items!). To help fill out the space in a big box, use Ziploc bags. Seal them all the way, then open them up just enough to fit a straw through. Blow through the straw to inflate them, then reseal—a homemade air pillow!

A White, Salty Christmas

You can easily dust your Christmas wreath with "snow" by using salt. Go outside in the backyard with a large paper grocery bag and half a cup of salt. Pour the salt in the bag, place the wreath inside, and fold the bag closed. Then shake gently for 20 seconds and your wreath will look as good as new.

Save Energy This Christmas

Did you know that one strand of traditional Christmas lights running five hours a day for 30 days can add up to $10 to your electricity bill? This Christmas, make sure you use LED lights, which will only run you 12¢ for the same amount of time. LED lights also last much longer!

Free Tree Stand

Instead of buying a stand for your Christmas tree, simply fill a bucket with sand. You can still water it, and you won't have to deal with the hassle of readjusting the stand so the tree isn't crooked.

Watering Your Christmas Tree

If you have trouble getting a watering can to reach underneath the lowest bows of your Christmas tree, throw several ice cubes into the base each day to easily keep it watered.

—Fran Kaiser, Shalimar, FL

Easy Christmas Decorating

Put those unused holiday ornaments to good use by using them for an inexpensive centerpiece. Simply pick your favorites and put them in a clear punch bowl, and add tinsel or pine sprigs around the base. It works great with those solid-colored orbs we always seem to have so many of!

Frost Your Windows

If you want your windows to look like they've been touched with frost this holiday season, just mix 1 tablespoon Epsom salts with 1 cup beer, then brush onto the window with a small paintbrush. When you're ready to remove the frost, just wash it off with ammonia and water.

Film Canister Ornaments

It's easy to turn film canisters into little Christmas treasure boxes. Any scraps from the arts and crafts table (glitter, sequins, bits of wrapping paper, mini buttons) can be applied with a hot glue gun to decorate the outside. Fill with little candies or toys from the five and dime store. Miniatures have a certain holiday magic and kids never seem to grow tired of them. To make into hanging ornaments, simply knot a ribbon into a loop and glue to the top.

—*Rachel Federman*

Walnut Treats

For a holiday treat, carve the nuts out of split walnut shells and place fortunes or little prizes inside. Glue back together and decorate with sparkle paint. When the shells are dry, collect them in a basket for a unique centerpiece and a fun activity one dark night of the advent. Pass around the table after dinner and let family members take turns reaching for a walnut and cracking it open to find out what's hidden inside.

Make Your Own Poppers

These are a favorite Christmas tradition in our house. We cut paper towel tubes into three pieces and then load them up with candy, little toys, and tissue paper crowns. Then we use wrapping paper to cover the tubes completely, leaving extra paper on each end that we tie up with ribbon. Everyone gets a popper with his or her place setting for Christmas dinner. Our kids love to show guests how to yank from the sides, so that the poppers actually pop!

Handmade Gift Soaps

Soaps never seem to lose their appeal as holiday gifts. They're useful and don't add clutter to people's houses (something we're always trying to avoid in ours). You can make your own by grating white, unscented soap it into a bowl with warm water. For color, add a few drops of food coloring. Next, add a drop or two of an essential oil (lavender or rose are lovely), then knead like pizza dough and make into little balls. As an alternative, use candy molds for fun shapes. Leave them to dry on wax paper for a day or so.

Frugal Christmas?

If opening presents is going to take drastically less time than usual this year, fill the gap by starting some new Christmas traditions. Make a popcorn string for the tree, cut out sugar cookies with different-colored sugars for decoration, or try this game to make gift-opening take longer (it's a favorite at our gatherings): Find as many holiday present rejects as you have people playing—all those candles with scents you can't stand, weird gifts from office gift exchanges, or your silliest finds from the dollar bin at Target. Wrap each one and have each guest pick a gift. Go around the room clockwise, starting with the youngest person. Before opening their gift, guests can decide to trade with someone else (even if that person's gift has been unwrapped). After one round of gift opening, have one more round of trades, with players deciding if they want to keep their current gift or switch with someone else. You'll be surprised which gifts people actually like, and "you'll have a laugh" at the expense of the person left with the worst one.

Coasters: More than Just Drink Holders!

Keep an eye out during the year for cool drink coasters that are served at bars. These cardboard circles and squares are great for gift tags and ornaments. Simply punch a hole through the top, insert a ribbon, and hang!

Easy Ornament Storage

The best container we've found for storing Christmas ornaments is an empty case of wine or liquor (no comment on how we came across this!). Keep the cardboard dividers inside, and you have a handy place to ball up your ornaments with newspaper and keep them safe until next year. These boxes are also great for storing rolled-up artwork and posters.

How to Keep a Poinsettia Blooming

Poinsettia plants are gifts that keep on giving, if *you* give *them* a little extra care. After the last of the Christmas decorations are packed away, bring your poinsettia plants down to the basement (or elsewhere) where it's cool and dark. Then keep them like prisoners, giving them very little water, until they're almost dried out but not quite. Toward the end of April, bring the plants back out, trim them down about halfway, and give them lots of water and sun. You'll be amazed at how well they re-bloom. When nights are warm enough for just a sweater, we sometimes plant them outside in a sunny spot to enjoy from the deck all summer long. Then bring them back inside in the fall, where they still get full sun and lots of water. **Just remember that poinsettias can be toxic to pets.**

The 365 Days of Christmas

Eventually, you do have to give in and take down the Christmas tree, but before it goes out the door, pull off a few handfuls of needles that you can keep as simple potpourri. Little cloth bags are readily available in craft stores, or you can make your own out of old nylons. Just cut a scrap into a square, place the needles inside, bundle up, and tie with a ribbon. There's no reason not to enjoy that woodland scent all year long.

Clean and Easy Tree Removal

The holidays have been over for weeks, but you've been dreading the removal of your Christmas tree, which has been shedding pine needles pretty much ever since you bought it. To get a dead tree out of your house without too much mess behind you, find the biggest, strongest garbage bag you can. Open it up so you can see the bottom, then place on the floor next to your tree. Once you free the tree from its stand, place the trunk squarely in the middle of the bag, then work your way around the tree, pulling the bag up as far as you can over its branches. (This is often easiest as a two-person job, with one person holding the tree and one person moving the bag.) Even if you can't get the bag all the way over your tree, you can still hold the bag in place while you carry the tree out to the curb. By the time you get there, there will be a huge pile of needles at the bottom of the bag that never made it onto your carpet.

Auld Lang Time

Here's an original idea for a cheap New Year's Eve decoration: Gather all the devices you use to tell time—stopwatches, alarm clocks, calendars, pocket planners, even the little hourglasses from board games—and place them on a tray next to the champagne bowl. Tell all your guests to set their alarms for midnight and do the same with the items you've collected.

> ### ● Who Knew? CLASSIC TIP
>
> Wondering how much food to make for your big soiree? Wonder no longer. At a cocktail party (no dinner served), 10–12 bite-sized portions per person is a good bet. If you're also serving a meal, figure on 4–5 bites per guest. For dip, figure 2 tablespoons per person (plus veggies or crackers for dipping), and for cheese, get 4 ounces for each person.

Housewarm with Houseplants

Clippings from a houseplant make great (and free!) housewarming presents. Cut your plant at the "knuckle" (or joint) section of the stem, then place in a cup of water until it grows roots. To present it, wrap the bottom in a wet paper towel and place in a plastic bag, tying it up with ribbon. Or plant in an old mug!

A Party Is About the People...

...Not how much money you spent on it. Before you throw a huge bash, write out your priorities in terms of what you think is most important to spend your money on (for example, the least on decorations and the most on food). Then figure out how much you're willing to spend on the highest item on your list, and work your way down. Friends always ask, "Can I bring anything?" and you shouldn't be afraid of asking your good friends to bring a dessert or appetizer. And don't forget—potlucks and picnics are cheap and always popular.

Party Photo Pleaser

When taking photos at night, sometimes the flash from your camera can leave an ugly glare on people's faces (making sure they'll never let you post the pics online!). Get rid of glare by taping a tiny piece of white coffee filter over the flash. The scene will still light up, but won't be as harsh.

Card Table Trick

This simple trick offers peace of mind when several folding tables are placed together to form a bigger table. Use cleaned-out coffee cans as holders for adjoining legs from different tables and rest assured that your grandmother's hand-blown glass punch bowl is safe.

Cork Control

Uh oh, you were uncorking a bottle of wine, and didn't do a very good job. You're not above drinking wine that has a little cork floating in it, but you definitely don't want to serve it to guests! Simply hold a coffee filter over a carafe and pour. It will filter out the cork pieces and your reputation will be saved...for now.

● Who Knew? CLASSIC TIP

Here's a great way to display dip on your table. Cut off the top of a bell pepper, then hollow it out and spoon your dip inside. You can also use a sturdy bread like pumpernickel as a hollowed-out dip container. Put spinach dip inside, then cut the bread you removed into large cubes and use for dipping.

Be Creative With Ice

If you're serving punch at a party, pour some of it into ice cube trays and freeze. This way, you can keep the punch nice and cold without diluting it. This also works well with wine, iced tea, or any number of other beverages. If you want to get really exotic, mint leaves are a great thing to make ice cubes out of—just fill the ice tray with water like normal and then stuff the leaves so that they rest below the surface.

Keep the TV Going

During parties, our giant TV suddenly becomes a dead spot in the room (when normally it's the center of attention!). Pop a movie into the DVD player and let it run on mute. Play a scary movie if it's a Halloween party, or a Christmas classic if it's a holiday party. Or play movies from your teenage years or favorites amongst your group of friends. And if it's your birthday, of course, it's your pick! Once you've picked your theme, pile the rest of your DVDs that fit it on top of the player and change the movie throughout the night.

Easily Label Drinks

Keep a handle on whose drink is whose by pressing window decals onto the sides of glassware. This is a perfect trick for a party that takes place around a holiday, when you can use festive decals that are easy to find at party stores.

Ice Bucket Solution

It's nice to keep an ice bucket next to your drinks on the table, but once the ice melts you're left with a few cubes soaking in a puddle of water. To fix this problem, place a colander on the top of your ice bucket and fill *it* with the ice. Water will drip through the bottom, and the ice will be easier to grab with some tongs.

—*Cynthia Ferris*

No-Spill Party Drinks

We love anything that gives us more time to talk to our company and cuts down on hosting duties during a party. One simple way to hand out drinks—use muffin trays instead of flat trays. You can easily carry two dozen glasses without breaking a sweat and even younger family members will be able to help.

The Secret to Day-Ahead Salad

It's so much easier to prepare food a day ahead for a dinner party—but what to do about the salad? Making the salad before guests arrive usually leads to a soggy mess, but here's a tip to allow you to make most of the salad without it going soft. Gather lettuce and any of the following ingredients: broccoli, cabbage, carrots, cauliflower, celery, cucumbers, onions, peppers, and radishes. Chop them up and place them in a large bowl. Then completely cover all your ingredients with water and keep the bowl in the refrigerator until you need it. Then add tomatoes, croutons, and any other toppings and enjoy a crisp, delicious salad.

Who Knew? CLASSIC TIP

Nothing gets the summertime party going faster than firing up the backyard grill. Just make sure you keep all that smoked and grilled meat coming—it's unforgivable to run out of fuel before the last kebab is bobbed. Even without a gas gauge, there is a way to figure out how much fuel you have left. Here's what to do a day or two *before* the flip-flopped masses are set to arrive. Boil water, then pour it down the side of the tank. Place your hand on the side: The cool part has propane inside, the warm part is empty.

Great Grilling

To get the most out of that grilled flavor everyone loves so much, add a few sprigs of your favorite herbs, such as rosemary, thyme, and savory, directly to the top of the charcoal as you grill. It will infuse whatever you're cooking with mouthwatering flavor.

Butter Corn With Ease

If you're serving bread with your barbecue, use a slice to easily butter your corn. Spread a generous amount of butter onto the bread, then gently wrap it around your corn. Twist the cob until the butter has gotten into every crack, then enjoy perfectly buttered corn and bread with melted butter.

A Makeshift Fish Cage

If you have two small wire racks, you can easily cook a fish (and impress your friends) on your outdoor grill. First, find toaster-oven or cooling racks and some fireproof wire. Oil the racks, then put the fish between them and tie the racks together. Grill the fish on one side, then flip your newly constructed basket with large tongs or a spatula. This makeshift cage will keep delicate fish from breaking apart.

Save Some Beer for the Bugs

The next time you're having a party in your garden, place a few cans of open beer around the perimeter of your yard—insects will be more attracted to the beer than to your guests.

BBQ Squeeze

A Sunday afternoon barbecue is one of our favorite summer traditions. The not-so-great part? Clean-up. One way to make it easier is to eliminate the entire barbecue sauce brushing routine, which is arguably just a way for guys to flex their muscles as they prepare for a big fire. Instead, use one of those disposable sport water bottles with the squirt top to store the sauce and squeeze while cooking as needed. Keep in the fridge when not in use.

Having a Picnic?

Include some sprigs of fresh mint in your picnic basket when eating al fresco. Bees and wasps don't like mint, so add some to your plate to keep it stinger-free.

The Secret Storage Secret for Coolers

Before stashing away your cooler for the winter, stuff it with a few balls of newspaper. The newspaper will absorb any lingering odors, so it won't be a mildewy nightmare when you open it back up in the spring.

You Can Catch More Wasps With Honey Than Vinegar

If you can't beat 'em, join 'em (kind of). At your next picnic party give stinging party crashers a treat of their own—a sugar-covered grapefruit. They'll go for the fruit and stay away from your guests.

Party Like It's Wednesday Night

If your children's birthday parties are putting a hurt on your budget, there's a simple solution—have the party during the week instead of on a weekend. Sure, everyone wants a weekend party, and that's why restaurants and other popular birthday locales charge a lot more for Saturday and Sunday events. They'll be only too happy to accommodate your request for a weekday party, and it might even be easier for you, too—just offer to pick up your child's playmates from school that afternoon and have them picked up from the party later. Your child will have just as much fun as they would at a weekend party, maybe even more, since it's a rare weekday treat. A great, but rarely utilized, location for a summer party is your local minor league baseball park. Tickets are cheap, kids will love interacting with the mascot, and there's no need to stay the whole game—five innings or so should suffice. The team might even offer you discounted group tickets and flash your child's name on the scoreboard.

The Perfect Candle Holder for Kids' Cakes

Life Savers are an excellent accent for your child's birthday cake. Not only do kids enjoy sucking on them, but they are perfect for holding candles! Use the regular size (not the jumbo kind that come individually wrapped in bags), put them on top of the cake, and then insert the candle in the middle. The candy will hold the candle straighter and is easily disposed of if wax drips on it.

Make Ice Cream Shapes for a Perfect Dessert Plate

Here's a fun and unique way to serve ice cream next to cake. Buy a pint-size container of your favorite ice cream, then slice right through it (cardboard and all) with a serrated knife, making ice cream "rounds" that are about 1-inch thick. Peel off the remaining cardboard, then use cookie cutters to make various shapes. Store them in your freezer in between pieces of parchment paper until you're ready to serve. And if you don't use the entire pint of ice cream, the top will still sit flush against your "short stack" to keep it fresh for later.

Tablecloth Substitution

Your daughter's party is about to start, and you just realized you don't have a plastic tablecloth on which to serve the cake. Don't worry, your dining room table isn't ruined yet. Just use the mat from your Twister game. It's covered with colorful dots, and food wipes right off.

Pass the Present

Here's a cheap and easy game for a kids' party that's become a favorite of our kids. Before the party, gather up enough party favors for each child who will be playing, then add a "special" party favor for just one child. Put the favors in a box and wrap it with an old scrap of wrapping paper. Then wrap it 6–12 more times (depending on how many guests you're expecting). When you're ready to play. Sit the children in a circle and start up some music. While the music plays, the children pass the present around to their right. When the music stops, the kid holding the present gets to unwrap a layer of wrapping paper. The game continues until the last child unwraps the present, and discovers the special prize for herself and the ones for everyone else.

All's Fair in Love and Piñatas

When it comes to piñatas, the spoils go to the bullies, but not if you separate the candies and prizes into Ziploc bags for each guest before stuffing them inside the papier-mâché animal. The kids will still get a rush of excitement when the piñata drops, but the game won't dissolve into an "Are we having fun yet?" moment when they start fighting over Tootsie Rolls and Milky Ways.

CHAPTER 12

Tricks for Getting Organized

Scrunchies Saved

Stop hunting around the house every time you need a hair band! Get a toilet paper tube and wrap the bands around it. Keep it in your bathroom or on your dresser and you'll never be without a ponytail holder again.

—Jackie Bavel, Manahawkin, NJ

Extra Storage for a Three-Ring Binder

If your kids are like ours, they have all kinds of problems keeping their school supplies organized. You can help remedy this by taking a heavy-duty Ziploc freezer bag, punching holes so that it fits in their three-ring school binder, and filling it with pencils, erasers, and other easily misplaced items.

Shoe Box Dividers

Keep bureau drawers under control by using shoe boxes to separate underwear, socks, tights, and whatever else gets stuffed in there when company comes.

Sewing Board

If you use a sewing machine often, mount a small bulletin board on the wall next to it. Then fill it with pushpins or straight pins. That way when you've got your hands full, you can use the pins to hang extra thread, buttons, bobbins, and other miscellany on the board until you need it.

Cut Your Clothing Clutter

Are you afraid you'll be buried in a fabric avalanche every time you open your closet? It's time to take control of your wardrobe. Going through your clothes and figuring out what you have and what you don't need has a lot of money-saving benefits. First of all, you can take unwanted clothes to a resale shop and either make some money or exchange them for new clothes. Second, you'll have a better handle on what clothes you need for the season, cutting down on duplicates and making impulse buying less likely. If you tend to buy a lot of items that are similar to each other, try organizing your closet by color, so when you pause by that black polo shirt at the store you'll remember just how many black short-sleeve shirts you already own.

Organize Those Bunches of Cords

Don't throw away empty toilet paper rolls! Use them to store the millions of cords running behind your entertainment center. Not only will the rolls keep the cords untangled, but if you also write which appliances the cord belongs to on the roll, you just might be the most organized person in your neighborhood.

Who Knew? CLASSIC TIP

Use an old egg carton to sort small items like nails, screws, and nuts. It can even be used for earrings!

Keep Track of Computer Logins

In these modern times, everyone is registered for more websites than they can count, making it next to impossible to remember all of one's usernames and passwords. Instead of forgetting these all the time, just create a computer document listing all your logins and passwords, and place it on your desktop. Whenever you sign up for a new site, it'll take about 10 seconds to add the new login to the document.

God's Gift to Organization

Clear plastic storage bins may be the greatest thing we have going for us. If you feel like your house is constantly cluttered, go to your nearest organizational store, superstore, or even a dollar store and stock up immediately. But before you go, take a look around your house to find empty areas for some covert storage. Buy long, flat bins for under the couch and you can store board games, video games, and DVDs. Buy tall, stackable ones for keeping items in a closet. And buy whatever fits best under your bed to maximize this perfect space for storing off-season clothes. Make sure to keep some where it's easy to reach—we have one that's simply for all the *stuff* we find in our living room that needs to be put back elsewhere in the house.

Old Cassette Cases Are Good for Something!

Looking for a container to store iPod earbud headphones where they won't get tangled? Coil the cord and then place them inside an old cassette case. Your headphones will be safe, and your friends can admire the *Flashdance* soundtrack decoration on the outside. So retro!

Meds on the Go

For the perfect container for keeping medicine with you in your purse or pocket, try a contact lens case. Since it comes with two handy sections, it's easy to store different pills in different compartments and label them, if necessary.

Remote Remedy

If you're always searching for the remote control, pick one designated place for it and try to always return it to that spot when you're done watching television. You can always keep it on the same end table, or attach self-adhesive Velcro to it and to your TV and affix it there. If you have two (or three, or four, or five) remotes, keep them together in a small basket by your favorite chair.

Organize Your Yarn

Doing some knitting? Keep yarn from getting tangled, especially if you're working with two strands at a time, by running the ends of the rolls through straws. If you pull the yarn through straws as you knit, they'll straighten out each strand.

—Missy Miller, Loveland, CO

How to Hide Your Hiding Spaces

Here's a quick and ingenious way to make a cover for under your sink or a small table that will hide anything underneath it. Take an old pillowcase or two and cut through the seams on the top, bottom, and unopened side. Then run a ribbon or piece of elastic through the hemmed portion on the end where you formerly would have stuffed a pillow. Wrap the ribbon around the tabletop or the base of the sink—you may need to string more than one pillowcase on to get full coverage. Tack or tape the string to the wall or the back of the table, then stuff all your power cords, cleaning supplies, or anything else you want out-of-sight underneath!

Pantyhose Problems?

Is pantyhose overrunning your sock drawer? Place each pair in its own resealable sandwich bag. Write any pertinent information (like the size, or whether or not it's control top) on the outside. If they're still taking up too much space, place them in a plastic storage bin under your dresser or somewhere else out of the way.

Bag It!

One of our favorite organizational tools is a hanging shoe organizer. These canvas contraptions are made to allow you to store your shoes on the back of a door, but their individualized compartments make them perfect for storing anything. Keep one in the bathroom for bobby pins, make-up, and lotion; one in your kitchen for spices; and one in the TV room for rarely used remotes and video game controllers. We keep one in each of our children's rooms, so that when we yell, "Clean up your room!" they have a handy place to stow toy cars, action figures, and the 20 million other little things that find their way onto their floors.

Solve Linen Closet Madness

Easily keep your cloth napkins and other matching linens together when you store them by using binder clips to keep like kinds together. You'll never have to dig through the closet looking for a lost place setting again.

Who Knew?

In a survey of 400 adults, 384 of them said they could save time every day by becoming more organized. What are some tweaks you could make to make your day run more smoothly?

Declutter Your Desk

If your desk seems cluttered, make sure you're taking advantage of the space above it. Install a shelf or two for books and folders, and make sure to attach some hooks on their undersides. Hang small baskets on the hooks and now you have a hiding place for paperclips, pens, glue stick, tape, and the hundred other things that are taking up room in your office space.

Get Rid of Menu Mayhem

If you live in an urban area, you probably get a take-out menu stuck under your door every day. To get rid of the clutter caused by having menus stacked up in a drawer, on a table, or practically all over your house, pick a storage method and stick to it. We use a sturdy, waterproof pocket folder for our menus, but you can also use a magazine holder, an inbox, or an old box with the flaps cut off. If you have a three-hole punch handy, you can even store them in a three-ring binder. Whatever you decide, go through your menus first and get rid of any duplicates. Also throw away any menus that serve similar food to a restaurant you order from regularly—once you find your favorite Chinese joint in the area, you're unlikely to try the mediocre one from the next neighborhood over. Make sure to tell your family where your menus now reside, and next time someone says, "Time for takeout," dinner really will be a breeze.

The Key to Keys

You'll never fumble with the wrong key again if you color-code them with a dot of nail polish. Just apply a thick coat of a different shade to the top of each key.

Finding the Card You Need: Priceless

A Rolodex is so old-school, but not if you use it in a new way. How many gift cards or store credits expire before you use them? What about those self-multiplying rewards cards? They slide all over the place in your wallet, and are always out of sight when you make a purchase. Organize them into a Rolodex so you'll never leave home without the right one again.

Clothespin Your Way to Organization

Glue one side of a sturdy clothespin to the inside of cabinet doors, the front of your washing machine, and elsewhere around your home. Hanging clothespins are great for holding plastic shopping bags, and plastic shopping bags are great for holding trash, clean rags, cleaning supplies, and more.

—*Katie N., Philadelphia, PA*

Getting a Handle on Pan Lids

Forget buying one more specialty-organizing device and instead use the time to actually organize. A dish rack or V-rack (meant for roasting) both make great containers for sorting pan lids in the cabinet. Act now and do away with banging and rummaging for good. Simply reach for the lid you need!

What Uses Can You Think of for a Giant Magnet?

Magnetic strips made to hold knives in your kitchen are useful in many other ways as well. Use them to hold keys, nail clippers and other bathroom must-haves, office supplies—even family photos with a magnet.

Jewelry Organizing Secret

This organizational tip is also a great bedroom decoration. Buy a bulletin board and lots of sturdy push-pins, then use them to hang your bracelets, necklaces, rings, and hook earrings. With all your jewelry on display, you'll be able to more quickly decide what you want to wear, and it won't be a tangled mess. You'll also get a chance to look at beautiful pieces that may not make it into your regular rotation.

—Devorah Klein, Sliver Spring, MD

How to Hide a PIN

Here's a question we often get asked: "Where's a safe place to keep PINs for bank cards and the like?" The answer isn't so much *where* as *how*: Hide them inside a fake phone number. For example, if your PIN is 1234 (and hopefully, it isn't!), scribble 347-1234 on the inside of your day planner or somewhere else accessible. Would-be thieves won't know it's the number they're looking for.

Make Bed-Making Easier

Want to know the quickest way to a perfectly made bed every time? Stitch a small *x* in the center of your flat sheet and blankets, then line them up with the center of the headboard. Presto!

—Stefanie Pole

Pillowcase It

Our closets are kind of a mess, but we manage never to misplace part of a sheet set. That's because after washing and folding them, we put them right inside one of the pillowcases, which is a convenient way to make sure everything stays in one place.

> ### ◑ Who Knew?
>
> Did you know that there is a National Organization of Professional Organizers? Called NAPO for short, it has more than 4,200 members.

Quick Serve

If your kids are like ours, they tend to grab whatever snacks are most easily accessible in the fridge. We've solved that problem and encouraged healthier eating by keeping a sandwich basket right in front, containing all the ingredients necessary for a quick meal—deli meats, cheese, condiments, and so on.

Medicine Cabinet Organization

If you have a metal medicine cabinet, mount a magnet inside it, and you'll be able to place nail clippers, tweezers, safety pins, or other handy items at your fingertips. And if your cabinet is made of metal, just glue the magnet inside.

Bountiful Bathroom Storage

Those three-tiered baskets that you usually find holding fruit in the kitchen are also perfect for bathrooms. Store brushes, hair gel, band-aids, or whatever else is taking up space in your medicine cabinet. If hung out of reach of your kids, it's also a great place to store shaving supplies.

Great Tip if You've Ever Said, "Where's My Ring?!"

Screw a small hook into the wall near your kitchen sink. It will make a handy place to store your rings while you're doing the dishes.

—*Tawnya Crawford*

Make Your Own Closet

You're in desperate need of more closet space, but you can't afford a fancy armoire. Here's what to do: Find two old doors at a yard sale or scrap yard. Paint or decorate them how you please, then hinge them together. Place the doors in the corner of the room at a 90-degree angle to each other so that you make a "box." Use one as the door of your new closet, and the other to hang shelves and attach a bar to. Suspend a clothes line between them for additional hanging. It may not be fancy, but we bet your friends will be impressed!

Who Knew?

January is National Get Organized Month. Celebrate by organizing your entire house! Or at least clean out that junk closet.

CHAPTER 13

Make Cooking
A Breeze

Mom's Omelet Secret

The best omelet you will ever eat has mustard in it. Just add ¼
teaspoon fancy mustard for each egg, and mix in when scrambling.
The mustard will add a hint of mysteriously delicious flavor to the eggs,
as well as making them the perfect consistency.

—*Aggie Bossolina, Jupiter, FL*

Chop Up Your Veggies

When cooking, avoid crunchy vegetables by slicing them up a bit
smaller. If you chop your veggies into tinier pieces, they'll cook more
evenly throughout. As an added bonus, they'll finish cooking more
quickly, too.

Wilted Lettuce No More

When we grew up, making a salad with wilted lettuce was a sin on par
with serving moldy bread. Do your best to dry the leaves after you
wash them. Once you put them in the salad bowl, you can keep off
excess water by piling them on top of an upside down plate that's on
the bottom of the bowl. Moisture will still collect along the bottom, but
the lettuce will remain a safe distance away.

Quickly Ripen Tomatoes

To bring already-picked tomatoes from green to red, place them in a
closed paper bag with an apple.

Double Frosting

This simple little trick saves money and calories. You may not have time
to make your own frosting, but you can blend store-bought frosting
with a hand mixer to double the volume.

Spoon Slipping Solution

At our house, all of our wooden mixing spoons have a rubber band wrapped tightly around the top of the handle. Why? Because they keep the spoons from falling into whatever you're stirring. Wrap some rubber bands around your spoons and you can safely rest the spoon on the side of the bowl without it slipping.

Cleaning Utensils as You Go

This cooking tip operates on the same principle as a kindergarten paint session. Just keep a jar with warm soapy water on your counter and place whatever knife or other utensil you're working with in it when you're done with that part of the recipe. When you need it again, you don't have to stop what you're doing to wash it. A quick rinse will do. Then again, one of us (not naming names) saves time by just reusing dirty utensils for the rest of the night.

Get Rid of Fish Odor Before It Starts

When frying up fish in a pan, add a dollop of peanut butter. It won't affect the taste of the fish, but it will affect the odor—peanut butter contains a chemical that absorbs that stinky fish odor, so your whole house doesn't have to.

—Marlena Kahn, Steubenville, OH

Cup a' Joe with a Twist

Flavored coffee is such a treat, but most families can barely manage to keep enough of the regular stuff stockpiled. Luckily, it's easy to add your own flavors with ingredients you have on hand. Orange peel, vanilla extract, cinnamon, allspice, or ground-up roasted nuts can all be added to coffee grinds before you brew. To make six cups of coffee, you just need ¼ teaspoon of whatever flavor you choose. Experiment to get the proportions exactly right.

Fix a Salt Shaker

You love your antique rooster-shaped salt shaker, but every time you shake it over something way too much salt empties out. Easily fix this problem by painting over a few of the holes with clear nail polish.

Sweetest Corn

To make the sweetest, freshest tasting corn you've ever had, add ¼ cup powdered milk to the pot while you're boiling it.

Award-Winning Pies

You'll impress even Martha Stewart with this one. After you've crimped the crust, but before you place your work of art in the oven, go around the edge again, this time carefully lifting the crust up ever-so-slightly from the dish so it won't stick while baking. When you go to serve pieces "just like Grandma made" they'll come out in one clean swoop rather than insides slopped on the plate followed by hacked up pieces of the crust.

Strawberry Days

Hate the waste of lopping off strawberry stems with a knife but like to serve the delicious summer treats ready-to-eat? Try this: After washing, push the stems out from the bottom up using a plastic straw.

Getting Your Cake to Come Clean

Your beautiful cake is perfect except for one thing—you can't get it out of the pan! Lay out a sheet of wax paper and gently turn the whole thing over. Next, put a dishtowel over the pan and iron it with a hot steam iron. After a few minutes the pan should be ready for lift-off.

Keeping Pasta Warm

Here's a trick that will keep freshly cooked pasta warmer longer. Place a large mixing bowl underneath your colander as you drain the pasta. The hot water will fill the bowl and heat it up. Once the bowl is warm, dump out the water and put the pasta in the bowl instead. Then cover the bowl and take your time finishing the rest of your meal.

Husking Corn

The easiest way to husk corn is to cut off both ends, then roll the corn on your counter for a moment. The husk will then peel right off!

—*Sona Gajiwala, Chicago, IL*

Bag Your Fruit

If you have some unripe fruit that you'd like to ripen faster, simply place it in a plastic garbage bag. The gases released by the fruit will remain trapped in the bag, causing it to ripen more quickly. Make sure not to seal the bag airtight, though—a little bit of ventilation is necessary.

A Different Kind of Soup Stone

Have you ever had to throw out a batch of soup because you accidentally oversalted it? Not anymore! Potatoes contain starch, which absorbs salt, so all you need to do is peel a raw potato or two and toss it in the soup. Let the pot simmer for about 15 minutes before removing the potato, and your soup will be almost good as new.

Stuck Marshmallows?

It's time for s'mores, but when you take the marshmallows out of the cupboard, they're all stuck together! Separate them by adding a bit of cornstarch to the bag, then shaking vigorously. The cornstarch will absorb the moisture that is keeping them stuck together and break them apart.

Protecting Your Cookbooks

A well-worn cookbook is a good sign, but company shouldn't be able to guess your favorite recipes just by inspecting the splatters. So here is yet another use for one of the million plastic bags taking over your pantry: Use one to cover the binding and pages surrounding the recipe you are using. You can then lay a sheet of plastic wrap over the page you are on.

Who Knew?

Sugary or tomato-based BBQ sauces should be added only at the end of the grilling process, because both will burn easily.

Make Leftover Onion Last Longer

You've chopped up half an onion and you'd like to save the rest for later. Make sure the onion lasts longer in your fridge by rubbing the cut end with butter, then wrapping in plastic wrap.

Quick Fix for Curdling

If you've added too much citrus to dairy and caused it to curdle, add an ice cube to the mix and you'll be back in business in no time. The cold will actually reverse the curdling process.

—*Charles Strohm, Calgary, AB*

Pitting Cherries

For a quick and easy way to pit cherries, use a pastry bag tip. Just set the tip on a cutting board with the jagged edge pointed up, then firmly press the cherry down on top of it. Be careful not to cut your fingers!

Make Your Pans Last Longer

When cooking on a gas stove, the flame should extend no farther than two-thirds up the pan. (If it does, opt for a bigger pan.) Never leave an empty pan on a hot stove for more than a couple of minutes, and keep an eye out for shiny rainbow-colored marks on the pan. These are signs that you've been cooking at too high a heat.

Remove Rust from Your Knife

If your knife is rusty, it's time to chop some onions. Believe or not, onions will remove rust from metal objects. Plunge the knife into the biggest onion you can find, let it sit for a few seconds, then pull it out. Repeat this process until the rust has dissolved, then wash as usual and dry.

Stop Stove Disasters

Keep pots of pasta or rice from boiling over by adding a tablespoon of butter to the water when you add the pasta or rice.

Freshen Your Hands

Reach for the mouthwash when you're cooking with garlic, onions, fish or anything else that can leave a scent on your hands. Just pour a few tablespoons into your palms, rub your hands together, and the smell will disappear.

Grapes Are Easy

After rinsing newly purchased grapes, leave them in the colander for refrigerator storage. Grapes are actually helped by lots of cool air, and the holes in the colander will allow the air to more freely circulate around them.

—*Teddy Levy, Casper, WY*

● Who Knew? CLASSIC TIP

If you know to put toothpicks in a cake before covering it with plastic wrap for travel, you're halfway there. The only problem is that sometimes the toothpicks poke right through the wrap and defeat the purpose. The solution? Miniature marshmallows, of course. Our six-year-old loves to carefully place one marshmallow on the top of each toothpick (and then pop the rest in his mouth). Much better results than when we let him apply the actual frosting.

Separating Eggs

Even if you don't have an egg separator, it's easy to separate an egg's yolk from its white. Place the smallest funnel you have over a container, then gently crack the egg into it. The white will slide into the container, while the yolk will stay behind.

Fix a Cookbook Problem Before It Starts

Oops! You just spilled on your favorite cookbook. Don't despair. Simply blot the page with a paper towel and then insert a piece of waxed paper on the page before closing the book. The pages won't stick together.

Makin' Bacon?

Always rinse bacon under cold water before frying—it will reduce the amount the bacon shrinks when you cook it.

Smooth Grating

Problem: You want to break your addiction to buying pre-grated cheese in bags, but cleaning up the cheese grater is always a pain. Solution? Put the grater in the freezer or run it under cold water for several minutes before grating, and the cheese won't stick. You can also try spraying it with cooking spray before each use.

Goodbye to Dry Burgers

The secret to juicy burgers is simple. Just let them sit, covered, at room temperature for an hour before you cook them. This is safe to do as long as it isn't too hot (over 80°) where they will be resting.

If you're like us, scorched rice isn't exactly a rarity in your kitchen. To fix this common mistake, turn the burner off and place a slice of white bread on top of the rice, then replace the lid. Wait 4–5 minutes and the scorched taste will be gone.

Decrystalizing Honey

There's nothing more sweetly delicious than real honey, but we find it often gets thick and full of crystals after a little while in the cabinet. To get it back to its former consistency, simply place the open container in the microwave, then heat on high for 10 seconds and stir. Continue microwaving in 10-second increments and stir until it's back to its lovely, spreadable self.

Nice Ice Cubes

Yes, even ice cubes can be perfected. Do yours look like they've melted and refrozen a hundred times? Make them beautiful and clear by using water that you've boiled, cooled, then poured into the tray.

For That Last Bit of Ketchup

The last bits of tomato sauce, ketchup, salsa, or chutney left in their bottles and jars are great to use in marinades. Simply add some vinegar and oil to the bottle and shake. The liquid will pour out easily. Now add a little onion, garlic, and spices, and you have a marinade!

—*Lupe Velasquez*

Beating Egg Whites

When you're going to beat egg whites for a recipe, let the eggs sit at room temperature for 30 minutes before using them. The egg whites will then beat to a greater volume.

Who Put the Apples in the Cookie Jar?

Chewy, homemade cookies are one of the great pleasures in life. So it's hard not to get disappointed when cookies dry out and turn crispy in the jar. It turns out a few apple slices thrown in will keep them as chewy as the day they were made (or brought out of the box). If your cookies have already hardened, soften them back up by brushing them with a little bit of milk and heating them in a 225° oven for five minutes.

Storing Fresh Herbs

Fresh parsley and cilantro are crisp, flavorful additions to any dish, but they always go bad so quickly. Both will last for at least a couple of weeks if you store them in a jar. Just clip the stems of the herbs, and place them in a jar with water in it, stems down. Cover loosely with a plastic bag and refrigerate.

Mess-Free Mashing

The quickest way to "chop" nuts is to place them in a sealed plastic bag, then roll over them with a rolling pin. This is also a clean, easy way to break up graham crackers or vanilla wafers to make a pie crust.

Cork Your Soda

Lost the cap to your soda bottle? Use a wine cork instead! They're usually the perfect size.

—*Maria Delakis, Shaker Heights, OH*

Picking Up Persistent Ice Cubes

If you're trying to retrieve a stubborn ice cube from the ice cube tray, here's a surefire trick. Run your finger under running water for a second, then press it to the center of the cube. The ice will stick to your finger long enough for you to transfer it into your glass.

Who Knew? CLASSIC TIP

When you finish a stick of butter, don't throw the paper wrapper away. Instead, fold in half and store in a plastic bag. Next time you need to prepare a buttered bowl or pan, use the buttered paper—it's easy and neat!

Bungled Beaters

If your hand mixer isn't what it used to be thanks to jiggling beaters, hardened food in its sockets may be to blame. Take out the beaters and clean out the sockets with a toothpick or bobby pin.

Give Your Potatoes an Apple

To keep your potatoes from producing buds before you use them, store them in a bin with an apple. The apple will slow down sprouts before they start.

Extra Cooling Rack

Keep your cool during holiday baking days. When you're covered with flour, have no idea where the kitchen table used to be, and just pulled the fifth blistering hot tray of gingerbread men out of the oven, simply flip over cardboard egg trays (you'll need two, spaced a little bit apart) and set the baking pan on top.

It's Burger Time

When freezing burgers or chops, always separate with sheets of parchment paper before storing in freezer bags. The paper makes it easy to remove the meat when it's time to cook.

Slicing Chicken

Cutting chicken into bite-sized pieces for dishes like pastas and stir-frys is easier when it's half frozen. Place fresh chicken in the freezer for two hours before you start dinner for easy cutting. Or, place frozen chicken in the microwave and cook on the defrost setting for about five minutes, turning halfway through.

Secret to Easily Peeling Garlic

To get garlic cloves to separate from their skins, break apart each individual clove from the head and heat on high in the microwave for 5–10 seconds. This tiny bit of cooking should make them easily slip out of their skins.

—*Jennifer Nelson, Philo, CA*

For Carrots That Keep

Always store your carrots with the tops removed. The green parts will pull moisture from the carrots while they're in the bin.

Jar Problem?

It might be handy to have a man around the house, but you won't need one with these jar-opening tips. If you have a jar you can't open, first try putting on some latex dishwashing gloves. If it still won't budge, wrap a few rubber bands around the lid for extra grip. If that doesn't work, run some hot water and hold the lid underneath it, turning the jar so the water hits all the edges of the lid. Then tap the edges several times with a butter knife, dry the lid, and try opening it with the gloves again. As a final attempt, smack the bottom of the jar squarely with the flat of your palm, then immediately try the lid again. This will send an air bubble to the top of the jar to hopefully help your cause.

Perfect Rice, Reheated

Ordering in Chinese always left us with leftover rice, but it never tasted quite right when we reheated it. I finally perfected (OK, stumbled upon) the perfect microwaving method. Place the rice in its original container or in a microwave-safe bowl. Cover it, then microwave for one minute on medium (50 percent) heat. Stir, then re-cover and heat for another minute on high. Let sit for one minute more and you'll have perfect rice.

—*Brian Shelby, Brooklyn, NY*

Shower Caps in the Kitchen

Plastic wrap is perfect for covering bowls of rising dough, but if you leave the room for too long the dough will push the wrap right off, leaving it susceptible to germs in the open air. Solve this problem by switching out the plastic wrap for a plastic shower cap—the elastic will fit perfectly over your bowl, and the plastic will stretch enough to allow for expansion.

Overdone Spaghetti?

If you forgot your simmering pot on the stove and your noodles are limp and mushy, try this trick. First run them under the coldest water possible—this will stop the cooking process immediately, and make the starch inside them contract. If you're making a dish with tomato sauce, heat them back up directly in the sauce, as the acid will help them hold up even better.

For Pancakes That Are as Light as Air

Substitute club soda for water when making pancakes, and they'll be fluffier than clouds.

Breaded Cutlets: Hold the Crumbs

Breaded cutlets are less appealing when the breadcrumbs have all dropped off in the oven. One extra step is all you need. After coating with crumbs, let the cutlets dry on a baking rack for 10 minutes, *then* cook.

Use a Potato to Erase Food Stains

This is a great tip that was taught to me by my grandmother after a grueling day of Thanksgiving cooking: To remove food stains on your hands, rub them on a peeled, raw potato. They'll come off like magic!

—*Megan O'Brien, Lovelock, NV*

Born Again Chips

It's 2 a.m.—do you know where your chips are? Yes, but unfortunately, they've been there way too long. Microwaving, which turns bread to mush, has the opposite effect on chips. Just give them a whirl for a minute on a glass plate. Be careful when you bring them out; they may need to cool down a bit before you can eat them.

Say Goodbye to Stuck Dumplings

To prevent delicate dumplings from sticking to your steamer while cooking, first line the steamer basket with lettuce leaves. Sticky dumplings will be a thing of the past.

Designing With Chocolate the Easy Way

Adding a chocolate design to cakes, brownies, and other confections gives them a sophisticated touch sure to be appreciated by your friends. To easily use chocolate for decorating, place old candy, unwrapped, in a plastic sandwich bag. Microwave for 30 seconds at a time, turning until melted. Then snip off the corner and use like a pastry bag to write words and create embellishments.

Perfect Cake Slicing

Keep crumbling to a minimum when slicing a cake by dipping your knife in cold water between every slice.

Leave the Seeds

When using only part of a red, green, or yellow pepper, cut it from the bottom or the sides, leaving the seeds attached, and it will remain moist for longer. You can put the rest in a resealable plastic bag and use it 3–4 days later.

Cleaner Basting Brushes

There's nothing like a gooey, smelly basting brush to ruin your mood. Put a stop to it today! After your usual washing routine with hot water and soap, dry it off a bit by shaking. Here's the cool part, which might remind you of your eighth-grade science class. Pour coarse salt into a cup and place the brush inside. Any remaining wetness will be absorbed by the salt, leaving the bristles as clean as can be.

Truss With Floss

You might know that "trussing" means tying the wings and legs of a bird down for more-even cooking. But do you know the best string to use for trussing? Dental floss! Not only does it come in a small container, it's usually easy to get for free at your dentist's office. It's also very strong, and won't burn in high heat.

Storing Milk and Eggs

It turns out the refrigerator door isn't the best place to store your milk and eggs. Because the temperature fluctuates more there, your dairy products may not stay as cold as they need to to stay fresh for a long period of time. Instead, place them on a shelf inside.

Quick Baked Potatoes

Halve the oven time for baked potatoes by placing each medium-sized potato in a muffin tin on its end. Turn over after 10 minutes, and they'll be ready in a half-hour or less.

The Many Uses of a Pizza Cutter

Pizza cutters can be used for a lot more than just pizza. Use your pizza cutter to quickly slice tortillas, sandwiches, pancakes, omelets, brownies, and even stale bread to make croutons.

Hot Sugar!

You're making cookies, but forgot to soften the butter beforehand. Instead of the trial-and-error involved in attempting to soften (but not melt) butter in the microwave, zap the sugar instead. Mixing butter with warm sugar will soften it in a second.

—*Lindsay Herman*

All the Kings Horses Could Not Peel This Egg

We could have saved years of our lives if we had known this trick earlier, not to mention many a cranky morning. When your eggs are boiled, put them inside a container filled with cold water and close the lid. Give a good shake until the eggs crack. That little pesky skin will separate from the white and stay out of your way when you try to peel the egg.

Extra Foam, Please!

A frothy, foamy cappuccino at home can really cheer up the family on a long, rainy afternoon (decaf for the younger crowd). But you don't need to buy an espresso machine or spend hours holding the milk up to one of those little steamers. Instead, once the milk is heated, simply beat it with a handheld mixer. You'll know it's ready when those white, luminous peaks are nicely holding themselves up. Pour into a mug, spoon the foam, and add cinnamon or chocolate powder. Voilà.

Fish Fix

If you're cooking fish but it comes out too dry, brush it with a mixture of equal parts melted butter and lemon juice and some dried or fresh herbs. The butter will help make it moister, while the lemon juice will help it hold together and cause your diners to salivate—perhaps making them less likely to notice your cooking error.

Stuck Cookies

Are your cookies stuck to the cookie sheet? Remove them easily by working some dental floss in between each cookie and the sheet.

Shabby Chic Trivets

Hardware and home improvement stores have lots of ceramic tiles that can be adapted as mix 'n' match trivets. Choose from a variety of designs and colors to add unique accents to your table setting. It's easy enough to affix felt corners (peel and stick) underneath.

Banana-Peeling Secret

When peeling bananas, peel from the bottom up. This will eliminate the banana "strings" you get when peeling from the top down.

Reheating Pizza

The best way to heat up leftover pizza is in the toaster oven, but if you don't have a toaster oven you don't need to endure the soggy crust that results from microwaving a leftover slice. Just place the piece in a covered skillet and heat over medium-low heat until warm.

Bar Cookie Perfection

Want to know the secret to perfectly cut bar cookies? As soon as you remove your sweet creation from the oven, make a ¼-inch incision with a knife and outline your bars. Then once they've cooled, cut all the way. This will ensure that the edges of your cookies are as smooth as can be.

Another Way to Unstick Stuck Cakes

The bad news is that your cake is stuck to the bottom of the pan. But the good news is that it's easy to get out intact—you just need to heat the bottom back up. This is easily accomplished by submerging the bottom of the pan in hot water. Once the pan heats back up, use a knife to easily dislodge your still-perfect cake.

Lower-Calorie Sweetener

In spiced recipes like muffins and biscuits, try reducing the amount of sugar in your recipes by half and doubling the cinnamon. Not only will the cinnamon taste help retain sweetness with the least calories possible, it has also been shown to help control blood sugar levels.

⬤ Who Knew?

Spices and dried herbs keep their flavor better if stored in a cupboard away from heat, light, and moisture, all of which impair flavor, change color, and shorten life. Herbs and ground spices will generally retain their best flavor for a year. Whole spices last one year.

Butter Your Veggies

When you scrape out the last of the margarine from the tub, don't throw the container away just yet. Throw some vegetables into the tub, microwave it for a few seconds, and voilà!—instant yummy veggies.

Intoxicating Tenderizer

Do you tend to buy those tougher, bargain-priced meats at your local supermarket? If so, you can tenderize them without spending extra money on powdered tenderizer. Just let your meat soak in a can's worth of beer for at least an hour, and that should do the job.

Turkey Trouble

When you're stuffing that Thanksgiving turkey with dressing, you may have trouble with the stuffing sticking inside the bird after cooking. To prevent this, wrap the stuffing in cheesecloth before cooking. When the turkey is done, pull out the cheesecloth and the stuffing will slide right out.

Pancakes: Heinz's 58th Variety

If you're the family pancake chef, make your job a lot easier by thoroughly rinsing out a squeezable ketchup or salad dressing bottle. Pour the batter in and squeeze, and you'll have neater, rounder, and more precise pancakes. You can even store the leftover amount in the fridge for next time.

Cut Your Cake and Eat It Too

If you've got a delicate cake that falls apart and sticks to the knife when you cut it, use dental floss—yes, dental floss—to cut it instead. Hold the floss tight and give it a slight sawing motion as you move it down to cut through the cake. This trick also works for blocks of soft cheese.

Don't Let Apples Go to Waste

If you have a bunch of apples that are going to go bad soon, here's how you can use them up quickly: Cut them into wedges or smaller chunks, dump them in a saucepan, and sauté them in butter over medium heat. When that's finished, sprinkle a half sugar/half cinnamon mixture on top, and you've got a yummy treat that the kids will love. You can even use them as the start of a homemade apple pie!

Butter Softener

Whenever I need soft butter and all I have is hard, refrigerated sticks, I simply shave off the needed amount with a vegetable peeler. In a matter of seconds, the butter shavings will be soft.

—Grace Carrick, Arlington, VA

● Who Knew? CLASSIC TIP

Bread gone stale? Simply wet your fingers and flick some water on each surface. Then wrap in foil and heat in an 250° oven for 10 minutes.

Measuring Hint

When measuring sticky foods like peanut butter or cream cheese, first rinse the inside of the measuring cup with hot water. The food you're measuring will slide out easily into your bowl.

Getting Cutting Boards to Stay Put

Cutting boards that slip around on the counter are an obvious no-no, yet it's amazing how often we turn cutting a watermelon into an extreme sport in our house. We finally figured out that all that extra shelf liner in the pantry *did* in fact come in handy one day. We simply cut it to the right size to use as a placemat for the board and it never slipped again.

Corn's Up

According to the unwritten laws of *The Guy's Guide to Life and Cooking*, everything edible can be grilled, but even our little guys had to concede that grilled mac 'n' cheese just wasn't working. Grilled corn, on the other hand, really is good. The trick is to shuck it down to the last layer of the husk and cut off the furry edges with scissors. Pop those babies on the grill and watch for the moment when the husk starts to show the outline of the kernels and the top edges begin to peel down. The ears are ready.

Hand Me That Cob

Yes, there's a utensil specifically designed for pulling corn out of boiling water (tongs). But if you can't find them and the corn is just right, a potato masher does the trick quite nicely with a tiny bit of balance. And our 11-year-old says airlifting the cobs this way is great practice for the crane machine filled with toys at the arcade!

Perfect, Easy Deviled Eggs

Here's a method for making deviled eggs that's so simple you'll want to make them for every picnic you go to. After hard-boiling eggs, slice them open and place their yolks in a resealable plastic bag. After mashing them up through the bag, add the mayonnaise and the rest of the ingredients. Mash some more to blend, then cut off the corner of the bag and use like a pastry bag to easily dispense the mixture into egg halves.

Say No to Flour

Hate that white floured look your cakes end up with after you flour the edges of your cake pan before baking? Make it a thing of the past by reserving a small amount of cake mix, then using it instead of flour to flour your pans.

Bake Me a Cake

Remember the rest of the line from this nursery rhyme? "As fast as you can." Those pre-made mixes from a box are so easy, but you can recreate the effect *and* maintain bragging rights to a homemade dessert. Measure things out a few days before you plan to bake. Store the mixes in Ziploc bags (for dry) and plastic containers (for wet), making sure wet stuff gets into the refrigerator. Eggs should be added the day of. We find this trick especially great for holiday bake-offs when we like to give tins of various cookies to neighbors and friends.

The Right Pan at the Right Time

You shouldn't need a ruler in the kitchen. Yet when a recipe gives you cooking times for five different pan sizes, you wish you knew the actual measurements of your baking pans. And now you will. All you have to do is use nail polish to mark the dimensions on the bottom of each pan. Then put that ruler back in the home office where it belongs.

CHAPTER 14

Dogs, Cats, and Other Pets

Due Doggie Diligence

When you're choosing what kind of pet to buy, make sure to research the different breeds before selecting one—even Wikipedia is a big help. For instance, did you know that dalmatians are among the most high-strung dogs, while beagles will often scamper away because they're always following their noses? It's always best to select a pet that's been raised by a friend or a reputable shelter; avoid puppy mills, which tend to mass-produce poorly adjusted pets. Remember, too, that while purebred animals are supposedly status symbols, they're also much less hardy and more prone to diseases than mutts.

Who Knew? CLASSIC TIP

Never have to throw away an ant-infested bowl of pet food again. Simply sprinkle some ground cinnamon around the bowl, and the ants will stay away.

How to Handle Pet Hair

If you don't have the heart to banish your pet from the couch, here's a solution for removing all that hair from your sofa. Just put on some rubber kitchen gloves or surgical latex gloves and then wipe the hair into a pile with your hand. Discard it and then repeat the process. After you've gotten most of the hair, take a sheet of fabric softener from the laundry room and use it to pick up the rest—the hair will be naturally attracted to it. When that's done, use a vacuum cleaner to add the finishing touch.

Help Pet Food Stay Put

If your pet's food dish always ends up three feet from where it started by the time he's done eating, make it skid-proof. With a glue gun, make a thin strip of glue around the bottom rim. The hardened glue will make it much harder for the bowl to slide across the floor.

Untangle Fur

Pet owners know that matted hair can make brushing your animal a frustrating experience for you—and a painful one for them. To prevent this, rub your pet with baby powder prior to brushing. It'll be easier to remove the tangles, for which both you and your pet will be grateful.

Save on Your Pet's Care

We all love our pets and will go to any length to make sure they are happy and healthy, but this shouldn't mean taking out a second mortgage to pay vet bills. Look at your local shelter to see what services they provide. Many will spay/neuter and administer vaccinations and annual shots for less than half the price of your friendly neighborhood vet.

Mutt Munchies

If your dog is teething, you can create a cheap chew toy by soaking an old washcloth in water, twisting it into a fun shape, and leaving it in the freezer. Give it to your pup fully frozen, and when it thaws out, simply repeat the process. Be careful doing this with tiny dogs, though, as they can get too cold if they chew on frozen toys too often.

Ease Painful Pads

If your poor pet's pads are cracked or dry, the solution is simple. Gently rub a little petroleum jelly into her pads while she's sleeping. It will moisturize the area and is completely safe if your pet decides she wants to lick it off later.

Butter Up Pills

If you have trouble getting your cat to swallow pills, try rubbing them in butter first. It will make them taste better to your cat, and they'll slide right down his throat.

Rein in Pet Hair

Cleaning out your own brush is bad enough, but cleaning out the one that belongs to your furry companion can be a half a day's work. Instead of getting angry next time you snag your pantyhose, give them a second life. Cut strips of hose and lay them over your pet's clean metal brush, poking the pins of the brush through. The next time your cat or dog looks like he just stepped out of a salon after a heavy brushing, all you'll have to do is remove the scraps of material, throw them out, and replace with new strips.

Who Knew?

If you have both cats and dogs, you may be tempted to feed your cat dog food. Don't do it! Besides being highly insulted if he happens to see the can, your cat needs certain nutrients that are found only in food made specifically for cats.

Routine Is Key

If you've ever had your pet wake you up precisely five minutes before your alarm goes off so she can be fed, you know that animals are creatures of routine. Changes in behavior could be a sign that something is wrong with your pet. Just to be sure, you should take her to the vet if you notice changes in appetite, thirst, frequency of urination, energy level, hiding behavior, or anything else that seems strange to you. Your pet will thank you!

For Smelly Cats and Dogs

Sometimes, your pet is just plain stinky. If you're beginning to notice pet odor when you open your front door, it's time to take action. Add a bit of brewer's yeast (1 teaspoon for cats and small dogs and 1 tablespoon for bigger dogs) to your pet's food and your pet will secrete less of those unpleasant odors.

Get Rid of Fleas

You can remove pesky fleas from your pet's coat without having to pay for expensive flea collars or medications. Simply bathe your pet in salt water, and the fleas will stay way. You can also try steeping rosemary in warm water and using that as bathwater. Better yet, use a combination of the two.

Treat Your 'Keet

If you have a parakeet or other bird, make sure you have perches in various diameters. Birds' talons don't get a proper workout unless they have different things to grasp. Use tree branches or store-bought perches, especially those with a rough feeling, to keep your bird exercised and happy.

Beware Poisonous Plants

If your pet likes chewing on plants, beware: Some common house and garden plants are poisonous to animals. They include rhododendron, daffodils, crocus, lilies, poinsettia, holy, mistletoe, lantana, laburnum, taro, yew, cyclamen, foxglove, hyacinth, hydrangea, rhubarb, narcissus, and the pits of many fruits like apricots, plums, and peaches. If you see your pet eat any of these, take him to the vet immediately!

To a Cat, Anything (and Everything) Is a Toy

Cats love toys, and they aren't picky about where they come from! Don't spend money on expensive cat toys. Instead, use a balled up piece of paper, a cork, a jingle bell, or anything else they can bat around the house. To make the toy extra enticing, throw it in a tissue box that has the plastic part removed. Cats will love sticking their paws inside to try to fish out the toy.

Secret to Shiny Fur

To make your short-haired cat's fur extra-shiny, rub it down with a piece of silk, velvet, or chamois cloth.

Build a Doggie Path

If your dog tends to track mud into the house, you can confine that mess to one area by creating a walkway for him to use before entering. The best bet is filling a path with gravel, which helps keep mud off the pooch's paws and keeps the house cleaner.

Who Knew? CLASSIC TIP

When getting a "treat" for being good, most dogs are just excited about a special snack, not that it's in the shape of a bone. Instead of paying extra for dog treats, keep a separate container of dog food where you normally keep the treats, then give your dog a small handful when he's done something reward-worthy.

Scent of a Pet Owner

If you're going to be unable to pay attention to your pet for a while—such as when she's in a carrier on a long trip—put an old, worn T-shirt (the best are ones you've recently exercised in) inside the pet carrier with her. Your scent will help ease your pet's worries.

Pet Mess

If you're training a new pet, here's the best way to get accidental wet spots out of the carpet. First soak up as much of the pet mess as possible with paper towels. Then combine 2 cups warm water, $\frac{2}{3}$ cup vinegar, and 2 teaspoons dishwashing detergent. Mix everything together, then blot the stain carefully with the solution, making sure not to apply excess liquid. Rinse it off with tap water and dry it with paper towels. When the carpet is completely dry—usually the next day—kill off the lingering smell by sprinkling a heavy dose of baking soda on the spot and letting it sit for one hour before vacuuming up.

Stave Off Shedding

Even regular brushing can't get every last stray hair off your pet, but a dryer sheet can. Run a dryer sheet over your pet's coat and static will cause any loose hairs to be picked up.

Fat Cat?

If you have trouble getting your cat to play with toys for exercise, make him or her work a little for food! First you'll need a cylindrical container—a yogurt container (with the yogurt and foil removed) that has a top for granola or candy works well. Cut a hole in one or both ends and re-enforce with masking or duct tape, to make sure there are no sharp edges in the plastic. Then put some dry food inside and put it in front of your cat. Cats love the noise the food makes when rattling around inside, and will continue to bat at the toy to get the food to come out.

Provide Ice Cubes During Transit

You're taking your pet on the plane, but you're worried about her getting water while you travel. Instead of filling a water dish with water, which can splash out during transit, put a few ice cubes in the dish. Once your pet's cage is settled in cargo, the ice cubes will melt, giving her some much-needed refreshment.

—Art Gallagher, Burnside, CT

A Bath for Your Goldfish

Before you clean out your goldfish's bowl, first prepare a salt-water bath for him. Even though goldfish are freshwater fish, salt will help your fish absorb much-needed electrolytes and kill any parasites on his fins. To get the salt water ready, run tap water into a bowl and let it sit for a day to allow the chlorine to evaporate (you should do this when filling his freshwater bowl, too). Add a teaspoon of non-iodized salt and mix until it dissolves. Then let Goldy go for a swim in the salt water for approximately 15 minutes.

When the Cat's Away Your Plants Will Be Happier

Here are two ways to keep feline visitors away from your indoor garden. Make a protective circle of crushed-up pine cones around the stems of your plants and mist the leaves with a combination of water and a few teaspoons of vinegar.

Prevent Sunburn

Did you know that light-colored animals can get sunburn, too? Guard against this by dabbing a bit of SPF 15 sunscreen on your pet's nose and the tips of his ears.

Eliminating Cat Smell

If the smell from your in-heat housecat's spray has more than nine lives, try mixing one cup hydrogen peroxide with ½ tablespoon baking soda and two squirts liquid dish soap. Pour into a spray bottle and use wherever Fluffy has left her trademark. (Be sure to spot-check as you run the risk of bleaching certain materials.)

Easy Dog Toy

Dog toys are expensive and can be made from harmful materials. In the colonial era, kids made their own dolls from rags. A canine version will make Fido just as happy as any designer plush toy. All you need to do is braid together three old dishtowels. Before you start, cut two strips off the side of two of them. Then use these to tie the tops and bottoms of the braid together.

Traveling With a Pet?

To make pets calmer while traveling with them in a car, add a few drops of Bach's Rescue Remedy to their water. Its all-natural ingredients will help pets stay calm just as well as it helps humans do.

Get Rid of Ear Mites

A great household remedy for ear mites is to rub a cotton ball soaked in 1 teaspoon baking soda that has been dissolved in 1 cup warm water. Of course, if you see a pet scratching his ears, you should always take him to the vet first, just to be sure.

Time for a Bath

You've finally trained your dog how to be good while getting a bath in the tub, but his tiny hairs always slip through your drain's catcher and clog up your pipes. To keep this from happening, stuff some steel wool into the opening (but not too far down). It will catch every hair from even the furriest of creatures. When you're done bathing, make sure to fish the steel wool out immediately.

Fido Being Finicky?

If you've bought a new brand of food and your dog doesn't want to eat it, put a piece of beef jerky in the bag and reseal it. By the next day, the smell will have worn off on the food, making it seem much more appetizing.

Birds Get Lonely, Too!

It may seem silly, but not to your bird—put a mirror in his cage to make sure he doesn't get lonely. The bird will see the reflection of himself and think it's another bird to keep him company. Of course, the other solution is simply buying your bird a real feathered friend!

Who Knew? CLASSIC TIP

Is your dog leaving brown spots on your lawn where he decides to pee? Put a few drops of vinegar into his water bowl every time you refill it and brown spots will be a thing of the past.

Does Your Cat Have a Weak Stomach?

If you have a cat who frequently vomits, you should (of course) take her to the vet. Unfortunately, your vet might tell you that some cats just throw up a lot. (Why do we love them so much again?) If your cat frequently vomits, it could be because she's eating too fast. Try leaving dry food out all day, to let her eat at her own pace. But if she becomes overweight, this might not be an option. Another trick to try is pulverizing some mint with some fresh catnip and seeing if she'll eat it—mint is good for calming stomachs.

Removing Ticks

You and your dog just enjoyed a fun romp through the forest, but now the poor guy has ticks in his fur! To more easily remove them, first wet a Q-tip with rubbing alcohol. Dab it on the tick, and he'll loosen his grip. You should then be able to pull the tick straight off your dog.

Bad Breath Bomb

If your cat or dog has horrible breath, try adding some fresh chopped parsley to his food.

Easiest Way to Clean a Fish Tank

Having fish is fun, but not when you have to periodically replace the water. Make your job easy with the help of some old pantyhose and a wet/dry shop vac. Place two or three layers of pantyhose over the nozzle of the hose and secure it with a rubber band. Remove your fish to a safe location, then stick the hose in the tank and start sucking. The dirty water will find its way into the vacuum, but the rocks won't make it through the nylon.

Ant Problem Solved

Petroleum jelly will keep ants out of a pet food dish. Simply rub a small amount on the rim around the bottom of bowl.

Get Rid of Litter Box Odor

If your cat's litter box smells like, well, a litter box, rinse it out and add a half-inch of white vinegar in the box. Let it stand for half an hour, then swish it around, rinse, and dry the box.

Keep Small Animals Calm

If you have a rabbit, guinea pig, hamster, or other small pet who lives in a cage, try refilling his water dish by sticking a turkey baster through the bars. It will allow you to give him something fresh to drink without scaring him by opening the door and moving things around.

Easier Than a Bath

Washing a pet can sure be a hassle—especially if it's a cat. Save yourself the trouble (and several scratches) by using cornstarch instead. Sprinkle cornstarch on your pet's coat, then work it into his hair. It will soak up grease and odors, and even fluff up his fur.

How to Discipline a Cat

Unfortunately, cats rarely respond when you tell them "no." So to make sure they have a reason to not repeat bad behavior, spray them in the face with water from a spray bottle when you catch them being bad. If this doesn't work, try spraying them with air from a compressed air can (usually used to clean electronics and computer keyboards). Cats hate the feeling of air on their faces.

● Who Knew?

It seems like a silly habit of guilty "dog parents," but it's true: Leaving the TV or radio on low in the room next to your pup will keep him calm while you're away.

Scaredy Cats

All cats will run and hide if they hear a loud noise, but some cats seem particularly flighty. If your overly anxious cat runs when she hears regularly occurring noises like shut doors, loud steps, or even sound effects from the TV, here's how to help. Begin by tapping a wooden spoon very gently against or pot or pan while he is eating. Make sure the sound is loud enough that he notices, but not so loud that he gets scared. After you've done this for a couple of days, you can begin slowly increasing how loudly you tap. Once your quiet tap is a loud bang and your cat is still calm, change the surface you're tapping to wood, or try to incorporate a sound that has easily spooked him in the past—just make sure to begin quietly and work your way up again. Finally, begin introducing these sounds into your cat's daily life. Eventually he won't even notice that clap of thunder from outside.

Get Groomed for Less

The busiest days at the pet groomer's are Friday, Saturday, Sunday, and Monday. Find a groomer who offers discounts on Tuesdays through Thursdays, or ask your groomer if she will offer you a discount for coming midweek.

Come Boy, Come!

If your dog simply won't come when called, it might be time to start from scratch. Once a dog has decided that a word doesn't mean anything to him, it's much harder to make him understand that "come" means "come to me," not "do whatever you want." Pick a different word like "here" or "move," and begin your dog's training over again by standing several feet away, saying your new word, and offering scraps of food when he obeys. Your friends at the dog park might think it's weird when you shout, "Draw nigh, Rover!" but it's way better than having him run the other way.

Pacify a Chewing Puppy

If your new puppy isn't adorable enough to make up for all those chair and table legs he's been chewing, head to your local vitamin or health food store and ask for some clove oil. Oil of cloves smells great to us but terrible to dogs. Wipe it on the legs of anything wooden and he'll stay away.

Pleasant-Smelling Litter

Don't spend extra money on scented cat litter. To keep cat litter fresh-smelling, simply mix a bit of baby powder into clean litter.

—*Peter and Sarah Bailey, Fitchburg, MA*

Lazy Lizards

If you have a lizard, you know how much they like to relax! But did you know that one of their favorite resting places is a hammock? Make one yourself by stringing up an old piece of cloth between two items in your lizard's cage, and you'll soon seem him taking a nap in style.

Lost Your Snake?

If you have a pet snake who's gotten away, help yourself find him with a little aluminum foil. Place the foil around the room and in potential hiding places. When your snake is done lying low, you'll be able to hear him slithering across the foil.

CHAPTER 15

Sanity-Saving Kid Tips

Numb the "Ick" of Taking Medicine

Nothing's worse than having to give a sick child medicine he can't stand the taste of. To make things a little easier, have him suck on a popsicle for a few minutes before taking the medicine. The popsicle will not only act as an incentive, it will numb his taste buds a bit, making the medicine easier to swallow.

Good Backpack Fix

If your child tears his backpack, there's no need to buy a new one. Just thread some floss onto a needle with a large eye, and use that to sew up the hole. It's sturdier than regular thread and will hold up well.

Don't Drop the Cup

If your children, like our youngest, have graduated past the sippy cup stage but still have problems getting a grip on "grown up" glasses, try putting five or six small rubber bands around the glass. That'll help them hold on, which means fewer spills for you to clean up.

● Who Knew? CLASSIC TIP

To keep melting ice cream from leaking out of the bottom of an ice cream cone, just drop a couple of mini marshmallows at the bottom before topping with ice cream. The marshmallows will act as a delicious plug.

Journey of 1,000 Untied Shoes

We carry emergency ChapStick around with us for the boys, but for their shoes, not their lips. A little rubbed on the laces around the knot keeps them in place, and means we get from the car to the rink (or football field, or school) in about half the time it would otherwise take.

Cheap Child-Proofing

Use a shower curtain ring to keep a toddler out of your cabinets. Just run the ring through two handles that are close by and latch.

—Randy Rodriguez, Waxahachie, TX

Rolling in Dough

Don't spend money on store-bought Play-Doh; make your own at home instead with the following ingredients: 2 cups flour, 2 cups water, 1 cup salt, 2 tablespoons vegetable oil, 1 tablespoon cream of tartar, and the food coloring of your choice. Combine the ingredients in a large saucepan and stir continuously over medium heat until a solid ball forms. Remove it from the heat, knead it until all the lumps are out, and you should end up with a finished product nearly identical to the real thing. Make sure to store it in a completely airtight container; you might even want to dab a few drops of water on the underside of the container lid before sealing it.

Bath Entertainment

For more fun at bath time, take all those little plastic toys your kids have gotten from vending machines and goody bags, and place one or two in each hole of a muffin tin. Then fill the tin with water and freeze. When it's time for a bath, pop one out and throw it in the tub. Your toddler will love watching it melt in their hands and then having a toy to play with.

Frozen Juice Box

When packing a sack lunch for your child, place a juice box in the freezer the night before and place it in the lunch bag while still frozen the next morning. It'll help keep the lunch cool, and as an extra bonus, the juice will be nice and cold when your child finally gets around to drinking it at lunchtime.

—Adriana S., Youngstown, OH

Make Your Kid Stand Out

If you know you're going to a crowded place, make sure to dress your children in bright colors so you can easily spot them. To make them stick out even more, buy each kid a cheap helium balloon and tie it around their wrist. Kids love balloons, and so will you when you realize you can see them from a mile away at the mall.

Who Knew?

Your teen or preteen may be more stressed than you think. According to an American Psychological Society survey, only 2–5 percent of parents said their child was highly stressed, while 14 percent of preteens and 28 percent of teens said they were.

Toy Parachutes

Make an old action figure fun again by creating a mini parachute. First, cut out a square from a plastic sandwich bag. Poke a hole in each corner, then thread a foot-long piece of dental floss through the hole, tying a knot at the end so the floss can't be pulled back through. Once you've threaded a piece of floss through each hole, tie their other ends around the arms or—dare we say it—the neck of the figurine. Now you're ready to launch.

Get the Dents Out of a Ping-Pong Ball

The sound of ping-pong balls being paddled all over the basement is worth every minute of keeping your kids busy! Unfortunately, they finally emerge from downstairs with tons of dented balls. To get the balls round again, fill a jar to the brim with warm water, then place the balls inside and close the lid so that they're submerged. In 20 minutes or less, the water's pressure will make them pop back into place.

Instant Indexing

Our kids, like many, are incorrigible procrastinators when it comes to schoolwork. When they need index cards at a moment's notice, however, a late-night trip to the store is unnecessary. Simply take an ordinary paper plate and measure out a 3-by-5-inch or 4-by-6-inch rectangle. Cut it out and use the first card as a stencil for the rest.

—*Nathaniel M.*

Interesting Art Project

Get creative with watercolors and candles—but perhaps not in the way you think. Give your child a white tapered candle and have her "draw" a picture on a piece of paper. She won't be able to see the drawing, of course, until she adds a little watercolor to the paper—and the picture will come to life. This is an especially good activity for two kids. Let them write "secret messages" to each other, then exchange the papers, apply some watercolors, and see what happens.

Teacher Appreciation

It can be a struggle to find the right gifts for teachers, and yet it's not hard when you think along the lines of something that will enhance their classrooms. Here are some ideas: books, magazine subscriptions, educational games, posters of material they teach (the solar system or animal kingdom, for example), art supplies, easy-to-care-for plants, and gift certificates to bookstores. Many teachers use their own money for classroom supplies, so this kind of gift will be especially gratifying.

Make Your Swing Set Safer

You've just bought your kids a new swing set, and you're peering out the window just waiting for one of them to fall off. Fear no more! Place carpet remnants or free carpet samples from a local store underneath the swings for extra padding. They'll kill the grass underneath, but your kids would have done that anyway.

Who Knew? CLASSIC TIP

Here's a great recipe for homemade bubble solution: 1 tablespoon glycerin, 2 tablespoons powdered laundry detergent, and 1 cup warm water (add a couple of drops of food coloring for colored bubbles). Use a wire hanger to make your own bubble blowing device, or stick a straw into the mixture and blow into it to create tiny bubbles that will float onto the surface and dissipate.

Make Ripping off Band-Aids Painless

Before removing a bandage from your child's skin, douse the area with baby oil. The baby oil will soak into the bandage and make it easy to remove without hurting her.

Eat Those Veggies!

If your child never wants to eat his vegetables at dinnertime, try putting out a plate of raw veggies like carrots, celery, and broccoli right before dinner. Since he'll be hungry (and probably pestering you in the kitchen), it will be more likely that he'll succumb to this healthy snack.

—*Terry Gallo, Breeding, KY*

Swap Out Your Toys

When you notice your kids getting bored with a toy (and they always do), don't buy them a new one. Instead, stash the disfavored toys away in a bag or box. Once you have several toys, swap with a friend for toys her kids have gotten sick of. Not only will you save money, you'll save on the clutter of continually purchasing new playthings for your kids.

Do It Yourself

Organized activities for your kids are great, but the expense of enrolling them can take a toll. Instead of paying for a pricey arts and crafts class, for example, simply search online for the necessary information and hold the "class" yourself. Instead of paying for swimming lessons, just take your kids to a relative's pool or a public pool. Spending on beginner-level instruction is often a waste, but if your child shows an aptitude for a certain activity or sport, *then* you can spend that money on more advanced instruction. If you have to cut down on activities or sports they're already involved in, ask your children if there are any they don't really like. You might find they're just playing soccer, for instance, because their friends are on the team.

Make Your Own Baby Toy

Here's a free, soft toy for your wee one: an old sock! Stuff it with old pantyhose, fiber fill, or even more old socks, then sew it shut to make a soft ball. Sure, it might not look as impressive as the $10 ones you'd buy at a toy store, but your baby won't know the difference!

Getting Rid of Lice Naturally

Nothing strikes fear in the hearts of parents like the words "lice outbreak." The harsh chemicals that are used to fight lice are almost as bad as the lice themselves. Luckily, there is a cheap, natural alternative, and it's as close as your refrigerator. Massage a liberal amount of mayonnaise into your child's scalp, then cover with a shower cap or towel and let it sit as long as possible (overnight is best—but with complaining kids you might have to settle for letting it sit through two movies and a round of video games). Then shampoo as usual, using a fine-toothed comb to snag any remaining lice bodies. To make sure you killed any eggs, repeat this procedure in one week.

Video Game Strategy

If your kids love video games, try to buy games that can be played over and over (such as puzzle games) rather than ones that aren't fun once you "win" them—you'll go a lot longer before you start hearing requests to buy a new game! When you finally do cave, make sure to buy used games whenever possible.

Homemade Glitter

If your kids need glitter in an emergency (and who hasn't had a glitter emergency?), you can make your own at home. Just take a cup of salt, add 10–15 drops of your favorite food coloring, and mix it thoroughly. Microwave on high for 2–3 minutes, then spread it out on a sheet of nonstick foil or wax paper to dry. If you don't use it all right away, make sure to store it in an airtight container.

Rainy-Day Shaker

Short of shaking vitamin bottles, this might be the easiest instrument a human can make. Put dry beans between two paper plates, then tape the plates together. Decorate with markers, crayons, sequins, or anything else you have on hand. Your kids will love creating rhythms with their new toys.

Make Your Own Ceramics

When they were younger, our kids always loved making ceramic objects out of clay. You don't need to sign them up for an art class, either: the clay is easy to make at home. Thoroughly mix the following ingredients in a bowl: 4 cups flour, 1⊠ cups salt, ¾ cup white glue, 1⊠ teaspoons lemon juice, and 1⊠ cups water. When you've got it all mixed together, you should end up with a pliable clay that can be either sculpted into different shapes or sliced with cookie cutters. When your kids are done molding the clay, let their creations sit overnight, allowing them to harden and air-dry. Then they can apply paint and/or glaze.

Exercise Weights as a Balancing Act

If your stroller has become unbalanced thanks to the hundreds of shopping bags you have hanging from the handles, use arm and ankle weights that are used for exercise to more evenly distribute the weight. Attach the weights (which come with Velcro) to the bars of the stroller right above its front wheels. Now when your child jumps out, you won't end up with your bags all over the sidewalk.

—*Donna Inklovich, Calumet City, IL*

Make Slides More Fun

If your kids have tired of that expensive playground set you bought them, make the slide even more fun by giving them each a large piece of wax paper. If they sit on the paper as they're going down the slide, they'll move much faster, and they'll never call it boring again (or at least not for a few weeks).

Homemade Swords

Here's a quick, homemade toy that will keep your kids busy for hours, if not days: Take a large piece of corrugated cardboard and cut it in the shape of a sword (use two pieces and tape them together, if necessary). Wrap the handle with electrical tape and the "blade" with duct tape. Your kids can practice their fencing skills against each other, and since they're playing with cardboard you won't have to worry about them getting hurt.

Take Off Temp Tats

There's nothing kids love more than temporary tattoos—until they decide they hate them. To easily remove a temp tat before it rubs off itself, dab some cold cream on the area, then wipe it off with a washcloth.

Getting Pen Marks Off Skin

Our kids drive us crazy by writing notes and drawing all over their hands (thankfully not answers for tests, as far as we know). The fastest way to get them ready for company: Green or black tea bags. You use the actual wet bag itself to dab at the stains, once you're done brewing a cup with it.

> ## ● Who Knew? CLASSIC TIP
>
> If you've got kids who never seem to know when enough is enough, add water to your hand soap. Your hands will get just as clean, but the soap will last longer! You can also find foaming soap dispensers at a lot of stores, which are also good for keeping the amount of soap you use to the minimum you need.

Cheap Fun That Lasts for Hours

If your young child likes building toys but you don't want to pay for expensive blocks, buy plastic cups in several different colors and use those instead. They're extremely cheap and just as fun to knock down!

Making Puppets

For a fun craft project, have your children make paper lunch bags into puppets. All you have to do is turn the bag upside down, then draw a face on what would be the bottom of the bag. Draw the mouth so that it's half on the bottom, half on the bag itself—that way, when someone puts their hand inside, they can open and close "the mouth." Give your kids extras from your sewing box such as trim, fabric scraps, and buttons to embellish the puppets.

Temper Tantrums Solved

When I'm taking trips with my children, I always bring along a bottle of bubbles. If (and when) a tantrum hits, I take out the bubbles and start blowing. This distracts them enough so that they calm down and I can actually speak to them! By handling over the wand and letting them help, I not only reward them for stopping the screaming, but it allows them to take deep breaths and become even more relaxed.

—Mary Bowers, Salt Lake City, UT

Perfect Bottle Holder

We're a little embarrassed to admit this, but when our boys were young we had the perfect holder for extra bottles for the babysitter: an old six-pack container. If you don't think it's funny to have "Heineken" written on the side, cover with contact paper, wrapping paper, or stickers. Your baby won't know the difference, and you'll make sure to leave with as many bottles as you came with.

Goodbye to Popsicle Drips

Keep messy melting popsicles from getting all over your kids' hands (and the floor) by poking the stick-end of the popsicle through a coffee filter before you hand it over. The filter will act like a bowl, catching any drips.

Popcorn, Without the Dishes

If you're serving popcorn to the kids but don't want to wash a bunch of bowls afterward, consider using coffee filters as disposable bowls.

Kids' Shoelaces Coming Untied?

If your children's shoelaces (or your own) often come untied, you may be tying them wrong. Bows that we tie with shoelaces work by using a square knot—and you may remember the adage "right over left, left over right, that's what makes a square knot nice and tight." Unfortunately, most of us do what's easiest for our hands—and that's tying both the beginning knot and the bow "right over left." If you look down at the shoes and the loops from the bows are pointing toward you rather than laying flat across the shoes from left to right, then you aren't tying a square knot properly! To fix this, simply reverse the way that you tie the beginning knot for your bow. In other words, if you normally cross the right shoelace over the left at the beginning, switch so that you're crossing left over right. It might take your hands a while to get used to it, but your bows will stay so well you won't even need to double-knot them.

Who Knew?

In a survey by the Early Childhood Investment Corporation, parents cited simply being with their children as the best part about parenting, and discipline as the worst part of parenting.

It's Camp Time

The best time to sign your kids up for camp is right after camp has ended. Many camps allow you to pay in advance for the next summer and save 5–10 percent. Ask at your camp as you're picking your kids up this year!

CHAPTER 16

Automotive Advice

Make the Most of That Expensive Gas!

With gas prices as high as they are, it's worth it to try to use the least amount of gas possible when driving. Here are some tips to get the most out of your mileage.

- ✦ Keep your tires inflated. It's much harder for your engine to get your car to move when your tires are even a little flat. Invest in a gauge, and make sure to keep them as inflated as possible without over-inflating.

- ✦ Go manual. If you're buying a new car and can't afford a hybrid, consider going with a stick-shift rather than automatic. Manually changing gears saves energy because your car is only using as much energy as it needs to—it's never in a higher gear when it shouldn't be. Being able to coast down hills also saves you tons.

- ✦ Stay under the speed limit. Your car will begin to lose fuel efficiency once it gets over 60 mph. One of the easiest ways to save money on gas is to always go the speed limit—and it's safer, too.

- ✦ Change your oil regularly. As oil ages, it gets thicker and harder to push through the engine, causing more energy to be used. By changing your oil regularly you'll make sure you get the best fuel economy possible.

- ✦ Remove excess weight. Take anything heavy out of your trunk or back seat that doesn't need to be there (kids don't count). An extra 100 pounds in your car can decrease your miles per gallon by 2 percent.

✦ Pick the best route. Stopping and starting and going up hills will cause you to use more gas. Consider taking a route that will allow you to make fewer adjustments as you are driving, even if it takes a little longer.

✦ Roll up your windows on the highway. Having the wind streaming through your hair might be fun, but it increases drag on the car and makes it take more energy to run. In this case, it's actually usually cheaper to run the AC.

✦ Group your errands. Obviously, if you're driving less distance by not traveling from home each time you'll save on gas, but the Department of Energy also reports that several short trips beginning from a cold start use almost twice as much energy as a single trip of the same length. Keep your engine warm and your car won't have to work as hard.

● Who Knew? CLASSIC TIP

If your windshield wipers are smearing your windshield while they work, wipe the blades with rubbing alcohol.

Educate Yourself Before You Buy

After gas, one of the biggest costs associated with having a car is from the interest you pay on the loan. Before you go buy a car, get a loan in place first—the financing the car dealership will offer most likely won't have a rate that is as good. Know your credit rating, and check with your employer's credit union or look online for deals on car loans. A good place to begin is a page that lets you compare rates and find out information on car loans. One site we like is BankRate.com. Click on "Auto" from the homepage.

Easily Remove Window Frost

Instead of scraping away frost from your car's windows and windshield, spray them with rubbing alcohol when you go out to start up your car. By the time you come back to drive, the frost will easily wipe away.

Keep Car Doors from Freezing

It's hard enough having to dig out your driveway and scrape off your car after a snowstorm. Save yourself the trouble of worrying about car doors freezing closed by spraying WD-40 in the lining. Once in the beginning of the winter should do it.

Condition Your Car

After washing your car, give it a second round just like you would your head—use hair conditioner! You might think we're crazy, but applying conditioner, leaving for five minutes, and then rinsing it off will give your car a just-waxed shine. As an added bonus, it will more effectively repel water!

For Supple Leather

If you car has leather seats, regularly apply a thin layer of baby oil to the leather and let it dry. This will prevent your seats from drying out and cracking.

Put the Brakes On

If an advertised price for fixing your brakes seems too good to be true, it is. Garages can't make a profit on $100 brake jobs, so rest assured that these places are either doing shoddy work, or are counting on sticking you with hidden extra costs. Whenever you get your brakes done, make sure to ask beforehand for an estimate of the final total cost, including all labor fees and other extra charges.

Get the Whole Part

Sometimes unethical mechanics will use cheap or knockoff parts—they're a lot more prevalent than you might think—and try to pass them off as the real thing. Whenever you're having parts replaced, make sure to insist on a brand-name part and ask to see the box it came in as proof.

Transmission A-OK

If you're not an automotive expert, you should be aware that small metal shavings in a transmission pan are a perfectly normal sign of usage. If a garage shows you a pan like this and uses it to pressure you into a new transmission, walk away. They're likely not being honest with you.

—J.D. Morse

Who Knew?

Only 5 percent of cars actually run better on premium gas as opposed to regular. Make sure to check your owner's manual to see what it recommends.

Don't Blow Off a Chipped Windshield

Never, ever ignore a chip in your windshield—get it fixed right away. A chip will often eventually grow into a crack, which will raise your costs from about $100 for a chip repair to $1,000 or more for a full windshield replacement. There are even companies that will repair the chip right there in your driveway; just do a Google search for something like "mobile windshield repair" near your home.

Turn a Visor Into an Organizer

Turn your car's visor into a handy place to store paper and other flat items by using rubber bands. Wrap several rubber bands snugly around the visor, then slip papers, CDs, or anything else under the rubber bands.

Covered in Tar?

You took a trip over some recently tarred roads, and now your bumper is covered in black spots. Get rid of tar with an unexpected item from your fridge—mayonnaise. Wipe on, wait five minutes, then easily wipe off both the mayo and the tar.

Take Two Aspirin for Yourself, Then Two for Your Car

If your car battery has died and you don't have jumper cables, don't get a headache just yet. First, try dropping a couple of aspirin tablets into the battery. The acid in the aspirin can provide it with just enough charge to get you to the nearest service station.

Free Floor Mats

If your car's floor mats need to be replaced, consider going to a carpet store and finding some samples to use instead. You'll always be able to find samples that are gray or another color to match your car, and they're free!

Time to Remove Those Parking Stickers

If your windshield is covered with parking permits and inspection stickers from years gone by, you'll love this tip. Pour nail polish remover over the decals until they're soaked. Then scrape with a razor blade and they'll come off cleanly in seconds.

Get Rid of Grease Stains

If your driveway or garage floor has become an easy place to do some Rorschach testing thanks to the grease, oil, and transmission fluid stains all over the place, take heart—clean concrete is only 10 minutes away. Spray any stained areas with oven cleaner, then let sit for 10 minutes. Rinse off with a hose and the stains will disappear.

Wait Till Monday

A mechanic friend (who shall remain nameless!) once confessed to us that he does his worst work on Fridays, because he tends to rush the job to get ready for the weekend. If it can wait, take your car in on Monday, when it will get the time it deserves.

Organize Your Pickup

Sick of things rattling around your truck bed? Divide it into several compartments for storage by using spring-loaded shower curtain rods. Brace the rods against the sides of your truck bed and each other. They'll keep larger items from shifting during flight.

Put 'Em to Work!

Want to know how to never have to pay for a car wash again? Make the kids do it! All you need is a bucket, a few squirts of car-washing detergent, and some sponges. Then put the kids in their swimsuits and get out the hose. Kids will love the water and suds, your car will get clean, and they'll be tired by bedtime!

Clean a Spot With Cat Litter

If your car has leaked oil in your garage, easily clean it up by applying some cat litter to the area (preferably the non-scoopable kind). Its super-absorbing properties will make the stain disappear in a day.

Make Your Battery Last Longer

Epsom salts can extend the life of your car battery. Just dissolve an ounce of Epsom salts in 1½ cups warm, distilled water and fill each battery cell.

Patch Up Your Upholstery

Oh no, your kids tore a hole in your car's seat. (Okay, so it wasn't the kids, it was you.) Instead of getting an expensive upholstery replacement, use an iron-on patch instead. Hold the patch in place with a few straight pins while you iron. If you don't have a long enough extension cord to bring the iron into your car, set the iron on one setting higher than the directions on the patch recommend. When it heats up, unplug it and quickly bring it out to the car.

Remove the Rack

We bought a mini-van that has a luggage rack, but we find that we almost never use it unless we're on a long vacation. If that applies to you, too, then you should remove the rack until you actually need it. Driving with the rack on top increases wind drag and helps kill your gas mileage. Removing it can be a real money-saver.

—Francesca R., Portland, OR

Find the Cheapest Gas

If you're on the road and know you're going to need gas soon, have the person in your passenger seat send a text message to gas@fuelgo. com. Just type your zip code as the body of the message, and they'll text you back with the lowest fuel prices in your area.

Who Knew?

All told, Americans drive over 245 billion miles per month.

It's Clean-Up Time

After working on your car, easily clean grease and oil off your hands by rubbing a bit of baby oil between them, then washing as usual with soap and water.

Tip for Car Buyers

If you're in the market for a new car, make sure you test drive it at night. Driving in the dark will give you an opportunity to make sure its lights work, and will draw your attention inward toward its dash, making sure you take in all of its interior features and whether or not you like them.

Buy a Program Car

Program cars are cars that are driven by people who work at a car dealership, and are sold after they reach 100,000 miles. Since it's often car mechanics themselves who drive these cars, they're always kept in good shape. Ask your local dealerships if they're selling their program cars and you can save big.

Keep Your Battery Clean

To prevent your car's battery from corroding, wipe down the battery posts with petroleum jelly once every couple of months.

Is It Time to Change Your Car's Air Filter?

A clean air filter can improve your car's mileage by up to 10 percent, so make sure yours is replaced regularly. Your car's filter should be changed at least every 8,000 miles, but if you live in a sandy or highly polluted area, you should change it more often. A good rule of thumb is to simply have it changed when you get your oil changed.

Know What's Under Warranty

Did you know that by law, emissions controls for your vehicle have an eight-year/80,000-mile warranty? When purchasing new parts for your car, check with the manufacturer to make sure you can't get them for free first.

Muffle a Motorcycle

If your motorcycle is too loud (yes, there is such a thing), stick a number-3 grade steel wool pad into the muffler.

—Jason Selway, Blacksburg, WV

Get Your Old Parts Back

When visiting a mechanic to have a part replaced, always ask for the worn/damaged part back. This way, you'll be sure it was actually replaced and that you're not getting a bum deal.

Don't Wait Until Empty

You should always fill up your gas tank before it dips below a quarter of a tank. Always having a little bit of fuel will ensure your car's fuel injection system stays healthy.

Removing Bumper Stickers

We hate to break it to you, but John Kerry and John McCain lost their elections. Get those old bumper stickers off and bring your car up to date. Rub cold cream on the stickers and wait 10 minutes. Then say goodbye to your former favorite candidate and peel the bumper stickers right off.

When Accidents Happen

Been involved in an accident? The best thing to do is to leave the vehicles where they are and call the police. Whether anyone is ticketed or not, your insurance company will usually require you to complete a police report, which will help them decide which party is to blame. But if the damage is minor and you either don't have time to call the police or have to move your car out of traffic, you should document what happened. Use your cell phone's camera to take as many pictures possible of the accident, so you can prove what happened later.

Impromptu Shovel

Stuck in the mud or sand with no way to dig yourself out? A shovel may be closer than you think. Just detach your hubcap and use it instead.

Cleaning Off Break Dust

To remove break dust—that fine, black powder—from your car's tires, spray on a bit of cooking spray or vegetable oil, then wipe right off.

The Perfect Parking Spot

If you have as much stuff stacked up in your garage as we do, you'll love this tip for making sure you don't run into it when you pull in. First, drill a hole through the middle of a tennis ball, then run a long piece of clothesline through it and knot the end so it won't pull through. Safely and successfully park your car in its ideal garage location, then tie the other end of the clothesline to the rafters of your garage so that the ball is hitting your windshield. Next time you pull in, you'll know when to stop without having to slowly inch your way in.

—*Bill B., Davenport, IA*

Stop Ice Before It Starts

To keep your car's door locks safe from ice during the cold winter months, place a refrigerator magnet over the lock. You can even take an old magnet (that 2008 calendar from a local realtor, perhaps) and cut it into pieces that fit perfectly.

It Pays to Restart Your Engine

If you are waiting for longer than 30 seconds in your car, turn off the engine. You use more fuel idling after 30 seconds than you use to restart your car.

● Who Knew?

Half of respondents in a 2009 *Consumer Reports* survey said that they need a new car, but are putting off buying one. Most cited financial trouble as the reason.

Is Your Child Safe?

Nothing is more important than the safety of your child, so make sure your car seat has been installed properly. If you've read the directions a hundred times and are still unsure, head over to your local police station. Most police officers are trained on how to properly install a car seat, and will be happy to check yours to make sure you've done the job correctly.

CHAPTER 17

Don't Sweat it! Home Repair

Do It Yourself

Before you call a repairman, try basic household fix-its yourself by getting a general manual, looking for information online, or simply following the instructions that come with replacement parts like door-knobs and faucets. You'll be surprised how many of these repairs are easy enough for you to do yourself.

Wooden Dent Removal

As long as the wood hasn't broken apart underneath, you may be able to fix dents in wooden floors or furniture. Here's how: Run a rag under warm water and wring it out, then place it on top of the dent. Apply an iron set on medium heat to the rag until the rag dries out. Repeat this process until your dent is gone.

Easy Way to Smooth Caulk

Caulking can be tricky business—it's hard to get perfect lines, but if you try smoothing them down with your finger, it sticks, creating an even uglier sight. When you need to smooth down caulk, try using an ice cube instead. The cold will help set the line, and it won't stick to the ice.

● Who Knew? CLASSIC TIP

When painting steps, paint every other one as you work your way down. When those are dry, go back and paint the rest. This way, you'll still be able to use the stairs while you're paint is drying (as long as your careful!).

Silence Squeaky Faucets

If the handles of your sink shriek when you turn them, try this simple fix. Unscrew the handles and rub petroleum jelly on all the threads. The jelly will keep them lubricated and (hopefully) squeak-free.

Clean Up a Spill With a Straw

You're trying to make a repair in a drawer or somewhere else with a tight corner, and you keep dripping glue that's nearly impossible to wipe up. Solve your problem by folding a drinking straw in half. The v shape is perfect for getting into tiny corners and crevices.

Untangle Twine

If you're working with a ball of twine that keeps getting tangled, find two baskets and overturn one to make a cage. Place the ball inside and run the end of the string through the cage. The ball will be caught inside while the string unspools freely.

Unhelpful Holes?

If a hole in your wall (or whatever else you're working on) is too stripped to hold a screw, dab some glue on a tiny piece of steel wool (which can be cut with scissors) and stuff it into the hole. Once the glue dries, you can screw in your screw without a problem.

—*Jian Liu, Charlotte, NC*

Patch It Up

To make a simple putty for quick patches, combine a tablespoon of salt with a tablespoon of powdered starch. Mix them together with just enough water to make a paste. Apply while still wet.

Rid of Rust

If you're trying to keep something rust-proof, here's a solution you can make. Combine two cups petroleum jelly and half a cup of lanolin in a microwave-safe bowl and heat the mixture until it melts together. Stir frequently, and make sure to apply to the rust-prone item while the mixture is still warm. Remember, don't wipe it off; allow the paste to dry on the item.

Pipe Down, Pipes

If your water pipes are banging and pounding, you may be able to get rid of the noise without paying for a plumber to visit. First, turn off your main water valve, which is usually located near the water meter. Turn on all your water faucets, set them to cold, and let them drain until dry. Then close them again. Turn your main valve back on, then turn each faucet back on as well. After making spitting and coughing noises for a few moments, they should now flow freely with no noise coming from the pipes.

Beware the Caulk

When caulking the edges of your bathtub, keep in mind that the caulking will often expand and crack the first time you fill the tub with hot water. To combat this, fill the tub with water *first*, then caulk away.

● Who Knew? CLASSIC TIP

Sanding wood and want to know if it's completely smooth? Slip an old nylon stocking over your hand and run it over the wood. If there's a rough spot, the nylon will snag.

Sandpaper Your Ladder

Most stepladders are perfectly safe, of course, but if you want to amp up the non-skid surface of the rungs, there's an easy way to do it. Just paint the steps of the ladder and, before it dries, sprinkle fine-grained sand on top. The sand will stick to the ladder and create a sandpaper-like surface.

Crack Goes the Ceiling

If you have a crack in your ceiling but you can't quite afford to re-plaster yet, you can fake it with some readily available household supplies. Take one part white glue and one part baking soda, mix them together thoroughly, and then dab the paste onto the crack using your fingers, a Q-tip, or similar object. If your ceiling isn't white, you can try mixing different food colorings into the paste until you get exactly the right shade.

Fill a Hole in Your Vinyl Floor

If there's a small hole in your vinyl floor, here's how to patch it up without anyone noticing the spot. Find a tile that is the same color, or better yet, one that you've saved for a replacement. Make some vinyl shavings from the tile using a cheese grater, then mix them with a small amount of clear nail polish. Dab the nail polish into the hole and let dry. Voilà! Your floor is like new again.

Painting?

Even if you clean your paintbrush thoroughly, the bristles are likely to be stiff after they dry. Keep them soft and flexible with ordinary hair conditioner. Just add a tablespoon of conditioner to a pint of warm water, and after cleaning the brush, dip it in the solution for a few minutes.

Paint Tray Problem Solved

The easiest way to clean a paint tray after you're done rolling on paint in a room is to never get it dirty in the first place! Instead of using plastic wrap or foil, put the paint tray in a plastic bag and pour the paint on top. Once you're done, simply turn the bag inside out and throw away.

Keep Drips Away

Maybe we're just messy painters, but when we paint a room that rim around the paint can is never a big enough trough to catch the paint that has slopped over the edge—eventually it fills up and runs down the can. To solve this problem, we make several holes in the bottom of the rim with a small nail and hammer. Now the paint drips back into the can rather than running down the side.

A Different Way to Get Rid of Excess Paint

Another way to make painting neater is to wrap a wide rubber band around your open paint can from top to bottom. The rubber band will run right over the opening to the can, and you can use it to wipe the excess paint from your brush instead of the edge of the can. Then when you're done painting, wrap the band around the paint can the other way, at the exact level that the paint is at inside. That way, you won't have to open the can to see how much paint is left.

Paint Odor Remover

To get rid of that overwhelming paint odor after you've redone a room, place a bowl or two of ammonia, vinegar, or onion slices in the room. They will absorb the smell of the paint.

Finding Imperfections

Filling and sanding every hole in the wall before you paint can be enough of a pain, but sometimes it's hard to find every crack, hole, and imperfection. Make your job easier by turning off the lights in a room, then slowly running a flashlight over the entire surface of the wall. The light will cast different shadows in these areas, making them easier to see than in the daylight.

Warm Your Paint

Did you know that enamel paint spreads more smoothly when it's warm? To get it up to a higher temperature, place it in a warm bath before you use it.

Brush-Shopping Secret

We'll usually tell you to go for the cheapest option, but when it comes to paint brushes, quality matters. To make sure you're buying a high-quality brush, look at the tips of the bristles. If they have a lot of split ends, they'll spread paint more evenly.

⬤ Who Knew? CLASSIC TIP

The fastest way we've found to clean a paintbrush is in a solution of ½ cup liquid fabric softener and 1 gallon of warm water. Stick the brush in a bucket of this solution, then swirl it vigorously for 20 seconds.

Wall Hole Solution

Before spackling small holes in your wall caused by nails, first cut a Q-tip in half and insert in the hole, stick end first. Then spackle as you normally would. This will completely fill the hole and make sure you won't have to go back for a second pass.

Make Your Door Stop Sticking

Your bedroom door has expanded, and realigning the hinges didn't work. Instead of taking the entire door down to sand the bottom, try this trick instead. Place enough newspaper under the door until it can just barely close on top of them. Then tape a piece of coarse sandpaper on top of the newspaper, and open and close the door until it glides over the floor without a noise.

Stud Finder Substitution

Looking for a stud and don't have a stud finder? Use an electric razor instead. Most razors will change slightly in tone when going over a stud in the wall.

Prevent Leaks With Floss

Instead of using expensive Teflon tape to preventing leaking between pipes and other parts that screw together, just use dental floss. Wrap the floss around the item's threads and you'll have a tight connection.

Screwy Screws

If you're having trouble with your screws falling off your screwdriver as you're trying to get them into the wall, first poke the screw through a piece of plastic wrap. Hold on to the wrap while you're screwing, then pull it away when you're finished.

Removing Old Wallpaper

Putting up new wallpaper? Here's a great trick to quickly and easily get rid of the old stuff. First, score the paper with a utility knife by cutting slashes through several parts of the paper. Then, dab on a mixture of half water and half liquid fabric softener. Leave on for 10–15 minutes, then watch your old wallpaper peel right off.

—*Lora Boudinot, Woodridge, IL*

Make Hanging Wallpaper Easier

Take your wallpaper out of its roll a few days before you hang it and re-roll it the opposite way. This will make it less curly and easier to hang.

A Better Fix for Wallpaper

If your wallpaper needs a fix-up in a small area, don't use scissors to cut off the replacement pieces. Instead, tear if off with your hands. The ragged edges of the new piece will blend in better than a straight edge.

A Home for Your Soldering Iron

If you regularly use a soldering iron, place several pieces of steel wool in an old coffee can. When you're done soldering, you can easily place the iron tip-down in the can to make sure you don't burn your work area.

Who Knew?

American homeowners spent an estimated $109.7 billion on home improvements in 2009.

Moving Large Items

Moving a large appliance or piece of furniture? Make your job easier by first placing carpet scraps (carpet-side down) under each corner—or do the same with flattened, waxy milk cartons. Either way, the piece of furniture will slide easily along your floor. If you're moving something in the kitchen (like a refrigerator), try squirting liquid dish detergent all over the floor. Watch your step, because it will be very slippery! So slippery, in fact, that your large appliance will just glide to the other side of the room.

How to Remove Superglue

Superglue's claim to fame is that it sticks to everything—and is impossible to get off. But if you accidentally get some on your work project or, heaven forbid, your fingers, there is one substance that can get your out of your "bind." Soak the corner of a soft cloth or paper towel in nail polish remover, then hold it on the area until the glue dissolves. Be aware, however, that nail polish remover will eat away at varnish and other finishes.

Impromptu Sawhorse

Need a sawhorse? Don't worry, it isn't time to cash in on that favor from a handy neighbor just yet. Instead, turn a sturdy ladder on its side. It works almost as well.

Replacement Cap

If you lose the tiny cap to your glue or caulk tube, stick a screw in there instead! We actually prefer long screws to caps, because they'll clean out the narrow area in the tube and make sure the glue or caulk doesn't harden between uses.

Repair a Scratched Floor

If you've scratched your floor while doing some home repairs, it's time to ask your kid for help. No, really! Go to his box of a million different-colored crayons, and pick the one that most closely matches the color of your floor. Cut off half the crayon and place it in an old take-out container (or something else you won't mind getting crayon all over). Melt the crayon in the microwave, then spread the hot wax into the crack. Wax your floor and it will look like new.

Fix a Squeaky Floor

If that squeak in your floor is about to drive you mad, you may be able to easily repair it yourself. Most squeaks are caused not by the floor boards themselves, but by the support beams that hold up your floor, called joists. If a joist gets too dry, it will shrink, causing the boards under your floor to rub against them rather than being held flush. To fix a squeak, first find the joist closest to it using a stud finder or a nail. Joists are usually located 16 inches apart and run lengthwise from the front to the back of your house. Once you find the joist, drill a number 8 wood screw through the floor into it. This should fix your problem.

A Handy Holder for Tape

If you use tape a lot near your work bench, make searching for rolls a thing of the past. Attach a toilet paper holder or a wall-mounted paper towel holder to the wall, and you have an easy holder for tape rolls.

Hold Screws More Tightly

If you're using a flat-head screwdriver and are having trouble keeping the screw on the end, try rubbing each side of the screwdriver with a piece of chalk. The chalk will increase the friction and give you a tighter hold.

—Jim Dwyer, Gettysburg, SD

Rein in Remodeling

If you're planning a big remodel of your home but don't want to spend a bundle, try to keep toilets and other major plumbing appliances like kitchen sinks where they are. These types of improvements can cost around $1,000 apiece, and could be a major portion of your renovation budget.

Add Marbles for Easy Painting

Before stirring paint, place a few old marbles in the can. They'll stir the paint so well you should just be able to give it a good shake to remix the paint before its next use. To make shaking and storing even easier, first empty the paint into a plastic jug with a funnel.

CHAPTER 18

Decorating Done Easily

Two Thumbs Up: Movie Poster Decorations

For fun wall decorations for kids' rooms or a family room, frame movie posters from your family's favorite movies. Try asking at video stores or movie theaters to see if you can have their posters when they are done with them. Often, they'll just give them to you for free. If you're looking for an older movie, you can also find them inexpensively on the internet. Just type in the name of the movie and the word "poster" into Google or another search engine. Another inexpensive decoration option is buying old magazines and hanging vintage ads and photo spreads in frames.

Glossy, Decorative Leaves

For an easy decorating project, gloss colorful autumn leaves. The whole family can collect them together and spread them out on newspaper inside. To gloss, combine equal parts milk and water and paint over the leaves or brush over with a clean rag. When the leaves are dry, use them to adorn indoor plants, fill a vase with them for an eye-catching centerpiece, spread them out on the mantle, or place them underneath candles to catch the drips.

Bargains for a Buck

Your local dollar store can be a boon for home decorating, even if you're not using the items for the purpose they were intended. A cheap, small plate can become a candle holder, while a teacup or bowl can be used as a pot for indoor plants.

—Carol Ann Laplante, Omak, WA

Suitable for Framing

Instead of spending tons of money on impressive, expensive frames, give your photos a personal touch. Buy the cheap frames at the store and repaint them yourself. Not only will they look almost as good as the expensive kind, but you can customize them to perfectly match your home decor.

Matching Not Necessary

You've probably noticed this at the restaurants you frequent, but it's becoming more and more acceptable nowadays—even hip—to eat your meals on vintage, mismatched chairs. Instead of spending a fortune on a dining-room set, go for the mismatched look and hunt for your chairs at thrift shops and used furniture stores.

Don't Discard Dingy Dressers

If your furniture is weathered or out of style, that's not necessarily a reason to replace it. There are plenty of ways to spruce up old dressers, chairs, and tables. Everybody loves quilts, so why not drape one over that old chair that needs reupholstering? You can also try using colorful fabrics on the fronts of nightstand and dresser drawers. Just get some scrap cloth from your last project or from a fabric store, and attach it to the dresser drawers with a staple gun. To have even more fun with it, we like to paint part of the piece and color-coordinate it with the cloth we're using.

A Beautiful Vanity Accent

To turn an old picture frame into a lovely tray for your vanity, take out the glass and pry off the arm that allows it to sit on a shelf. Reinforce what is now the bottom of the tray with a piece of cardboard and a nice fabric of your choosing.

Who Needs Frames?

To make a fun display for your favorite photos, hang twine in a corner and place clothespins on it like a clothesline. Then clip on photos, artwork, or your children's drawings to show off.

Bring Back a Treasured Vase

Just because there's a crack in your grandmother's old vase doesn't mean you can't use it for fresh flowers anymore. Just line it with one of those clear plastic bags you get in the produce section of your grocery store, and your problem is solved. It makes for simple cleaning as well! Just dump the water out, then throw away the bag with the dead flowers in it.

A Place for Firewood

Instead of buying an expensive container to hold firewood and kindling next to your fireplace, use a ceramic flower pot instead. They're cheap and easy to find in tons of different designs.

—Lamar Wallace, Shiprock, NV

Table It

If you have a room whose decor seems disorganized or mishmashed, place a dark brown or black piece of furniture, like a table, in the center. The darker item will attract the eye and focus people's attention.

Don't Rip Up That Carpet Just Yet

If you're thinking of getting new carpet put in, consider getting your old one professionally cleaned first. You'll be shocked at what a difference it makes, and it might change your mind about replacing the carpet. If there are still stains that even a professional cleaning won't remove, a strategically placed rug or chair can hide them.

Handled With Style

If your cabinets are getting old and worn, you can make them look nearly new just by replacing the knobs and handles. A good variety should be available inexpensively at your local hardware store. They'll make your kitchen or bathroom look brand new!

Read All About It

For something new and interesting to decorate your coffee table, why not coffee-table books? Choose a few of the most interesting ones from your collection (including this one, of course) and leave them out for visitors to peruse. If you really want to go the extra mile, you can also select a couple of random, heavy doodads to use as bookends.

Color Coordinate

You can easily create an attractive tabletop display by color-coordinating. Gather whatever objects you have that are the same color, and they'll catch the eye more easily. If you have more than one space to fill, create different displays using different colors for each.

Mirror, Mirror on the Wall

Do you have an old, dusty picture hanging in a place of prominence on your wall? Has it finally worn out its welcome? If so, replacing it with a large mirror can help brighten and reinvigorate your room.

Ditch the Drapes

Here's the thing about drapes: They're expensive and unnecessary. High-quality shower curtains are much cheaper and can serve the same purpose. Nobody will be able to tell the difference!

Raise the Rod

Who knew your windows will appear larger—and will let a little more light into the room—if you just raise the curtain rod a few inches? You'll be surprised how much of a difference this makes.

Make Your Own Clock

An easy way to add custom knickknacks to your home is to buy clock mechanisms from your hardware store. These do-it-yourself clocks are just the hands and the motor, so you can add them to household items and turn them into clocks. Add them to tins, plates, photos with a cardboard backing, or just about anything else in your home. All it takes is a little creativity!

Fun Addition to a Child's Room

Here's a great decorating idea for a child's room: Make a magnetic chalkboard out of the wall! This can be easily accomplished by purchasing a can of magnetic paint and a can of chalkboard paint, both of which should be available at your local hardware store and will run you about $15–$25 apiece. Mark off the area that you're going to paint with masking tape, and remember that it can be any shape or size. Then paint several layers of the magnetic paint, waiting for each layer to dry before adding another layer on top of it. Finally, paint on a layer of the chalkboard paint and let it sit for 2–3 days. With the help of some magnets, you'll be able to hang your child's artwork on the wall, and she'll be able to doodle to her heart's delight.

● Who Knew?

According to *Nursing Standard* magazine, clowns are the worst possible choice you can make for decorating your child's room. They surveyed 250 pediatric patients and found that every single one of them hated being in a ward with clowns painted on the wall.

Repurpose Old Furniture

If your country kitchen is running out of room, consider a dresser. Even though you're used to bureaus being only for bedrooms, it can be a valuable addition to a kitchen for storing napkins, utensils, and more. Repaint the dresser in colors to match your kitchen and you'll have guests asking where you got your newest piece of kitchen furniture.

Jazzing Up Outdoor Plants

Sure you can stick with plain flowerpots for your outdoor foliage, but here are some ideas for days when you're feeling more inspired: Pretty watering cans, an old mailbox, a leather boot, crockery from a second-hand shop, a broken teakettle, or a dresser drawer. You'll need holes in the bottom (cut or drill as appropriate) of whatever items you choose, and you might want to add little stones as well.

How to Light Up a Room

If you have the interior decorating bug, but don't have much to spend on home accents, here's an easy way to add ambience: Use Christmas lights. They're great over a doorway, winding up a large houseplant, along a counter, or out on your patio, and you'll be surprised how many compliments you'll get for this simple technique. They're especially great to implement in January, when all the holiday decorations are half off!

Get Flowers to Bloom

If you've tried cutting their stems at an angle and changing their water but the flowers in your vase just won't bloom, try a hair dryer. Put a diffuser on it and set it to low, then point it at your bouquet and slowly sweep it back and forth for five minutes. The warmth simulates the sun, which may get your shy flowers to open up.

A Better Way to Hang a Poster

Kids love to put up posters on their walls, but kids being kids, of course, those posters will often sag or fall off completely when the thumbtack holes get torn. To prevent this, just place a strip of tape—electrical, packing, or strapping tape will work—on each corner of the back of the poster *before* tacking it to the wall. The tape will be unseen once the poster is hung, but it will reinforce the tack holes and the poster will stay on the wall considerably longer.

Fix a Tilted Frame

If you have a picture frame that won't stop tilting, simply stick a bit of something sticky behind one of the corners. Two options are "sticky tack," which can be found at office supply stores, and mounting putty, which can be purchased in hardware stores.

—*Tamara Joseph, Saginaw, MI*

Dust Ruffle Alternative

A dust ruffle is one item that can safely be consigned to the "things you really don't need" category—unless you're trying to hide everything you've stored under the bed. Make your own with a sheet or tablecloth. Only the sides of the bed that show need to have something hanging down over them. A more streamlined option is simply to cover the box spring with a fitted sheet.

Furniture Floor Samples

Let's be honest. If you have kids or pets, your furniture is going to be banged up. So why not get deep savings on furniture that already has a few dings on it? Almost all furniture stores sell floor samples of their merchandise. Ask a sales representative if the store is willing to sell the floor samples; often, stores have sales specifically for floor samples and the salesperson can tell you when that happens. Otherwise, they may only be willing to sell the floor sample if it's the last piece left. Ask if you can leave your phone number for when the rest run out, and don't be afraid to bargain on the price!

Jar Displays

Have some beautiful clear jars, but don't know what to do with them? Try putting photos inside! Add marbles, rocks, colored sand, or other decoration at the bottom, then bend the photo ever-so-slightly so it fits the curve of the jar.

Who Knew?

When asked what kind of decorating style they prefer in a survey, 27 percent of respondents said "country style."

It Beats Buying Limited-Edition Prints

If you've got lots of bare wall space that you need to fill, there's a way to fill it cheaply and attractively. Buy a pile of cheap frames at the store, and then head to your nearest used bookstore to find a discounted art or photography book on a subject that interests you. When you find an image you like, use a box opener or X-Acto knife to cut the image out of the book cleanly. (Instead of a book, you can also use your favorite wall calendar from a year gone by.) If all the images you use come from the same book, the pages will all be the same size, which will enable you to arrange the frames in a cohesive way on the wall.

Cool Tips for Cut Flowers

Who doesn't love a bouquet of flowers displayed in a vase? Unfortunately, it's not always easy to keep your display looking fresh and beautiful. You probably know that you should keep your flowers' water fresh and regularly cut their stems, but here are more ideas to keep your flowers lasting longer and your bouquet at its best.

✦ To keep your cut flowers smelling fresh, make sure you remove any of the stem leaves that will be underwater in your vase. If left underwater, leaves rot quickly.

✦ If you've perfectly arranged a vase of flowers that's filled to the brim, water it without disturbing your design by filling a turkey baster with water, then slipping it between the stems.

✦ A drop or two of bleach can keep fresh flowers "alive" longer. This always struck us as odd, until we stopped to think that you use bleach to kill bacteria, viruses, and germs in general. Why not flower germs? You can also add aspirin and a little sugar.

✦ To prevent flowers from wilting, gently spray the undersides of petals and leaves with a little bit of hairspray. It really works!

✦ If you're cutting flowers from your garden, do it first thing in the morning. Flowers have more moisture then and will last longer if cut early in the day.

✦ Ever have the problem of a beautiful bouquet spreading out too much in the vase? It ends up looking rather sad and scrawny, but here's a simple fix: Use a hair elastic to hold stems together.

✦ If the opening of your vase is too large, make a grid by crisscrossing clear tape over the top. Then stick stems into the individual holes created by the tape.

✦ Your flowers may be indifferent to the inebriating effects of vodka, but you should feed it to them all the same. Pour a small shot of the cheapest vodka you can find into the vase, and your bouquet will stay fresh longer.

✦ To easily transport cut flowers, slip a balloon over the faucet and fill it with some water, then pull the opening over the stems of your flowers and secure with a rubber band. It's an unmessy way to let them have a drink in transit.

Internet Art

Hanging any image you'd like on your wall is as easy as a color printer and some internet-searching know-how. To find images that won't be too small or fuzzy when you print them out, go to Images.Google.com and click on "Advanced Image Search." Enter a the subject of your desired picture (for example, "moon") in the box labeled "Related to any of the words" and select "Large" next to "Image size." Even "large" images won't be poster-sized, but they'll still have enough pixels per inch to make sure it's not blurry when you print it out.

Another Tip for Hanging Frames

When a picture refuses to hang straight, wrap clear adhesive tape around the center of the wire to prevent it from slipping sideways.

● Who Knew? CLASSIC TIP

Store your candles in the freezer. Once you light them, they'll go hours before they start dripping.

Decorate With Fruit

Fill a large, glass bowl with citrus fruit for a bright centerpiece that's especially good for the dining room table. Use whatever is on sale—lemons, limes, oranges, or a mixture.

Spice Up a Bathroom

Want to add a little style to your bathroom? Replace old, boring shower curtain rings with pretty ribbon that matches your curtain. Just run it through the grommets and tie a bow on top of the rod.

Kitchen Decorating Idea

A fun and vintage-looking decoration for a kitchen is framed seed packets. Dig through whatever is available at your gardening store, then carefully slit the top to let the seeds loose. Center the empty pack on a matte or solid-color background, then glue with rubber cement or white glue. Frame, then hang on the wall for the perfectly themed picture.

Hang Pictures Easily

To get rid of the guesswork that comes with putting a nail in the wall to hang a picture, try this easy trick. Place a dab of toothpaste on the back of the frame on the hook or string (whatever will touch the nail). Then hold the frame up to the wall, position it carefully, and press it against the wall. The toothpaste will leave a mark that you can hammer a nail through, then wipe away.

Dress Up a Bedroom

If you love the look of lace, add some to your bedroom or guest room with this inexpensive trick. Buy a rectangular lace tablecloth that is 70-by-90 inches, and you can place it directly on top of your existing comforter. You'll have friends asking how you could afford to dress up your bed with lace!

Sliding Solution

If you're finding it hard to keep a floor rug in one place, buy some self-adhesive Velcro strips. Attach to the floor and to the corners of the rug and your skidding problems will be over for good! This also works great for keeping cushions on chairs.

—Robert Lepovetsky, Camp Hill, PA

Make Your Room Look Bigger (and Brighter!)

To make a ceiling look higher, all you need to do is change the lighting. Floor lamps that have the shade below the light bulb—like halogens—reflect the light onto the ceiling, which will make it look farther away.

Postcard Pizzazz

For beautiful art at cheap prices, try the gift shop of an art museum. They sell a wide variety of prints from their collection (and sometimes famous works as well) available in several different styles. Our favorite gift shop buy, however, is art postcards. Buy some cheap, black plastic frames, pop your postcards inside, and you have a lovely mini art display for your wall.

Liven Up an Already-Bright Room

For a sunny room that gets a lot of light, try this neat decorating trick: Fill clear bottles with water and add food coloring, then place on the windowsill. The sun will filter through them, casting brightly colored shades and shapes reminiscent of stained glass around the room.

Color Matching

If you're shopping for accessories to match a color on a bed spread, couch, or piece of art, taking a photo often doesn't cut it. Especially if you print it out on your home printer, the variance in color from the photograph to the actual article can be dramatic. Instead, go to a paint store and pick up paint swatches that you think are close in shade. Then go home and find the closest match. Mark that color, then bring the swatch to the store instead.

Striping Solution

Looking to add some character to a room by painting stripes on the wall? Make it easy by first adding "stripes" to your paint roller. Run masking tape around it in several places to mat down the roller. When you paint, the masking tape won't touch the wall, leaving clearly defined stripes behind.

See Your Carpet for What It Is

When shopping for carpet, make sure you do more than just leave your swatches on the floor. When you've narrowed your decision down to a few different shades, take them outside and get them a little dirty! You may surprised how well dirt is hidden—or revealed—on each sample.

Make Your Flowers Taller

Got some nice flowers whose stems are too short for the vase you want to put them in? Take a clear plastic straw and cut a segment off, then slide it over the bottom of the flower stem. Your floral display will now stand tall!

CHAPTER 19

Jeanne's Best Beauty Secrets

The Truth About Moisturizers

If you're looking for a way to cut back on cosmetics, the first place to start is with your moisturizer. Whether it's night cream, day cream, anti-aging lotion, or anti-wrinkle solution, it's all pretty much the same. Pick a moisturizer with an SPF of at least 15—other than that, go with a less expensive brand with a fragrance you like. Your wallet will know the difference, but your face never will.

Save on Shower Necessities

Transfer your shampoo, conditioner, and body wash into pump bottles. Your products will not only be easier to dispense, but you'll make sure not to use too much. One pump is all you should need!

—Alexis Raizen-Rubenstein

Who Knew?

The average American woman spends more than $1,000 per year on beauty products. Read this chapter carefully to see how you can save!

Make Your Bath Luxurious

Don't spend a bundle on bath salts. Instead, make your own by combining two cups Epsom salts and two drops essential oil. Essential oils can be found online and in vitamin shops, health food stores, and in some drugstores. Find your favorite scent, then add it to Epsom salts for a relaxing bath.

Trick for Puffy Eyes

Fix a puffy under-eye area by rubbing egg whites on it. As the egg whites dry, you'll feel the skin get tighter. Leave on for a few minutes after it dries, then rinse off with cool water. You can also try applying a few slices of cucumber or potato to your eyes and leaving on for 15 minutes.

Brighten Skin Naturally

Rubbing a slice of pineapple or papaya onto your skin will help remove dead skin cells. Leave for five minutes, then rinse off with water. Alternatively, use olive oil mixed with salt for an abrasive action.

Callus Be Gone!

Get rid of ugly, unwanted calluses by dabbing them with chest rub, then covering them with bandages and leaving overnight. Repeat this procedure several days in a row and your calluses will disappear in no time. Believe or not, chest rub is also good for curing toenail fungus!

Surprising Use for a Coffee Bean

To freshen your breath, try sucking on a coffee bean. It's much cheaper than a breath mint, and tastes great to us coffee addicts!

Tiny Purse? Tiny Powder!

You're headed out for a night on the town with that fantastic new clutch you found, but once you shove your cell phone, wallet, and keys in there you barely have room for your lipstick. So what do you do with the powder compact you were counting on for touch-ups? Simply take some of those pieces of pressed powder that inevitably break off of the mass and keep them in a tissue. When it's time to refresh, rub the tissue across your face.

Make Perfume Last Longer

Before putting on a splash of your favorite scent, rub a pit of petroleum jelly on your skin. It will keep your fragrance from fading.

Fast Dry for Nail Polish

You have just enough time to touch-up your nails before you leave—but not enough time to dry them. Make your nail polish dry more quickly by spraying your final coat with cooking spray. The oil will help them dry faster, and moisturize your cuticles, too!

Who Knew?

When shopping for perfume, hair spray, nail polish, and other cosmetics, keep an eye out for phthalates on the ingredient list. Phthalates can be absorbed through the skin and have been found to damage the liver and reproductive system. They have been outlawed in Europe, but they're still legal in the US, so make sure you check the label before you buy.

Don't Dare to Neglect Hair Care

If you want to strengthen your hair, make sure to brush or comb it thoroughly each night. This will increase circulation in your scalp, loosen dry skin, and help moisturize your hair with your body's natural oils.

Keep Dandruff Away

Aspirin may help reduce dandruff if you crush a couple of tablets and add them to your normal shampoo. Just make sure to let the shampoo sit on your hair for 1–2 minutes before washing out.

Hand-Brewed Shampoo

It may surprise you to discover that beer has practical uses other than guzzling, but it's true. One of the best ones is enlivening flat hair. Mix three tablespoons of your favorite brew with half a cup of warm water, and after shampooing, rub the beer solution into your hair. Let it sit awhile before rinsing it off, and your hair will get that lively bounce back.

Blondes (Usually) Have More Fun

Ever heard the one about blonde hair turning green in a swimming pool? We've seen it happen. Thankfully, there is a solution: our 40th president's favorite "vegetable." Coat your hair with tomato ketchup and let it sit for a half an hour or so before you rinse it off. Then follow with your regular hair washing and conditioning routine. Remember to use up those packets stockpiled from fast-food places!

Summer Scalp

Hot summer sunshine can increase sweat production and make your scalp look and feel much greasier. To counteract this problem, try more frequent washings with a small amount of shampoo, and use a much lighter conditioner than you use in the winter.

Helping Oatmeal Help You

Have you ever noticed that oatmeal is often a main ingredient of bath products? Well guess what—you have that very same oatmeal in your kitchen! Unfortunately, it's not as easy as just throwing some into a hot bath. First, grind the oatmeal down in a blender or coffee grinder to expose its inner skin-soothing qualities. Then place it in a piece of cheesecloth with a few drops of your favorite scented oil. While you're running your bath, hold it under the faucet, or tie it with a bit of string. You'll have a luxurious oatmeal bath, and even a little sachet you can use as a washcloth to help you exfoliate your skin.

Foot Bath Formula

If you need a good soak in a foot bath, here's a soothing recipe to use. Pour a gallon of water into whatever container you use for foot soaking, and then add 1 cup lemon juice, 1 tablespoon olive oil, and ¼ cup milk. Mix thoroughly, stick your feet in, and relax!

● Who Knew? CLASSIC TIP

Instead of buying expensive shaving creams or foams, try shaving with hair conditioner. (Buy the cheapest kind.) The conditioner will soften the hair and provide a layer of protection between your blade and your skin. You'll even find your shave is closer.

Brighten Your Nails

If your fingernails have become stained by wearing dark nail polish, here's a quick fix: Plop a denture-cleaning tablet into a glass of water and soak your nails for a couple of minutes. The stain will come right off.

Moisturize Your Cuticles

To keep the cuticles of your nails super soft, pour mayonnaise into a small bowl and keep your fingers submerged in it for five minutes. Keep the bowl covered in the fridge and take it out three or four times a week to repeat this admittedly strange beauty routine.

Freshen Feet

Stinky feet? Keep them fresh by sprinkling a bit of cornstarch into your shoes once or twice a week. The cornstarch will absorb moisture and odors, making you unafraid to slip off those uncomfortable dress shoes under your desk.

Too Much Perfume?

Oops! You accidentally put on way too much perfume, and you're afraid the restaurant you're going to will smell like someone just let off a flower-scented bomb! To make your perfume less strong but still a little fragrant, dab a bit of rubbing alcohol wherever you applied the scent with a cotton ball. Your friends will thank you!

Natural Acne Fighter

Sprouting pimples like they're going out of style? Try this neat trick to clear up your face. Cut a raw potato in half and rub the flat end over your face. Leave the juice on for 20 minutes before rinsing off. The starch in the potato will help dry out your oily skin.

Wrinkle Cure and Face Massage in One

When you're feeling too lazy to hit the gym, work out your face instead! Doing facial exercises can help keep your skin looking fresh and young. Begin with this exercise for tired eyes: Simply look up and down with your eyes closed. Then move on to massaging your temples, which not only feels nice, but also helps relieve headache tension and can help prevent wrinkles. Pulling your skin from the eyebrows outward is also a good wrinkle-preventer. Exercise your cheeks by rubbing them in circles, chewing gum, and blowing on an instrument or into a straw.

Who Knew?

Sophia Loren once said, "Beauty is how you feel inside, and it reflects in your eyes. It is not something physical." If one of the most beautiful women in the world thinks so, it must be true!

The Best Place to Store Soap

If you've just purchased a new bar of soap, take it out of its box or wrapper and place it in your linen closet. Being exposed to the air will make the soap harden slightly, which will help it last longer. Meanwhile, it will freshen your closet while it's waiting to be used in the shower.

Make Your Own Liquid Soap

Shower gel can get expensive, so make your own from the cheapest bar soap you can find. Grate two bars of soap of your choice with a cheese grater and add to 2½ cups warm water. Add a soothing oil of your choice (baby or almond oil work well), as well as rose water or an essential oil like eucalyptus or marjoram. Refill an empty soap dispenser and shake. (You may need to shake each time you use it.)

—*Emma Louise Haydu*

Who Needs a Soap Dish?

Instead of letting your soap sit in standing water on your soap dish, put it in a mesh bag (like the kind you would get a bunch of onions in) and tie it to your faucet or an in-shower towel rod. The water will run right through.

How to Clean Your Iron

If your curling or straightening iron is getting a little gross from caked-on hair product and other dirt, head to the kitchen and reach for some oven cleaner. Spray it on, then let it sit for an hour and wipe off. Then wipe the iron with a damp cloth and make sure to let it dry before you use it again.

A Pool No-No

Never wear silver jewelry in pools, because chlorine can cause pitting, small indentations in the surface. It's not a particularly good idea to wear gold jewelry in chlorinated water either, so make sure to leave your valuables at home before heading to the pool.

Fix Broken Jewelry

If a stone has popped out of a piece of your jewelry and you were lucky enough to save it, you can easily put it back in place with a tiny dab of clear nail polish.

To whiten your teeth naturally (and cheaply), mash 4–5 strawberries with ½ teaspoon baking soda. Brush onto your teeth with a toothbrush and let sit for 10–15 minutes. Then rinse out and brush your teeth as usual, making sure no strawberry seeds got caught between your teeth. Repeat this process every night and you'll start to see results in 3–4 weeks.

Treatment for Tired Feet

To rejuvenate tired feet, treat them to this home spa treatment. Massage some butter into your soles, then wrap your feet in warm, moist towels and let sit for 10 minutes. When you unwrap them they may smell a little like popcorn, but they'll be soft and feel great.

Natural Toner

Toner is a final layer of beauty product to use after cleaning your skin. It will help you get a fresh look, reduce puffiness, and tighten your pores. To make your own all-natural version, combine a quarter of a cucumber (no need to peel) with 1½ tablespoons witch hazel and 1 tablespoon water (distilled if you have it) in a blender. Add a little lemon juice and blend until smooth (which should only take a minute). Push through a mesh tea strainer and throw out the solids. Store the toner in the fridge, and when you're ready to use it, dab on your face with a cotton pad or ball. It can be used daily and should last a few weeks. Enjoy! Once you try it you'll never go back to the store-bought kind.

Get Rid of Dead Skin

Another way to slough off dead skin easily is by applying mayonnaise over any dry, rough patches. Let sit for 10 minutes, then wipe away with a washcloth that has been dampened with warm water.

Sylists in Progress

Get your haircut on the cheap by students who are studying to be beauticians. You may risk a less-than-professional 'do, but it's probably better than having a friend do it. Student haircuts are also great for kids, whose simple cuts are usually hard to screw up. To find a beauty school near you that offers cuts and styles at low prices, go to BeautySchoolDirectory.com.

Trim on the Cheap

If you're used to getting an expensive haircut, it's hard to switch to a bargain salon such as Supercuts. But what you can do to save yourself hundreds of dollars a year is to get a hairstyle that doesn't need a lot of upkeep. When you need a trim in between cuts, go to an inexpensive salon. While hair stylists at the bargain salons sometimes can't give you the fancy cut you want, they can usually handle a simple trim, following the path of your normal stylist. If you just need your bangs cut, ask at your usual salon if they offer free bang trims in between cuts.

Your Hair Won't Know the Difference!

For a cheap alternative to hair gel, try a light hand lotion instead. If you have a short cut, it works great to weigh down curls and frizzies, and costs less than half the price of hair gel. Hand lotion is also great as a hair product because you can find it in so many scents—you'll probably find one you like even more than your normal hair-care product!

Too Much Hairspray?

If you've gotten hairspray on your eyeglasses, just wipe them down with rubbing alcohol and you'll be seeing clearly again.

Cheap Make-Up Remover

For an inexpensive way to remove mascara, eye liner, and shadow, try baby shampoo. It contains many of the same ingredients as eye-make-up remover, and works just as well. Dispense a small amount on a tissue or cotton ball, rub over closed eyes, and rinse with water.

Strong Foundations

Some of the most expensive kinds of make-up are foundation and powder. Make them last longer by buying a shade darker than your natural shade, then mixing it with moisturizer (for foundation) or baby powder (for powder) until it matches your normal color. You'll have more than twice as much, and you'll never be able to tell the difference!

● Who Knew?

Many forms of make-up are sensitive to the sun due to their preservatives. Make sure to keep your make-up away from the window to ensure it lasts as long as possible.

Watch Your Wardrobe

The biggest thing people do wrong when trying to hide their weight is to buy loose-fitting clothes. The truth is, baggy clothes will just make you look bigger. Instead, find an outfit that accentuates the positives—whether that's your hourglass hips, great legs, or beautiful neckline.

Getting clothes that are tailored, but not tight, will not only draw attention where you want it to, but will let people know that you're still confident about your appearance—which is way sexier than losing a few pounds around your waist.

Play Up Your Best Features

The whole point of jewelry is to enhance your beauty. So if you're self-conscious about your neckline, by all means steer clear of a dramatic choker. Try bracelets and elegant headbands instead. If those daily crunches are starting to pay off, wear a flashy belt or a bright scarf wrapped around just above the hips to draw attention to your slimming waistline.

Keep Static Away from Stockings

If you've ever had your skirt or slip stick to your pantyhose due to static electricity, you'll love this tip. Just spritz a little hair spray on your nylons and they'll not only be free of static, they'll be less likely to run.

—*Francie J. Shor*

Quick Bracelet Fastening

Having trouble getting that bracelet on? Make fastening easy by attaching the bracelet to your arm with a bit of tape. Then clasp, pull the tape off, and go!

Make Shoes Shine

After polishing your shoes, spray them with a bit of hairspray. People will wonder how you got them so shiny!

The Trick for New Shoes

Cobblers will stretch out your new shoes for you, but there's no need to pay their price. Do it yourself by wearing your new shoes around the house and out to run errands for a few days, and wear two pairs of thick socks with them. The extra padding will stretch out the shoes until there is plenty of room for your feet, and will also make your feet less likely to get blisters when you're ready to wear your new shoes out on the town.

—*Betsy Beier, Viroqua, WI*

Two-Minute Slimdown

You don't need to purchase a shaper and certainly not a corset to make yourself look five pounds slimmer. Try leotards, tight-fitting tank tops, leggings, and spandex running pants. The trick is to layer them underneath your nice outfit so you don't get the "Are-those-pajamas-you're-wearing?" look. You'll feel firmed up and pulled-together, at least until you catch sight of your hair.

Who Knew?

Never paint your nails on a wooden table. Even one drop of nail polish is hard to remove, and nail polish remover will strip the varnish. Paint your nails over newspaper and you'll make sure to avoid an expensive repair bill!

Get Rid of Static

If brushing your hair makes it practically stand on end, run your brush under cold water before running it through your hair.

Fight Dandruff With Thyme

If your scalp is getting flaky, try treating it with a mixture of 2 tablespoons dried thyme and 1 cup water. Let the water boil, then add the thyme and wait 5 minutes. Remove from the heat and let cool, then strain out the thyme and pour the water on your hair and scalp after you've washed and rinsed it. To let it work, don't rinse it out for 12 hours—but don't worry, your hair will dry fine (and smell delicious)!

Another Way to Combat Chlorine Coloring

If you're a fair-haired person and an avid swimmer, you've probably noticed that the chlorine in pools can wreak havoc on the color of your hair—often turning it green! If you want your old hair color back, just dissolve a half-dozen aspirin in a bowl of warm water and rub it into your hair. Let it sit for 20 minutes and then wash it out with tap water, and your hair will be good as new. Alternatively, you can rub cider vinegar into your hair *before* jumping in the water, which helps prevent color change.

Help Dry Hair

Suffering from dry hair? Here's a surefire way to make your hair moist again. Mash a banana and mix with a teaspoon of almond or olive oil. Rub the mixture into your hair and scalp, and let sit for 20 minutes. Rinse off and shampoo and condition as usual. You'll be surprised at the results!

Face Masks for Every Skin Type

Face masks aren't only good for your face, they're also a relaxing treat. Make girls' night even more interesting by making your own! With these homemade face mask recipes, you'll get the same results as store-bought masks, and they're easy too!

◆ Simple avocado: Just mash up a ripe avocado (the fruit shouldn't be tough, and it give a little when touched). Apply to your face and let it dry for 15–20 minutes. Add some cucumbers to your eyes for extra relaxation! Rinse with warm water.

◆ Go bananas: Bananas are great for oily skin. Mash one banana with a teaspoon of honey and a couple of drops of lemon juice. Apply to your face and let sit for 15 minutes before washing with a cool washcloth.

◆ The solution for dry skin: Mix one egg yolk with a teaspoon of honey and a teaspoon of olive oil. Leave on your face for as long as possible, then wash off. The vitamin A in the egg yolk is great for your skin!

◆ Exfoliant: Mix ¼ cup brown sugar with 1½ tablespoons whole or 2 percent milk. Rub into your face, then leave on for 10 minutes. The brown sugar will exfoliate while the milk will moisturize. Tastes pretty good, too!

◆ Clay: You won't believe it till you try it, but clay cat litter is actually the exact same clay that's found in some of the most expensive face masks on the market. Find some cat litter labeled "100 percent all-natural clay" and mix it with water until it gets to the consistency you want. Adding a couple drops of scented oil will also help make it seem less like you're applying cat litter to your face. Wash the mask off after it hardens.

◆ Skin soother: This face mask is perfect for sunburned or irritated skin. Combine ¼ cup full-fat yogurt with 2 tablespoons oatmeal. Mix vigorously for one minute, then apply to your face. Leave on for at least 10 minutes, then wash off with warm water.

Getting Your Eyebrows Waxed?

The next time you get your eyebrows waxed, bring a container of eye drops with you. Applying the solution to your brows after your wax will greatly reduce the redness that comes with it.

For That Last Bit of Mascara

You've just spent more time than you'd like to admit perfecting your make-up when you realize you're out of the finishing touch—your mascara! Don't despair. You can still get a little bit more out of the tube. Tightly close the cap and run the mascara under hot water for 15 seconds. The water will heat up the mascara on the sides of the tube, allowing it to flow more freely. Unscrew the cap and stick the brush back in a few times and you'll have enough mascara for one more night on the town.

CHAPTER 20

Simple Solutions for Better Health

Exercise the Easy Way

Oftentimes, surveying the latest home exercise equipment or worrying about which gym to join are just excuses to put off actually getting in shape. Start getting in shape *today* by using your stairs (if you have them) and cans of food as hand weights. You can march in place anywhere, do squats while waiting for the pasta to cook, and rotate your arms while talking on the phone with a headset. If you do have some equipment, but want access to more, try circuit training with a neighbor—you have a bike and treadmill, she has a weight machine and rower. Trade every other day. Even without any machines you can create your own little circuit, setting up stations to do sit-ups, push-ups, jumping jacks, and even a few yoga poses if you're feeling adventurous.

Original Hiccup Cure

When "Boo!", drinking upside down, and holding your breath don't work, try this to get rid of your hiccups. Insert a Q-tip into your mouth and gently dab the back of the throat under the soft palate. You're trying to hit the uvula, which requires good aim, a diagram, or both! If this doesn't work, try putting sugar under the tongue and letting it dissolve, or swallowing a tablespoon of lemon juice.

Instant Hand Sanitizer

To avoid spending money on expensive hand sanitizers, make your own at home with these ingredients: 2 cups aloe vera gel, 2 teaspoons rubbing alcohol, 4 teaspoons vegetable glycerin, and 15 drops eucalyptus oil. Mix the ingredients well and you should be able to use it the same way you'd use the commercially made version.

Foot Bath for Health

If you find that you're susceptible to athlete's foot, here's a trick that will keep that nasty fungus at bay. Once or twice a week, soak your feet in a hot bath with two cloves of crushed garlic mixed in. The garlic will kill athlete's foot before it starts, and you won't be afraid to walk around in sandals. To treat a case of athlete's food that has already begun, try soaking your toes in mouthwash. It may sting a little, but the nasty fungus will be gone in just a few days.

Binder Clips to Build Strength

If you suffer from arthritis, try this trick to make it easier to open jars and perform other daily tasks. Take a medium-sized binder clip and push back the wings with your thumb and index finger. Hold for 5–10 seconds, then move on to each finger of each hand. Do this a few times a day and it should help your grip.

Back Pain? Check Your Wallet

If you're a man who suffers from back pain, your wallet may be to blame. Sitting on a bulky wallet can cause your spine to become misaligned and your muscles to compensate. Try carrying your wallet in a front pocket (where it's also safe from pickpockets) or make sure it's as thin as possible.

Homemade Heating Pad

Don't spend your money on an aromatherapy pillow! Instead, add uncooked, long-grain rice to a sock and tie it shut. Whenever you need a little heat after a long day, stick it in the microwave on high for 1–2 minutes and you'll have soothing warmth. To add a little scent to the pillow, add a few drops of your favorite essential oil to the rice.

Keeping Finger Bandages Dry

You put a Band-Aid on your finger to cover up a scratch, but you still have to go through your day full of hand-washing, child-bathing, and dishes-doing. To keep the bandage dry while you work, cover it with a non-inflated balloon—any color will do!

The Fish That Don't Kill You Will Make You Stronger

Eating some fish will seriously jeopardize your health because of the mercury content, but eating others will help you live to 100. Which are which? These types are safe and have lots of omega-3s for a healthier heart: anchovies, Chinook salmon, farmed salmon, herring, Atlantic mackerel, sablefish, striped bass, Pacific oysters, sardines, albacore tuna, and freshwater trout. Swim clear of these five, which you should only have once or twice a month, or not at all if you're pregnant or under five years old: king mackerel, swordfish, marlin, tuna steak, and shark tilefish.

Vitamin A is a true wonder vitamin. Not only does it sooth and rejuvenate the skin, but it may also prevent sun damage. Eat liver, sweet potatoes, carrots, mangoes, and spinach (and drink lots of milk) to make sure to get your daily vitamin A.

Get Your Ducts in a Row

If you find yourself getting headaches or sinus trouble more often than you used to, it might be that your home's ducts simply need a good cleaning. Whenever air conditioning or heating is on, tiny particles that have accumulated inside the ducts blow out too, including mold, mouse droppings, and plain old dust. If you have sensitive allergies, a professional duct cleaning may be just what the doctor ordered.

Help for Stings

Believe it or not, meat tenderizer works wonders on all sorts of stings—bee, wasp, even jellyfish. That's because it contains papain, which helps break down the proteins in venom. Make a paste with the tenderizer by adding a few drops of water at a time, then rub on the affected area.

After-Sun Soother

Lots of people swear by aloe lotion, but green tea is a cheaper option and just as effective for treating sunburns. Use a washcloth soaked in tea that has been cooled in the refrigerator as a compress on your tender skin. (Some people say topically applied green tea may even protect against skin cancer.) This is also a great way to ease a sunburned scalp. After washing and rinsing your hair as usual, pour the cooled tea over your scalp. Your poor skin will thank you!

A Different Kind of Ice Pack

If you're a vodka drinker, you're well aware that it doesn't solidify in the freezer. For this reason, it's also a great tool for making your own homemade gel ice pack to use on aches or injuries. Just pour two cups of water, one-third cup of Smirnoff, and a few drops of green or yellow food coloring (so everyone will know not to eat the contents) into a heavy-duty Ziploc freezer bag. Put it in the freezer for a while, and you've got an instant ice pack. If you don't keep vodka around, you can simulate the same effect with liquid dishwasher detergent. (If you do use detergent, though, make absolutely certain to label the bag so nobody ingests it.)

Desk Discomfort

If you find sitting at your desk is causing lower back pain, try slightly elevating your feet. And old phone book is perfect for the job.

Three Cheers for Turmeric

Making tumeric—a Southeast Asian relative of the ginger root—part of your diet can pay off in many different ways. It reduces cholesterol, and lab tests have indicated that it may also inhibit tumors. It's also a natural antibacterial agent and helps detoxify the liver. You can mix the powder into drinks or baked goods, or even sprinkle it on ice cream!

Bug Bite?

A great way to treat mosquito bites is with a dab of ammonia, which stops them from itching. In fact, ammonia is the main ingredient in many of the itch-relief products currently on the market. You can also try a dab of rubbing alcohol.

Get Rid of Chiggers

There may be nothing more disgusting in this world than chiggers. After picking them up in the forest, chiggers will lay eggs in the folds of your skin, causing a poison ivy–like rash. If you think you've been exposed to chiggers, take a hot bath. The heat will cause the larvae to die, making your pain (and disgust!) short-lived.

Rub Away the Bloat

Feeling bloated? It could just be trapped gas. Encourage it to move by gently stroking from your right hip up toward your ribs, then across the bottom of your rib cage and down toward your left hip. Repeat several times.

Cure for Canker Sores

Hydrogen peroxide may help reduce and relieve canker sores. Simply mix one part peroxide with one part water, then dab on any affected areas several times a day or swish around in your mouth for as long as possible.

Sun-Lovers Take Note!

Don't wait until you are out in the sun to apply a protective lotion to your skin. Sunscreen needs time to work, so smooth it on about 20 minutes before you go outside, and don't be stingy with it—use liberal amounts and reapply after doing any swimming.

Drink Up to Stop Stiffness

If you find you're often stiff after exercising, you probably just need more water. Dehydration is a major cause of post-exercise muscle soreness. Drinking water regularly while you work out should keep water levels high enough to combat pain.

Lose Weight Without Lifting a Pound

Hot, spicy foods can help the body burn up calories. Using spices like cayenne pepper and chili powder elevates the body temperature, which makes the heart beat faster and requires more energy.

Slightly Less Sugar

You can reduce your children's calorie and sugar intake by diluting their apple and orange juice with a bit of water. When you open a new bottle, empty a quarter of the juice into a pitcher, then fill the original juice bottle back to the brim with water. It'll still taste delicious, but the kids will get less of a sugar rush, and the juice will last longer to boot.

—Rosemary Deibler, Harrodsburg, KY

Sanitize a Cut

You just got a nasty cut on your hand, but don't have anything to clean it out with before you put the bandage on. Luckily, there's something in your medicine cabinet that you may not have thought of—mouthwash. The alcohol-based formula for mouthwash was originally used as an antiseptic during surgeries, so it will definitely work for your cut, too.

● Who Knew?

If you're over 50, taking 400 IU of vitamin D every day will reduce your risk of osteoarthritis in your knees.

Pepper Yourself for Pain

Cayenne pepper contains a substance called capaicin, which stimulates the brain to secrete endorphins, which are peptides that help block pain signals and reduce chronic pain, such as that from arthritis and a bad back. If you suffer from pain, try sprinkling a little cayenne pepper into your food.

Keep the Doctor Away

If you need medical treatment but can't afford a doctor, consider a walk-in clinic. Walk-in retail clinics can be found in many drug and even department stores. You'll see a nurse or nurse practitioner and may get everything you need, with the convenience of the pharmacy on-site. Besides the quick service and low cost, you'll appreciate the extended evening and weekend hours. Remember that these clinics are meant for minor illnesses and injuries such as colds and flus, sprained muscles, pinkeye, burns, and ear infections. If your situation goes beyond the scope of the clinic, you'll be advised to see a doctor.

—Samantha Chumley

Drink Tea for Better Bones

The caffeine in coffee is thought to deplete calcium levels, contributing to osteoporosis, but the same isn't true for tea, which actually has the opposite effect. Drinking tea can reduce fracture risk by 10–20 percent, probably because of its estrogen-building isoflavonoid chemicals.

Cold Cure

Stuffy nose? Don't spend money on decongestant—head to your fridge instead. Cut the "root" end of two scallions and carefully insert the white ends into your nose (being cautious not to shove them too high!). You may look silly, but your nose will start to clear in a couple of minutes.

Reflexology: Health in Your Hands

Take your health into your own hands (literally) with reflexology, which is the practice of applying pressure to the feet and hands to help ease pain and prevent disease. For instance, if you experience eye strain, you can pinch the webbing between your fingers or toes to help alleviate it. For colds, press about halfway down the side of your thumb. It may sound crazy, but it's been practiced in Asia for years, and China has recently been recruiting reflexologists to cut down on health care costs. For learn more, visit your local library or Reflexology-Research.com/whatis.htm.

Sore Throat?

To cure a sore throat in a day or two, mix equal parts vinegar and honey and take one tablespoonful every two hours.

—*Ruth Leibenguth*

Root Out Nausea

Ginger root, taken as a powder or in tea, works directly in the gastrointestinal tract by interfering with the feedback mechanisms that send sickness messages to the brain. Take some when you're feeling nauseated to help alleviate your symptoms.

Headache Pain

Many headaches are caused by dehydration. Before you reach for the pain reliever, try drinking two or three glasses of water or an energy drink like Gatorade. You may find you're back to normal in no time.

Toothpaste Hero

A white, pasty toothpaste (not a gel) like original Colgate should be a part of everyone's medicine cabinet—and not just for clean teeth. This kind of toothpaste can be used to clear up pimples and even as a salve for burns. Simply dab a small amount onto affected areas and leave overnight.

● Who Knew? CLASSIC TIP

Having trouble sleeping? Before you turn to the prescription medication, try valerian root. Used in sleep remedies for generations, valerian is a natural sleeping aide.

Soothing Back Pain

If you have chronic back pain—especially associated with arthritis—or other sore muscles, try adding yellow mustard to a hot bath. Add a few tablespoons for mild pain, and up to a whole 8-ounce bottle if the pain is severe. The bathwater may look strange, but your aching back will thank you.

Watery Eyes?

If your eyes are itchy, try this quick fix to cut down on your misery: Rub a small amount of baby shampoo on your eyelids. It should reduce your symptoms dramatically.

Steam Away a Cold

Steam is a wonderful household remedy for colds, especially with some aromatherapy oils mixed in. Try pouring hot water into a bowl and breathing in as you lean over it. Stick your tongue out as you do it—this will open the throat and allow more steam through, which prevents membranes from drying out. Add aromatherapy oils to the water that are especially known to alleviate the symptoms of congestion, such as black pepper, eucalyptus, hyssop, pine, and sweet thyme.

Alleviate Neck Tension

Been leaning over your work too long? Try this to help a hurting neck. Inhale and raise your shoulders up to your ears, pulling them as high as they will go. Then let go with an "ahhh" and drop them slowly back down. Repeat several times to release muscle tension.

Get Rid of Toenail Fungus

If you have yellow toenails, you may have a fungus problem. Get rid of this unsightly affliction by soaking your toes in mouthwash for 10–15 minutes each evening.

Are Your Eyes Causing Headaches?

Less-than-perfect eyesight can trigger headaches because the muscles around the eyes squeeze in order to focus. If your headaches come on after reading or working at a computer, make sure you give your eyes a rest every 15 minutes by focusing on a distant object for at least a minute. You may also want to get your eyes examined to see if you need glasses.

Hangover Cure

Party too hard last night? Just spread a little honey on your favorite crackers. The honey provides your body with the essential sodium, potassium, and fructose it needs after a raucous night out!

Hard Cheese for Healthy Teeth

Serve hard cheese like romano and aged cheddar as an after-dinner snack. They'll help scrub your teeth of acids found in other foods, and the calcium inside helps make teeth stronger.

Pummel Pollen

If you have a pollen allergy, try to keep these sneeze-inducing allergens out of your home. Take a shower immediately after doing any yard work to get rid of pollens you may have carried in on your hair and skin, and throw your clothes in the laundry basket. Animals can carry in pollen, too. After taking your dog for a walk or letting your cat out, wipe them down with a wet rag or baby wipe.

Olives for Healthy Joints

People who eat the most olive oil and cooked vegetables are about 75 percent less likely to develop rheumatoid arthritis than those who eat the fewest servings. So use olive oil in your cooking, and consider buying some gourmet olive oil that you can mix with pasta and eat as-is.

Get Rid of Headaches

An old-fashioned and effective way to treat headaches is to cut a lime in half and rub it on your forehead. In a few minutes, the throbbing should subside.

● Who Knew?

It's official—children have known it for years, but scientists now admit that eating ice cream can actually make you feel better. Eating a spoonful of ice cream lights up the same pleasure center in the brain as winning money!

When Bees Strike

When you're stung by a bee, carefully grasp the stinger and pull it out as fast as you can. The less venom that enters your body, the smaller and less painful the resulting welt will be. Ice the area immediately to reduce the swelling. If it still hurts, try cutting an onion in half and applying the fleshy side to the sting. It should help ease the pain.

High Blood Pressure?

If you have high blood pressure, and particularly if you take cholesterol-lowering drugs, make sure your diet is high in Co-enzyme Q10 (CoQ10). It can help lower blood pressure and protect against heart disease, breast cancer, and gum disease. Good sources include organic meat and eggs, rice bran, wheat germ, peanuts, spinach, broccoli, mackerel, and sardines.

Satisfy a Sweet Tooth

Trying to lose weight but keep craving something sweet? Keep a bunch of grapes in your fridge and grab a handful when the hunger hits. Grapes release sugar quickly, so they are great for satisfying your sweet tooth. If you don't feel like the grapes are hitting the spot, wait 10 minutes and see how you feel before reaching for the candy!

Nuts for a Healthy Heart

Nuts are rich in unsaturated fats and vitamin E, which have been linked to a reduced risk of heart disease. Nut-eaters are a third less likely to suffer heart disease than others, so get some trail mix and get to munching!

Headache Help

If you tend to get headaches in the late mornings, late afternoons, or after a long nap, they might be due to low blood sugar, also known as hypoglycemia. These headaches can be helped by eating foods that release sugar slowly, such as bananas, whole grains, and oats.

Natural Remedies for Motion Sickness

If you get nauseated every time you ride in a car, boat, or train, take some lemon wedges with you. Suck on them as you ride to relieve nausea. You can also try sucking on a piece of ginger or drinking ginger tea.

Sore Throat?

Aspirin does more than just relieve headaches! If you have a sore throat, dissolve two non-coated tablets in a glass of water and gargle. Just make sure to note that this only works with aspirin—don't try it with other pain relievers like ibuprofen.

CHAPTER 21

Stain-Fighting Miracles and Other Laundry Wisdom

Save with Steam

Save time and money by steaming your clothes at home rather than taking them to a dry cleaner. Choose a steamer with 1,200 to 1,500 watts of de-wrinkling power—anything above that may cause a short circuit, and anything under that may not be effective. Hang suits, shirts, and skirts on a shower rod and steam several items at once. You may find it doesn't take too much longer than dropping them off at the dry cleaner's!

A Detergent Secret from a Professional

We'll never forget a friendly repairman who, while fixing our washing machine, told us, "You know, you only need half of the detergent that they tell you you need." If you do as much laundry as we do, this tip will save you money right away. If you miss the smell of lots of detergent, add an extra half of a dryer sheet to the dryer. You can also use half the amount of dish detergent in your dishwasher!

Not Your Mother's Mothballs

Mothballs have that telltale old attic smell and even worse, they contain a carcinogen. Use a pretty-smelling natural potpourri made of rosemary, mint, thyme, ginseng, and cloves for the same effect. You want about eight times as many cloves as the other ingredients, since they are what actually keeps the moths away. You can also add lemon peel and tansy. Store in little sachets, which you can buy in a craft store, or tie up in old rags. If you have moths on an item of clothing, put it in your freezer for two days and then clean as usual.

Keep Clothes Color-Fast

The secret ingredient to keeping your clothes from bleeding in the washing machine may surprise you—it's pepper! Throw a teaspoon of ground pepper into the washing machine with your dirty clothes and they'll be less likely to bleed and more likely to keep their bright colors longer.

For Wrinkle-Free Sheets

Though we like wrinkle-free linens as much as the next person, we simply don't have the time to iron bed sheets like our mothers used to. Still, there are a few things you can do to stop wrinkles before they start. Believe it or not, drying your sheets in the dryer can actually increase and set wrinkles. Instead, fold the sheet into quarters or eighths, snapping it and smoothing it out after each fold. Then place the last fold over a clothesline. The fabric is so light, it will easily dry, with only a few wrinkles still intact.

● Who Knew? CLASSIC TIP

Trying to get an ink stain out? Try spraying ultra-stiffening hairspray on the spot, then laundering as usual. Hairspray will usually remove the stain.

Restore Worn Velvet

If your velvet dress, shawl, shirt, or—dare we say it—pants are getting a shiny mark from too much wear, you may be able to remove it. Try lightly spraying the area with water, then rubbing it against the grain with an old toothbrush.

Say Goodbye to Ring Around the Collar

If your dress shirts are getting stained around the collar, wipe the back of your neck with an alcohol-based astringent before you get dressed in the morning. The alcohol will prevent your sweat from leaving a stain.

Suntan Oil Spill

You had a great time at the beach, but you accidentally got suntan lotion all over your wrap. To remove this stubborn stain, cover with liquid dish detergent and rub in. Then turn your kitchen sink on at full blast and run under cold water.

Paint Stains

Got paint on your clothes? Unfortunately, it's often impossible to remove. Before you give up completely, however, try saturating the stain in a solution of one part ammonia and one part turpentine, then washing as usual.

Give Buttons Some Wiggle Room

When sewing on buttons, place a toothpick between the button and the garment. This will ensure you're not sewing it too close to the fabric.

—*Joyce Barone, Hoboken, NJ*

Help Sweaters Stay in Shape

Be careful when drying sweaters! Common laundry advice, but it usually stops there. You can't throw them in the dryer. You can't let them hang and fall out of shape. So what *are* you supposed to do? Once pantyhose have lost their shape, run the legs through the arms of your sweater so the waist is up at the sweater's neck. Use a hanger with clips to grab the ends of the pantyhose (the feet) and hang.

Hiding Marks on White Canvas Shoes

Uh oh, your new white canvas shoes just got a big, black scuff on them. The best way to get them looking like new again is to dab a bit of liquid white-out on the stain. You won't be able to tell the difference when looking down from above.

Who Knew? CLASSIC TIP

Nothing stinks on your clothes like gasoline! To remove the odor, place the offending clothes in a bucket of cold water, and add a can of cola and a cup of baking soda. Soak overnight, then line dry outside if possible. If there is still any odor left, just wash as usual and it should be gone.

For Dye-Bleeding Blunders

If you open the washer and everything's vaguely the same color as your new red shirt, don't despair. Skip the dryer and soak any garments that have been accidentally dyed in the wash in a bucket of rubbing alcohol, then rinse. Repeat the process until your clothes are their original color, then wash as usual.

What to Do with Grass Stains

Try a little corn syrup to remove stubborn grass stains from clothing, instead of those expensive pre-soaks. Just rub the syrup into the stain and launder as normal.

Easy Way to Thread a Needle

To quickly thread a needle, spray the end of the thread with a bit of hair spray. It will stiffen the thread and make it much easier to get through the eye, leaving you ready to darn all those socks.

Make Mending Easier

If you're mending a hole on a sleeve or pant leg, it's easy to miss a stitch when the fabric gets all balled up. Make your job easier by rolling up a magazine and placing it inside. It will partially unroll as far as the sleeve or leg will let it, creating just enough tension to hold the fabric in place.

Who Knew?

When given a list of household appliances in a survey, people rated their washing machine as the number one appliance they can't live without. Following the washing machine were their microwave, dishwasher, DVR, and coffee maker.

Neat Pleats

Bobby pins keep the shape of pleats so you won't ruin them with the iron (and we know you iron every Sunday night at least).

Never Throw Away a Needle

If your needle has grown dull, sharpen it up again by running its tip back and forth on an emery board several times.

—*Patricia S., West Plains, MO*

Stitching Sheer Wear

It's fun to work with sheer materials for curtains and lingerie, but they can be very unwieldy when you're using a sewing machine. If you first sew them to paper (which you'll rip off as soon as you're done), they will stay smooth. Make sure to use needles made for lightweight fabric and fine thread.

Keep Your Clothes Lasting Longer

Once you've found the outfit of your dreams, make sure it lasts! Here are some tips to prolong the life your favorite clothes.

+ Many of your clothes can be worn several times before you wash them, especially sweaters. Most items get more wear and tear from being in the washing machine than they do on your bodies!

+ Turn knitted clothes and T-shirts with designs on them inside-out when washing and drying.

+ Synthetic fabrics wear faster, while naturals like linen and wool will last longer.

+ When pre-treating a stain, try to wash the item within an hour after applying the stain remover.

+ When ironing clothes, especially dark ones, iron them from the inside. Make sure to use distilled water if you use a steaming iron to prevent stains.

+ Line dry your clothes. Not only is air-drying less harsh, you'll love the real smell of sun-dried linens. If you don't have a clothesline, use hangers to hang shirts and pants on tree limbs! Just make sure not to put brights in the sun, as they made fade.

Quick Fix for Heavy Drapes

To give heavy drapes or bedding a fast fluff-up, run them on the delicate setting of your dryer with a damp towel.

● Who Knew?

It's important never to rub a fresh stain with a bar of soap. Many stains can set further when treated with soap.

Scorch Mark?

If you have a scorch mark on fabric, your quest to remove it begins in the kitchen. Cut the end off of an onion and grate about a fourth of it into a bowl using a cheese grater. Rub the stain with the grated onion, blotting it with as much of the onion juice as you can. Let it sit for 8–10 minutes, and if necessary, reapply the onion juice. Once the stain is gone, launder as usual.

Suede Stains

The emery board that you normally use on your nails can remove small stains from suede. Gently rub the file across the stain a few times to remove the mess.

Take Them for Another Spin

If you find your clothes are still dripping wet when you take them out of the washing machine, put them back in and set the cycle to spin. The extra spin time will wring them out even further, and use less energy than extra time in the dryer will.

Prevent Underarm Stains

Here's a great tip if you get those pesky yellow stains on the armpits of white shirts. Coat the would-be stained area on the inside of the shirt with a spray adhesive (available at your local craft store). The adhesive will seal the fibers, so that sweat and your deodorant can't get inside— or stain the cloth. You can also try sprinkling on a little baby powder before you iron the spot.

● Who Knew? CLASSIC TIP

To make your jeans last longer, iron patches on the inside as soon as you purchase them. Place the patches where the jeans usually wear out quickly, such as at the knees or the inner thighs.

Iron Woman

A great way to defend the purchase of a straightening iron for your hair is to point out the contribution it will make to the household: ironing those hard-to-reach places between buttons on a blouse or dress shirt!

Need to Iron a Straw Hat?

Rescue a straw hat by placing a damp cloth between the straw and a warm iron. Rest the brim underside up on the ironing board and press, rotating the hat. For flat tops, place cardboard inside and pack with crumpled newspaper before pressing.

Keeping Lace Lovely

Nervous about ironing lace items? Don't be. Before ironing, simply dip the lace in sugar water, and your item should emerge from ironing unscathed.

Remove Scuff Marks from Shoes

Just about any scuff mark can be removed with the help of some nail polish remover. Wet a rag with some, then rub on the scuff mark lightly but quickly. You may need to give your shoes the once-over with a damp cloth afterwards.

Grease Be Gone

Liquid dish detergent is made especially to get out grease—which is why it is perfect for removing grease stains from your clothes. Pretreat grease-stained clothes with a bit of dishwashing liquid, then launder as usual.

Revive Water-Resistant Items

Do you have a jacket, backpack, or tent that used to be water-resistant, but has lost its effectiveness over time? Set your hair dryer to its highest setting and blow air evenly over it. The warmth will reactivate the coating on the cloth that makes it repel water.

A Coat of Coffee Does the Trick

If your black cotton items are starting to look more like they're dark blue, wash a load of only black items. But first, brew a strong pot of black coffee, then add it to the rinse cycle.

Hand-Washing Tip

When you're hand-washing cashmere and wool, add a drop of baby oil to the water during your last rinse. The oil will make the fabric more pliable, so you can more easily move it back into its original shape for drying.

—*Cece Barrington, Shelby, NB*

Fix Frustrating Trousers

Keep the waistband of your slacks from curling up by ironing a strip of rug binding onto it. Problem solved!

● Who Knew? CLASSIC TIP

To make your clothes dry more quickly, throw a dry towel in with each load.

Tea Stains

Tea and lemon are best friends—even in the laundry room. Rub a tea stain with equal parts lemon juice and water. Just make sure the mixture only gets on the stain, using a Q-tip or eyedropper if necessary.

Blood Stains

Here's a unique way to remove blood stains, in case you've tried everything else and it's failed. Mix unseasoned meat tenderizer with a bit of water to form a thick paste, then apply it to the stain. Let sit for a half an hour, then rinse and launder as usual.

Brighten Your Whites

Add ½ cup lemon juice to the wash cycle of your washing machine to brighten your white clothes. They'll also smell wonderful!

Bird Got Your Leather?

If you were enjoying a nice day outside until a bird pooped on your leather jacket, don't go get your BB gun. Instead, rub a bit of petroleum jelly into the spot and let set for five minutes. It should rub right off.

How to Wash Lace

Even if you hand-wash it, lace can get easily tangled and torn when cleaning. To prevent this from happening, safety-pin the lace to a sheet or smaller cloth. Wash gently as usual, then unpin when dry.

Smelly Shoes?

Place a fabric softener sheet in your shoes overnight to get rid of any foul odors. This also works for hampers, gym bags, or anything else that needs a little freshening.

Even Smellier Shoes!

Here's another great tip for preventing smelly shoes. Take a couple of old socks without holes and fill them with scented cat litter. Then place them in the shoes when you're not wearing them. They'll suck up any moisture, and odor along with it.

The number one energy-sucker in your home is your hot water heater. Cut down on your bills by washing your clothes in cold water with a cold rinse.

Don't Give Up, Get Creative

If you can't get a coffee or tea stain out of a white tablecloth, there is one last solution. Soak the tablecloth in a bucket of strong coffee or tea (depending on the type of stain) for two hours. You won't get the stain out, but you will dye your linen a lovely earth tone!

Shiny Pearls for Life

Pearl buttons, whether they're real or fake, can benefit from a coating of clear nail polish.

Storing Leather and Suede

When storing leather and suede garments, don't cover them in plastic. These materials need a little breathing space, or they'll quickly dry out.

Spotty Situation

It never fails that the second our family is all dressed up in their Sunday Finest (which is definitely not every Sunday), a leaky pen materializes out of nowhere. Luckily this powerful fix is made from ingredients we always have on hand. Mix white vinegar, lemon juice, milk, and borax in a bowl (go heavier on the vinegar and milk, easy on the other two). Lay one paper towel over the stain and one underneath. Use a clean sponge to apply the solution to the stain gently (you don't want to rub it into the fabric). Rinse with cold water and repeat as necessary.

Gummy Mess

If you've gotten gum on your clothes, try rubbing them with egg whites using an old toothbrush. If that doesn't work, you can also try placing a piece of wax paper on the affected area, then ironing the wax paper. The gum should transfer from the cloth to the paper—problem solved!

Winterize Your Shoes

To protect your shoes from getting damaged and stained by too much rock salt in the winter months, coat them with hair conditioner and let it soak in. The conditioner will repel the salt, and help keep leather shoes supple.

⬤ Who Knew? CLASSIC TIP

Dab a small drop of clear nail polish on the front of a button to keep the threads in place and never lose a button again.

Mismatching Socks

When your kids' socks finally need to be thrown away (or turned into rags) because of holes, rips, or stains, make sure to keep their mates. Since you probably bought them in a pack, it's only a matter of time before another one just like it bites the dust. And if you end up with mismatching socks, your kids can still wear them around the house or to bed.

—*Debra R. Young*

How to Fix a Shrunken Sweater

If you've accidentally shrunk a sweater in the dryer, there may still be hope. Let it sit in a bucket of water with a generous amount of hair conditioner mixed in. The chemicals in the conditioner can untangle the fibers in your sweater, making them expand back to their original condition. If that doesn't work, it's time to cut up the sweater and make some new mittens!

Storing Sweaters

When putting away your sweaters for the spring and summer months, wrap them in newspaper and tape the sides. The newspaper will keep away both moths and moisture.

How to Save a Stretched-Out Sweater

Somehow, our boys always manage to stretch out the cuffs of their sweaters. If you have a sweater-stretching problem, too, use this quick fix to get them back into shape. Spritz the area with warm water, and then turn your hair dryer on it. The heat will cause the wool or cotton to shrink back into place.

Stuck Shoelaces?

If you can't get the knot out of your shoelaces, here's a simple trick to make the job easier. Just sprinkle your laces with talcum or baby powder. The powder will provide extra friction that will make them easy to untie in seconds.

CHAPTER 22

Don't Throw it Away: Second Lives for Ordinary Items

Plastic Hanger Covers

We hate throwing out *anything* at our house. Even plastic from the dry cleaners is turned into trash bags by tying a knot by the hanger hole. They're great for showing off pretty wastebaskets because they're clear!

Mouse Pads Without Mice

Extra mouse pads can do a lot more than take up space in a desk drawer. Put the ones that don't have a plastic coating to use in the kitchen as hot plates so you can keep the fancy trivets clean for company. Repurposed pads can also be used as shelf liners, mini placemats for kids, or kneepads for gardening and playing with sidewalk chalk.

Squeeze Bottles Still Have Air!

Save plastic squeeze bottles, but not to store things in. Wash them out and let them dry, and they make the perfect substitute for bottles of compressed air, which are used to clean out computer keyboards, electronics, and other tiny crevices. This works especially well with squeeze bottles with small spouts, such as lemon juice dispensers.

Oven Mitts for Your Car

When it's time to retire your oven mitts because they're covered in stains and burn marks, don't throw them away. Save them for use with your car. Oven mitts are great to use when handling hot engine parts or even as a washing mitt.

Coffee Can Lids

Instead of throwing away the lids to coffee cans, use them as a washable, greener alternative to parchment paper. Place them between slabs of burgers in the freezer or use them to set things on in the microwave while you're heating them up.

—Caren C., Red Bank, SC

Yarn Container

Yarn can get out of control very quickly (especially if you have cats), so keep each ball of yarn in a dispenser made from an appropriately sized soda bottle (cleaned out, of course). Cut a hole in the bottom big enough to slip the yarn through, then place your skein inside and string it out through the bottle opening.

Checkbook Covers Turned Organizers

When you receive new checks in the mail, don't throw away the plastic cover that often comes with them. Instead, use it as an organizational tool to store receipts, itineraries, or other papers that find their way into your purse or wallet.

What to Do with Wet Umbrellas

Need a cover to store your wet umbrella in while you're on the go? Look no further than the end of your driveway. The plastic bags newspapers come in are waterproof, and are the perfect size.

Shower Curtain Liner

When it's finally time to replace your shower curtain liner, keep the old one and use it for a drop cloth while painting or doing art projects.

Binder Clips

If you're one of those people who prance around town without a purse or giant bag, then we envy you, because we're sure we look like we're moving to another country most days. If you can pull off a fanny pack, more power to you. Otherwise, get that free and easy look (and feel) by pinching a couple of binder clips from the supply closet at work. Use them to fasten your keys and dollar bills to your pockets, belt or waistband. Look Ma—no hands!

Quick Fix for a Loose Button

After rifling through your clothes for a half an hour, you've finally decided on the perfect outfit to wear—but a button is loose! If you're about to lose a button and you're already halfway out the door, use a twisty tie instead. Just remove the paper covering, then twist it through the holes in the button and fasten on the other side of the cloth. Just make sure to replace with real thread later!

Makeshift Vase

When you're serving breakfast in bed, don't despair if you can't find a vase for that elegant touch of fresh flowers. Grab a toothbrush holder, which gives a mod look and holds the flowers up quite nicely.

Recycled Inbox

Cereal boxes make great stacking trays for your home office. Carefully cut off the top and back of the box, and you have an inbox waiting to happen. If you don't like the Total, Wheaties, and Chex look, spray the boxes with silver spray paint and let dry before using.

—David Dean, Fairbanks, AK

Repurpose an Old Candle

You've lost the wick of an old candle, and you were never really crazy about the scent anyway. Turn your old candle into a pincushion by simply sticking pins in the top or the sides. The wax will even help them slide more easily into cloth.

Venetian Blinds

Before you toss out that set of old Venetian blinds, cut out a dozen of the blinds to use as straight edges. They're great for home projects, because if you get any paint, varnish, or other material on them, you can just throw them away. We especially like them in lieu of using tape to make sure paint stops at the ceiling, because it's easier than trying to tape a straight line. As for the rest of the blinds, take the ladder-shaped strings that hold them together and give them to your kids. You'll quickly find that action figures and small dolls always have a use for ladders.

Garden Hose

Old hose finally kick the bucket? Before you throw it away, cut two portions that are each about a foot long, then cut a slit in them. They'll make perfect covers for the blades of ice skates.

DIY Comforter Cover

Even the sewing-challenged can manage to make a cover for their comforter using two sheets sewn together. Mix and match patterns if you'd like. Ours has a flannel sheet on one side, which makes it extra cozy. Don't forget to leave one side open (with a few buttons intact) so you can remove the cover for washing.

An Ingenious Way to Cover Up Ugly Toilet Bolts

If the caps to the bolts at the base of your toilet have cracked or gone missing, you've probably discovered that they're hard to replace. A perfectly suitable replacement are the protective caps used on some stick deodorants that need to be removed before you can apply the deodorant for the first time. So go buy a few new sticks of deodorant, and make sure to take a look at the cap color before you buy!

Winter Time-Saver

If you park your car outside during winter, you can save yourself scraping and wiping time each morning by wrapping your side mirrors and windshield wipers in old plastic bags.

Breath Mint Containers

The containers to Tic Tacs and other breath mints are perfect for storing tiny items like pins, needles, buttons, beads, and nails. Plus, they'll still smell minty fresh when you open them!

Keep that Carton

Don't discard that partitioned wine or liquor carton! Instead, cut the top off and keep it in the garage for storage of sporting goods, fishing poles, and other sundries.

Bottles for Boots

One-liter and other-sized plastic bottles are perfect for propping up leather boots. Just clean the bottles and place one in each of your knee-high boots, and you won't have to worry about them getting wrinkles from folding over.

Match Point Jar Opener

You've seen those nifty, colorful jar openers in cool houseware shops, but you might not realize you've got a bunch of tools that are just as effective lying around your garage or basement. Using an X-Acto knife, slice open an old tennis ball and you've got two handy openers —point, set, match. Now pass the olives.

Pantyhose and Other Nylons

If your tights, knee highs, or other nylon items have holes that can't be solved with the old clear nail polish trick, use them as extra stuffing in sagging throw pillows.

● Who Knew? CLASSIC TIP

It's hard to get more than a few wearings out of a pair of pantyhose, but luckily there are lots of uses for them once they get runs. Save them to use as dust rags, or use them to buff your shoes. We find they polish even better than a normal cloth.

Turn Extra-Large Tees into Extra-Stylish Tees

If you're like us, you have a million XL T-shirts that you've gotten from various organizations and events. Unfortunately, all of them make you look like a formless blob. Fix them into something you would actually wear by getting a little creative. To make a scoop-necked shirt that's perfect to wear over bathing suits or tank tops, cut off the piece of fabric that runs along the neck hole with a pair of scissors. Try the shirt on, and cut a little at a time until it fits your style and shape. To make a fitted tank top from your XL shirt, cut off the sleeves, then slice up the sides of the shirt and stitch them back together more tightly to fit your form. For instructions on how to perform these T-shirt surgeries and many more (most of which don't even require a sewing machine), check out the book *Generation T* by Megan Nicolay. (And make sure to get it for free at the library!)

Dryer Sheets

After you pull your clothes out of the dryer, save the fabric softener sheet! Tape it to your heat or air conditioning vent and it will freshen the whole room.

—*Marge Backes*

A New Use for Dustpans

Instead of throwing away an old dustpan (even a cracked one), wash it thoroughly and throw it in with your kid's sandbox toys. It makes a great scoop.

Wipes Dispenser Turned Organizational Tool

An old plastic cylindrical dispenser for baby wipes or disinfectant wipes is perfect for holding your child's chunky markers. (Cut to size if necessary.)

Homemade Exercise Weights

If you have teenage boys, odds are they'll sign up for a sport at some point that requires them to do minor strength conditioning at home. If you can't afford a set of weights, just take some empty plastic milk jugs and fill them with dry pinto beans. The result won't be perfect, but it'll be good enough to fake it.

Save Your Bottles

If you're looking for a cheap and practical toy for kids, thoroughly wash old ketchup, salad dressing, and shampoo bottles and let the kids use them to play in the swimming pool or bathtub. They're also a good way to wash shampoo out of hair at bathtime.

Make Your Own Watering Can

Don't spend money on a watering can unless it's for decorating purposes—it's much more practical to make your own. Simply wash out an old 1-gallon milk jug, then poke or drill very small holes below the spout on the side opposite the handle. Fill it with water, screw the top back on, and you have a homemade device to water your plants!

Perfect Storage Containers

Instead of throwing away the boxes that powdered laundry detergent comes in, we keep them to store household items. We have one in the garage for tools, one for my wife's sewing supplies, and we give them to the kids for toys. They're perfect because they're easy to carry and lined with waterproof wax. Just make sure to rinse them out first!

—*Eggbert Joliet, Toronto, ON*

Homemade Bath Pillow

To make your own bath pillow, reuse a household item no one seems to be able to get rid of: packing peanuts! Pour packing peanuts into a large, resealable freezer bag, then let out some of the air and seal. Place in the bath as a soft resting place for your head.

White-Out

There's still a use for old-fashioned liquid paper, so if you've still got it, don't throw it away. Use it as touch-up paint for white appliances, like your refrigerator. If your fridge has a ding but it's not white, try buying a small amount of touch-up paint from a car detailer.

Tops to Condiment Bottles

When you've used all the ketchup in a plastic squeeze bottle, throw the cap in the dishwasher and wash until the caked-on ketchup is gone. Keep it, along with other tops to condiment bottles, handy in the kitchen. When your current bottle gets all mucked-up, simply switch it out with a clean top and throw the dirty one in the dishwasher.

Who Knew?

Each day the population of the United States throws away enough trash to fill 63,000 garbage trucks.

Garlic and Onion Skins

Yes, there's even a second use for the skins of garlic and onions. Save them for the next barbecue and toss them into the fire just before grilling meats or vegetables. The flavor is terrific.

The Perfect Tie Holder

Don't throw away the little z-shaped hooks that come with dress socks—use them as tie holders! Slip them onto a hanger and they are perfect for hanging the tie that accompanies that particular suit. Who knew?

Butter Box

If the butter you buy comes in a flat box of four, don't throw away the container when you're done. These square boxes are perfect for stowing sandwiches! Now I can just put my lunchtime sandwich in my purse and head to work without worrying about it getting smushed.

—*Sarah Parkarvarkar*

Fun with Old Crayons

If your child has lots of little crayon pieces left over, turn them into a fun craft project by removing the paper and melting the pieces together in an old muffin tin. Your child will love the new, enormous crayon with unpredictable colors!

Clean That Jar

After your jar candles burn out, they can be cleaned out and reused for any number of things—including other candles. One way to clean a candle jar is by setting your oven to 200°, melting the leftover wax, and then pouring it out. An even better way, though, is to put it in the freezer for an hour and then pry out the frozen block of wax. It should fall right out.

Shower Caps

Shower caps that you receive for free in hotel rooms are perfect for wrapping your shoes before you pack them in your suitcase. The plastic cap will keep the rest of the items in your suitcase from becoming dirty.

Use Easter Eggs All Year Round

Instead of packing away those plastic Easter eggs for once-a-year use (or tossing them out altogether), you can keep using them throughout the year. For instance, instead of putting snacks in Ziploc bags in your child's sack lunch, put the snacks inside the eggs. They can be filled with M&Ms, Skittles, Cheerios, Goldfish crackers, and a variety of other things.

—Hadley Moore, Hartford, CT

Shower Curtain Rings

Got new curtain rings (or took our advice to change them out with ribbon)? Use the old ones to organize your coat closet. Hammer a nail into the wall, then hang a couple of curtain rings on it. They can be used to grasp items like gloves and hats, or you can run a scarf through one.

Dryer Lint

Instead of throwing away lint you've cleaned out of your dryer's screen, use it as kindling for your fireplace. It lights quickly and can be stuffed places paper can't.

Old Toothbrushes

There are many uses for an old toothbrush—the biggest being to clean crevices and other tiny spaces like the molding between bathroom tiles. Our favorite second life for an old toothbrush, however, has to be in the kitchen. Use an old toothbrush to quickly and easily remove the silks from a fresh ear of corn.

Who Knew? CLASSIC TIP

Forget about expensive plant food! Just save the water when you boil potatoes or pasta, let it cool, and use it to water your plants. They'll love the starchy water.

Six-Pack Containers

Six-packs are a must-have at a barbecue—and not just for the beer. Turn an old six-pack container into a holder and carrier for condiments like ketchup, mustard, and relish. You can even stick napkins and plastic utensils inside. To make it extra strong (and waterproof), wrap in duct tape!

Egg Cartons

Cardboard egg cartons are great to use when starting fires (in your fireplace or outside in a pit, of course). Fill them with bits of wood and pieces of paper that would be too small to use on their own, like receipts. You can also fill an egg carton with charcoal and use it to start your barbecue grill.

Produce Bags

The plastic bags you put your produce in at the grocery store are perfect for makeshift gloves. Slip your hands inside and fasten around your wrists with rubber bands.

Cardboard Boxes

Place the side of a large cardboard box near your door during snow storms so family members can pile their filthy, slushy boots and winter gear on top while keeping your home clean.

Velcro

Before you throw away something that has Velcro on it, first cut out the part of the article that has the "hooked" side of the Velcro. It's perfect for getting the little pills off of sweaters, scarves, and other clothing items.

Camera Saver

When packing, a plastic container for bar soap is usually the perfect size for stowing your digital point-and-shoot camera inside.

Eggshells

Even eggshells have a great use before you throw them away: getting rid of rings on hard-to-clean places in vases. Fill the vase mostly full with warm water, then add a drop of dishwashing liquid and the egg shells. They'll act as an abrasive to scrub off the stains.

Versatile Speakers

If you're getting rid of a computer, make sure to keep the speakers if they are detachable. Plug them into a portable CD player or mp3 player, and you have an inexpensive stereo for your kitchen, bathroom, or workspace!

—Christopher James

Tissue Box

An empty tissue box is great for holding plastic shopping bags that are waiting for their chance at a second life. As you place each bag in the box, make sure its handles are poking up through the hole. Then thread each new bag through the previous bag's handles. That way, when you pull a bag out of the box, the next one will pop right up.

Mittens

Mittens that you no longer use make great glasses cases! You can also use them during their "off-season" to hold sunglasses in the summer.

According to recent studies, between 2 and 5 percent of what we throw away each day is potentially reusable.

Coffee Cans

Coffee cans are the perfect container for more than just coffee. You can also use them to bake dough! Use like you would a loaf pan, making sure to grease them first, and only fill halfway if you're making a bread with yeast in it.

Candle Tubes

Looking for a container to store long, tapered candles in? Now you have one: The tube that Pringles potato crisps come in. It even has a lid!

Bottles for Candles

Here's another great use for used, clear 2-liter bottles. Cut off the tops and bottoms, then place the middle portions over candles that you're using outside. The plastic will act as a shield to keep wind away and the fire lit.

Fish Tank Water

Even old water from your aquarium can be used again. Use it to water your houseplants—they'll love the extra "fertilizer" the fish provided.

Repurposed Paintbrush

Before you throw away that old paintbrush, use it as a cleaning brush. Cut the bristles very short and use in hard-to-reach places like the corner of the tub.

A Comb for Your Broom

Use an old wide-toothed comb to get the lint and hair out of the midst of your broom's bristles. And always store brooms upside down to make sure the bristles stay straight.

Packing Peanuts Turned Beauty Product

Here's another use for those packing peanuts that you never seem to be able to get rid of. Save eight of them and use the next time you're painting your toenails. Insert one between each pair of toes to separate them and more easily give yourself a pedicure.

Unwanted Perfume

Someone gave you perfume as a present and although it smells nice, it's just not your bag. Instead of using it on yourself, use it to freshen rooms in your home. Squirt a small amount near light bulbs, and when you turn on the lights you'll turn on a lovely scent with them. You can also use perfume as a refill for a bottle that contains aromatherapy sticks.

Do You Play Guitar?

If so, you never need to buy a pick again! Instead, use the plastic fasteners found on bread bags. They work just as well, and they're free!

Cheesecloth

After you've used a piece of cheesecloth, don't throw it away. Throw it into a load of laundry, then use it as a dust rag. It will trap small particles in its weave, and won't leave behind a bunch of lint.

—*Fanny Lassiter, Pine Bluff, AR*

Get Creative with Wallpaper Scraps

You've just finished a big wallpaper job, and have at least a half a roll left. Use your extra wallpaper scraps to decorate accessories in the room. Cover the fronts of drawers or cabinets, even the backs of chairs! Wallpaper can also be used to cover notebooks, pencil cases, and other office supplies.

Yet Another Use for Packing Peanuts

Packing peanuts will take several decades to decompose, so you can make better use of them than throwing them away. Place them at the bottom of flowerpots before covering with soil and planting flowers and other plants. They'll keep the pot well drained and much lighter than if you had used rocks.

When a Pin Is a Button

Every now and then, we or our kids will receive a round pin with a removable back to commemorate an event, membership in an honor society, or an award. We never knew what to do with these pins (which look like tie tacks), until we discovered they can be used as a "replacement" button on jeans and other pants that have become too loose. If you've lost weight and your pants no longer fit, affix one of these pins to your pants next to the usual button that keeps them closed (you may want to secure the back with a bit of duct tape). You can then pull the other side of the fly tighter, looping the button hole through the new "button" that's farther away than the real one.

Tire Pool

If you have access to an old truck tire, there's no need to buy a wading pool for your small children! Just drape a shower curtain over the tire, making sure to push it down in the middle, and go get the hose!

—Sandy Curran, Pine Bluff, AR

How Tennis Balls Can Keep Your Pool Clean

Tennis balls can keep your pool clean, but not in the way you might think. Throw a few old tennis balls into the pool, and they'll absorb any oil that floats to the surface. In the summertime, that means plenty of sweat and sunscreen.

PART THREE

Making Your Money Go Further

We've given you plenty of tips for saving a bit of money here and there around the house, but what about the big stuff? Whether you're looking for ways to save on your yearly vacation, lower your energy costs, or spend less when you're at the store, we've got the solution for you. Better yet, this section contains hundreds of things you can get for absolutely free! And if that isn't enough, check out our chapter on ways you can easily make extra money from home. Finally, we're offering special deals from online retailers that are available to *Who Knew?* readers only. Read on and save!

Managing Your Money and Lowering Your Bills

Reduce Your APR

Ask and you shall receive! It sounds too simple to be true, but one of the first things you should do when attempting to reduce your debt is call up your credit card company and ask them to reduce your interest rate or annual percentage rate (APR). If you have had the card for a while and have routinely made payments on time, the company is usually happy to take this piece-of-cake step to keep your business.

Planning for the Future

When you get a bump in salary, put a higher proportion of it into your savings account. For instance, if you get a 4 percent raise, add 1 percent to your household budget and set aside the other 3 percent for your retirement account. You'll thank yourself later!

Make Sure You Know the Facts

Always read the terms of a credit card agreement before you sign up for the card. The fine print may be boring, but you owe it to yourself to make sure you're not getting a bum deal. Highlight any passages you don't understand, and find out what they mean by asking a lawyer or accountant; or simply look the phrase up in an internet search engine. Some agreements will try to scam you—one recent ploy is for companies to buy up your bad debt, then trick you into signing up for a card that already has the bad debt tacked onto the balance. (If this happens to you, you should insist on getting documents that prove that you are accountable for that debt or the interest, so don't agree to anything until you speak with that lawyer or accountant). Be especially careful if the offer seems too good to be true.

Neighborhood Changes Can Mean Lower Insurance

A big factor in how much you're charged for homeowners insurance is where you live. So if there have been improvements to your neighborhood or subdivision, such as storm drains being installed or a fire hazard being cleared away, make sure to alert your insurance company and see if they will lower your rates.

Which Cell Plan Should You Be Using?

Do you end up with lots of unused cell phone minutes at the end of the month? Visit BillShrink.com, where you can enter the amount you talk and text to find the best plan for you in your area. We found a plan that saved us $10 per month!

 Who Knew?

According to the Federal Reserve Board, Americans have $2.56 trillion in consumer debt.

Bring It Together: Debt Consolidation

Debt consolidation is a smart and relatively painless way to ease some of the hardship of having lots of debt. With debt consolidation, you can lower your monthly payments, and you may also be able to lock in a lower interest rate. The easiest kinds of consolidations to obtain are for student loans, but many banks also offer consolidation services for mortgages, and (if your credit score is good) credit card debt. There are different types of debt consolidation services, so make sure you know what you're getting into. Some services—often non-profits— contact the financial institutions you owe the money to and try to get your interest rates lowered. Then you pay them one lump payment each month, and they pay the companies for you. Other types of debt consolidation—usually through banks—basically just give you a loan to pay off all your other loans. Either way, debt consolidation can make your finances a little more manageable.

When Insurance Isn't a Good Idea

When purchasing a cell phone, never sign up for insurance or a warranty—and if you're paying a monthly fee for insurance, cancel it immediately. The insurance plan of many cellular providers has a deductible of up to $50 that you are responsible for paying, and the phone you'll usually receive as a replacement will be an already-outdated model from last year. The cost of taking your chances and buying a cheap replacement if necessary is much less than what your cellular company is offering you.

Better Budgeting

Trying to get a handle on budgeting? Visit FrugalMom.net/ blog/?p=364, which will not only walk you through how to better budget your money, but will also give you free, downloadable forms like a spending tracker to help get you started.

Up Your Credit Score

It's a tough time to get credit, so make sure your rating is as good as possible. Here are a few easy ways to raise your credit score.

✦ If you haven't already, get a free credit report by going to AnnualCreditReport.com or calling 1-877-322-8228. Don't be fooled by other "free credit report" sites, which often require you to pay a membership fee.

✦ Check your report for accuracy. On the internet, you can often click the item directly to dispute it. Make sure all of the addresses listed are current or former addresses, and that all loans and lines of credit listed are yours. If you're unsure, contact the customer service number on the report and ask for more information.

✦ Get rid of credit cards you never use anymore. See three or four credit cards for stores you don't frequently shop at? Even if you don't carry balances on these cards, one of the things that can lower your credit rating is the amount of available credit you have. Call the number on the back of the cards and cancel them!

✦ If you are listed as a secondary card holder for an account of someone who's racked up a lot of debt on the card, this can negatively impact your credit rating. If it isn't necessary for you to be on this credit card account, call the company and get your name taken off.

✦ You can request a free credit report once a year. Try to make a regular habit of requesting it and reviewing it as closely as you would your bank statement. The more quickly you notice a discrepancy, the easier it will be to get it removed from your report.

Meds by Mail

Before you reorder a prescription, find out if your insurance provider offers a pharmacy-by-mail service. Though it's not as easy as going to your local pharmacy, you can save up to 30 percent on some medicines.

—Emme Boutin-Robertson, Cambridge, MA

Smile: You're Saving Money on Dental Care

It's true: you can get that root canal you've been putting off *and* keep your retirement account. Find a dental school in your area to visit for regular cleanings and check-ups, and you'll save big. Be prepared, however, for crowded waiting rooms, long visits, and less privacy. While you're waiting, start dreaming about that cruise to Alaska.

Automatic Debit

Nothing's worse than getting socked with an unfairly enormous late fee for paying your bills a couple of days late. Say goodbye to late fees forever by setting up an automatic debit from your checking account. You can usually set up automatic debit by calling the company the account is with or visiting their website.

Gas Cards

Take an extra-careful look at credit cards offered by gas companies—most have a higher interest rate than average credit cards. Before you sign up, make sure to ask about their fraud protection, which is usually pretty weak. You may be better off using a "regular" credit card that offers rebates on gas purchases. Two good choices are the Discover Platinum Gas Card and the Chase Cash Plus Card.

Good Guidance

If you feel like you're in over your head with your debt, or if you simply want some answers about the most efficient way to pay it off and manage a budget, there is free counseling available to you. These one-on-one sessions are offered by organizations across the country who want to help people who are struggling with money problems. They also often offer consolidation loans and debt management programs. To find an agency that will work with you in person, over the phone, online, or via mail, call the National Foundation for Credit Counseling at 1-800-388-2227. This organization makes sure its members are accredited, not-for-profit, and generally on the level.

How Many Minutes Do You Have Left?

There are easy ways to keep an eye on how many minutes you've used on your cell phone each month. If you are a Verizon Wireless customer, dial #BAL (#225) and press call to check your balance. To check minute usage, dial #MIN (#646) and press call. To check text messages and data usage, dial #DATA (#3282) and press call. If you have AT&T, dial *BAL# (*225#) and press call. For minutes, dial *MIN# (*646#) and press call. Now you'll always know when you're about to go over your allotted minutes.

Entertainment Spending

The point of making a budget isn't getting rid of your entertainment spending, it's just prioritizing what you like to spend your money on.

Decide what your favorite activities are (as a family, couple, and by yourself or with friends). Then make sure you save enough to spend on the things you really enjoy. For instance, you may decide you'd like to give up going to the movies a few times a month so you can go to a concert. Or you might prefer to spend your money on a nice dinner rather than a couple of trips to the bar.

Make the Bank Switch

It may be a pain, but if you're getting socked with fees for your checking or savings accounts, it's time to switch banks. You should never have to pay monthly service charges, and many banks are now even offering cash for opening a new account. Make sure to visit several banks in your area and ask about their fees, interest rates, opening bonuses, and other perks like free checking.

Don't be Fooled by a Sneaky Bank

Many banks are desperate for your money these days, and they like to offer free stuff. Don't take their advertisements at face value, and make sure to read the fine print carefully. One major bank is currently touting, "Access to over 35,000 free ATMs! Never pay a fee again!" The fine print? Their offer is just a link to AllPointNetwork.com, where you can, in fact, get access to 35,000 free ATMs—without joining anything at all!

Are You Sure You Know What's on Your Phone Bill?

Phone companies are notorious for automatically enrolling you in a calling package filled with services you never use. Make sure to check your phone bills for extra charges such as voicemail, three-way calling, and call forwarding. If you don't use these services, cancel them to save! If you use your cell phone more than your home phone, you might want to consider stripping your land line down to the bare minimum or canceling your service outright.

A Must-Visit Site!

At LowerMyBills.com, you'll find a way to reduce just about any bill. Whether you're looking to refinance your home, consolidate your credit card debt, or just lower your phone bill, this site will give you the tools you need to compare different companies and calculate your costs. You can also sign up for an email newsletter filled with tips and deals.

Double Pay

Credit card interest is calculated based on your average daily balance over the month, which means you can reduce your charges by making more payments. Instead of paying, say, $300 at the end of the month, split that up into two $150 payments. That way, your average daily balance will be lower, and therefore your finance charges will be, too.

Cut the Cable

You can save money by disconnecting your cable TV service during the times of year that you don't need it. Going on a long vacation? Have a summer ahead filled with time-consuming activities? Just get rid of the cable during the time you won't be using it, and who knows, you might even be offered an enticing deal when it's time to re-subscribe.

Lead the Way for Your Friends

You're trying to keep your socializing budget under control, but your friends are constantly inviting you on expensive outings you can't afford! Instead of having to turn down invitations, take the initiative and be first to invite everyone out. This way, you can decide the place—something more in your price range. Better yet, host a potluck or movie night at your home.

A Visual Debt Reminder

If you're having trouble paying down your debt, try making a chart or graph of what you want to accomplish. Place it somewhere you'll see it often, and update it as you send in checks. Being able to track your progress will help keep you motivated!

—Linda Everett

Stop Paying For Unused Cellular Minutes

If you find yourself under-using your mobile minutes each month, consider canceling your current plan when your contract runs out and paying as you go instead. With pay-as-you-go phones, you pay an amount of money up front instead of getting a bill each month. Most plans will charge you 5–10¢ a minute, and offer discounts if you put a large amount of money—usually $100—on the phone. The good news is that you can also send and receive text (and sometimes picture) messages, and even surf the web on some phones. The bad news is that the minutes usually expire after a certain amount of time. Pay-as-you-go phones are great for phones that you pretty much only use in an emergency, and for giving to teens so that you can make sure they don't overspend. Ask at a cell phone or electronics store about pay-as-you-go phones and promotions.

Save Automatically

To help you save on a monthly basis, make it easier to contribute to your savings account. Banks allow you to set up recurring transfers, so set one up for each time you get paid. Putting even $50 into your savings account each time you get a paycheck will quickly add up, and you'll be glad you have it on a rainy day or when vacation time rolls around.

Be Vigilant about Your Car Insurance

When your auto insurance renewal comes in the mail, don't just write a check and send it in. Review your policy and make sure it's still the type of coverage you need as your vehicle ages year after year. When it gets to the point where your collision coverage premiums (plus the deductible) are almost the same as the value of the car itself, drop that portion of the coverage—you're only flushing money down the toilet.

When Health Insurance Goes Wrong

Those of us lucky enough to have health insurance love having to pay less for health care—as long as the system works. If (OK, *when*) you have problems with your health insurance reimbursing you for a claim, it can be so frustrating and even demoralizing that you're tempted to give up. Here are some steps you can take to make sure you get the money you deserve.

✦ Stay organized. Take notes when you are disputing a claim, and refer to them when you call the company. The representative will be more likely to take you seriously if you can state the dates you spoke to someone, what the claim or reference number is, and the amount it was for. Also make sure to have the date the service was performed and the date the claim was submitted on hand.

◆ Ask your doctor for help. If the insurance company is telling you the procedure wasn't necessary or "reasonable or customary," have your doctor's office write a letter or call the company to explain why it was.

◆ If you have a group plan, see if you can get the administrator of the plan (usually in your HR department) to help you complain to the company.

◆ Contact your state's department of insurance. If they won't help you go after the company, they can usually at least provide you with important information about your rights.

◆ Don't be afraid to go to court. If you feel you are unjustly being denied a claim, a court will probably think so, too. If the claim amount is less than $500, you will most likely not need an attorney, but if it is higher than that, many attorneys will take the case on a contingency basis (meaning they only get paid if you do) if it seems strong. Bring any literature from the company that seems to contradict why they have been telling you the cost wasn't covered—in most states, judges have ruled that policies have to be straightforward enough for a layperson to read them, not an insurance agent or lawyer.

Cheaper Tooth Care

Many companies don't offer dental insurance, but you can join a plan on your own for discounts ranging from 10–60 percent off. Check out DentalPlans.com or call 1-888-632-5353 to find a plan and dentist in your neighborhood. Certain plans may be used in combination with dental insurance you already have.

Waive It Off

It sounds too simple to be true, but you can often just ask credit card companies, utilities, landlords, and others to waive late fees. If you're a longtime customer with a good history, companies will often re-credit your account, especially if it was your first offense.

Share More Than Cookies with the Neighbors!

Do you and your neighbors both use wireless internet? A great way to save is to go in on an internet plan together. If you already have a plan, ask a neighbor you trust if they'd like to pay you for half the cost if you give them the password to your network. Especially if you live in an apartment building, you should be able to use the wireless internet hub you currently own, but if your homes are particularly far apart you may need to extend your network with a second hub or router.

Phone Cards: A Must for Overseas Dialing!

When making international phone calls, never dial directly. Instead, buy an international phone card at your local convenience store. Most specialize in a particular country or continent, and will allow you to talk for only pennies a minute. You can also go to AlTelephone.com, which works pretty much the same way, but gives you the option of prepaying online or being sent a bill.

Choosing the Card That's Right for You

Even if you're in the market for a new credit card, the amount of offers that show up in your mailbox can be daunting. And whether you anticipate your relationship with the card to be long and prosperous, or quick and a little irresponsible, how do you know which card is right for you? Here are some questions to ask before you decide.

✦ How long is the introductory period? Most cards start you off with a good deal, like a low APR or free balance transfers. But make sure to check how long the promotional rates last.

✦ What perks does it have? If you fly a lot, cards with air-mile programs can save you hundreds. Other cards offer insurance on purchases or car rentals. Figure out how much you think these extras will save you, and take this into consideration when you pick a card.

✦ What will your credit limit be? Most companies don't like to tell you what your credit limit is until you apply for the card, but before you sign, first ask them how much you are going to be able to spend. If you're good about paying your bill off, having a high percentage of credit left will help your credit score. But if you have trouble keeping yourself from maxing out, ask if you can lower the card's limit.

✦ What's the best deal you can get? Compare card offers and don't be afraid to negotiate. Visit CardWeb.com, where you can find hundreds of cards sorted by types of rewards, your credit history, and their brand. Call the phone number listed to see if you qualify for cards that fit what you need.

Negotiate Your Way to Savings

If you're lucky enough to live in an area that has more than one company providing phone, cable, or other utilities, use this to your advantage by lowering your payment amount—without having to switch companies! Find out what the competitors are charging by calling them or visiting WhiteFence.com, then call and ask for your rates to be lowered. If the first person you talk to says no, don't be discouraged and don't be afraid to ask to speak to a supervisor. If you call between 9 a.m. and 5 p.m. you'll be more likely to get an experienced supervisor on the phone who's willing to bargain.

● Who Knew?

Most banks are FDIC insured, but you should still make sure yours is. With an FDIC-insured bank, even if the financial institution fails your money will still be insured for up to $200,000.

Raise Your Deductibles to Lower Your Costs

You can save hundreds each year on your home and auto insurance by raising your deductibles. If you have more than one type of insurance with the same carrier, you may also qualify for bundled discounts. It's not in your insurance company's best interests to keep you informed about the lowest rates, so make sure you call them and ask.

Take Advantage of Employer Discounts

Your employer may offer more perks than just weak coffee in Styrofoam cups and free filtered water. In addition to the traditional retirement accounts and health care options, many employers—especially companies that have a national presence—offer many more benefits on a small and large scale. Check with your HR department to see if you can get pre-tax money for transportation or "flex-spending"—funds that you can spend on medical or other specified expenses. Many employers often have agreements with businesses and are able to offer their employees discounted movie and amusement park tickets, savings on cell phones and computer equipment, and cheaper rates at nearby gyms.

Change Your Due Dates

Here's an easy solution if you keep getting socked with late fees, or neglect to pay more than the minimum on your credit cards because the payment is always due at the same time as your rent. Ask your credit card company to change the date your payment is due. It might take a few months to kick in, but you'll be able to pay down the card more easily during the part of the month that isn't as much of a crunch.

It May Be Time For a Transfer

If you owe lots of money to one credit card and not-so-much to one with a lower interest rate, ask your credit card company if you can do a balance transfer. You may incur a fee, but you often end up saving in the end, and many cards offer them for free during the first year of your agreement. If you have two cards from the same company, ask if the card with the better deal allows "credit reallocation," which would let you transfer not only the balance from the other card but its credit limit as well, without even submitting you to another credit check.

What To Do When Collection Agencies Call

Nothing feels worse than having collection agencies calling you to try to collect on a debt. If you have old debt, it's time to stop feeling bad about it and confront the collection agencies or credit card companies head-on. Here are some tips for dealing with debt in collections, one of the worst kinds in terms of your credit report.

+ The first step is to stop ignoring phone calls and letters. It's hard, but you know it must be done!

+ It's important to remember the person you're talking to is just doing his or her job. If you're polite during the entire call, he or she will be more likely to help you out. Whatever you do, don't lose your cool.

+ The first tactic of most collection agencies will be to try to get you to pay the total amount at once. You should be aware that you can always set up a payment plan. Only pay as much as you think you can each month—never commit to more than you can pay and risk being unable to make payments.

+ Most collection agencies will settle for 40 to 60 percent of the total amount you owe. The more you can pay them immediately as a lump sum, and the higher you can make your monthly payments, the better! Don't be afraid to negotiate.

+ In local and state courts in many areas, lawsuits from collection and credit card agencies have been overturned. If you are being asked to pay more than 60 percent of the debt, the agency has been unable to show you proof that you owe the debt, or you otherwise feel like you're getting a raw deal, don't be afraid to go to court with the collection agency. Not only do you deserve to go in front of a neutral arbitrator, it will make the other party more likely to settle (because they won't want to pay lawyer's fees). However, it is vitally important that you stay apprised of court dates and show up to every one of them.

✦ Stay empowered! Remember the important thing: you're taking care of your bad debt. You deserve to be able to work toward clean credit, and to have the agency you owe money to be polite and respectful. Don't settle for less!

Save Money Fast On Homeowners Insurance

Did you know that most homeowners insurance policies will deduct 3–5 percent of your cost for adding simple security features such as a smoke alarm or dead bolts? You can often save a lot more if you're willing to install a more sophisticated security system. These systems can get expensive, but the savings (not to mention the security) may be worth it. Before you choose one, make sure to call your insurance company to see what kind of system they recommend. You may also be able to save if you are 65 or older.

● Who Knew?

Although households with no landline use an average of 332 more minutes per month on their cell phones than those with a landline, they still spend an average of $33 less per month on phone service.

CHAPTER 24

Energy-Saving Solutions

A Smarter Power Cord

One of the easiest ways to save money on electricity is to turn off electronics when you're not using them. To make it easier, get a power strip like the SmartStrip, which powers down devices based on one device's usage. For example, when you switch off your computer, the SmartStrip will cut the power to your monitor, printer, and scanner as well.

Quick Lesson in Refrigeration

You can make your refrigerator more energy efficient by understanding how it works. Refrigerators use energy to reduce the humidity inside, which helps cool foods. Therefore, any time you leave an open container of liquid inside, you're wasting energy. Make sure all your pitchers have lids, and make sure dressings and moist leftovers are well-covered. You should also always let hot foods cool before placing them in the refrigerator, so it doesn't have to use extra energy to bring them down to room temperature. Of course, be careful with cooked meats, eggs, and poultry—they shouldn't stay out for more than an hour.

Be a Night Owl

You may not realize that most electric companies charge more for power during the day than at night. Contact your local utility to find out whether this is the case in your area. If it is, make sure to do all your laundry, dishwashing, internet surfing, and other power-intensive tasks during off-peak hours. We noticed the difference on our electric bill, and you will, too.

Hand Wash Separately

Having an Energy Star dishwasher is energy efficient, but not when you are running it twice a day. Cut back on the amount of space you take up in your dishwasher by washing large pots and pans the old-fashioned way in the sink. By spending a little extra water to wash these items separately, you'll save a lot of water in fewer loads washed.

Look For Leaks!

According to the Environmental Protection Agency, a well-sealed home can be up to 20 percent more energy efficient. Most leaks occur in the basement or attic—look where you feel a draft or around wiring holes, plumbing vents, ducts, and basement rim joints. You'll be able to seal lots of leaks with a simple caulking gun, but for instructions on how to plug larger holes go to EnergyStar.gov and search for "plug leaks."

Shut Out the Lights

One of the easiest ways to waste money is by leaving lights on that aren't being used. Save your hard-earned cash by buying motion-activated lights for your home, especially for bathrooms and hallways. It may seem expensive at first, but they'll pay for themselves soon enough. You'll love seeing a smaller electric bill each month!

—*Kitty Lubin Rosati, Crested Butte, CO*

Keep It Humid

It's true that it's not the heat that makes you feel warm, it's the humidity. Humid air feels warmer than dry air, so in the winter, instead of cranking the heat, run a humidifier. This allows you to turn down the heat, save energy, and still feel comfortable. Live, leafy plants also help raise humidity levels.

Does Your Teenager Take 45-Minute Showers?

If you have teenagers, try giving them an incentive to take shorter showers—like five minutes added on to their curfew for every minute they shave off their showering time.

—*Salina Gonzalez, Minden, LA*

Who Knew?

According to the *Wall Street Journal*, shortening your daily shower by five minutes can save you $100 per year on water bills.

Easy Fix for a Stuck Thermostat

If your furnace and AC don't seem to be paying attention to your thermostat, don't call the expensive repairman just yet. It could be a simple case of your thermostat's connectors being dirty. Take off the casing, and run the point of an index card through the connectors to remove any crud. Stand back and cross your fingers, and your thermostat may be as good as new.

Keep Cold Appliances Cold

It may be time to rearrange your kitchen for energy-efficient savings. Keeping appliances that heat things up (like a stove, oven, or toaster) away from your refrigerator will make it easier for your fridge and freezer to stay cold, which can save you lots of money in the long run.

Know Your Hot and Cold Water Levels

Quit fiddling with the knobs on your shower when trying to get the water just right before you hop in. Find your favorite setting, then mark where the knob is pointing on the tile with a dab of nail polish. This water-preserving trick is great for kids, who can take a long time adjusting the water before they get in.

Use Lighter Paint

If you're trying to decide between deep or baby blue for your walls, you should know that lighter colors of paint will help you use less energy. They reflect the light and heat in a room better than darker hues.

Make Sure That Lint Screen Is Clean!

Removing the lint from the screen in your dryer may not be enough to make sure it is running as efficiently as possible. The fabric softener used in dryer sheets can get caught in the mesh, even if you can't see it. To be sure you're completely cleaning the screen, remove it and clean it with warm, soapy water and a brush. Leave it out to dry completely before placing back in your dryer.

The Easiest Way to Save on Water

If you pay for water, make sure to never use more than you have to. Only wash full loads of laundry and dishes, and don't leave the tap running.

Fuel Co-Ops

A fuel co-op is an organization that negotiates lower rates for your heating gas by buying in bulk. Even though you normally have to pay a membership fee, you can save big bucks on your heating bill by joining a fuel co-op, and you often don't even need to change from your current gas company. Most co-ops will offer you discounts if you're a senior citizen or on a fixed income. To find one in your area simply type "fuel co-op" and your geographic location (e.g., "New Jersey") into Google or another search engine.

A Hot Attic Means a Hot House

When running your air conditioner, make sure your attic isn't hot, which will warm up ceilings and make it much more expensive to cool your home. Open any attic windows, and invest in a fan that will suck hot air out during the day and pump cool air in at night.

Leaky Fridge?

If your refrigerator is more than a few years old, the rubber lining that runs around the door (also known as the gasket) could be loose. To find out, close the door on a piece of paper. If you can pull it out without it ripping, your gasket is loose. To figure out where, turn on a battery-powered lamp or flashlight and place it in your fridge. Turn the lights off in your kitchen and close the door. Wherever you see light peeking through, cold air is leaking! Try regluing your gasket or buying a new one from wherever you purchased your fridge.

Close Some Vents

Close the heating and air-conditioning vents in rooms in your home you don't frequently use, like a guest room or laundry room. If your vents don't have closures, simply seal them off with duct tape.

—*Barbie Rodgers, Wilmington, NC*

Buy Your Water Heater a Jacket

A water heater insulation jacket costs $15–$35, but it can cut the cost to heat your water dramatically. By insulating your water heater, you'll cut in half the amount of energy it needs to heat standing water, also cutting down on the amount you need to pay. To find out if you need a water heater jacket, touch the side of it. If it's warm, it's leaking energy.

The Venetian Secret

Be smart when using your heating or air conditioning. When the heat's on, open the blinds on windows that are exposed to the sun, and use a little solar heat to help out your furnace! When you have the AC going, close as many blinds as possible, so that the sun won't get in and warm your house more than necessary.

Fabulously Full Freezer

Your freezer is more energy efficient when it's full of stuff, so don't be shy about stuffing it as much as possible. When you're running low on food items, just fill a few empty juice cartons with water and use them to fill up the space.

Ensure Accurate Temperature

For accurate temperature readings, make sure to place your thermostat away from sources of artificial heat, like ovens, appliances, computers, or direct sunlight. An inaccurately high temperature at the thermostat will cause the rest of the house to be colder than you want it to be. Similarly, make sure that cold air, such as that from windows or wiring holes, isn't making its way to the thermostat either. Also, make sure your thermostat is reading the inside room temperature and not the outside temperature.

Savings with Each Flush

A great way to save water is to fill a plastic bottle or two with sand and put them in your toilet tank. You'll use a lot less water with each flush. Just make sure you place them away from the operating mechanism. Also, don't use bricks—they disintegrate and can damage your toilet.

—Brad Elgart, Winters, TX

Replace Those Shower Heads!

If the shower heads in your home were installed before 1994, you should seriously consider replacing them with their modern, energy-saving equivalents. Check out your local hardware store for low-flow alternatives, and remember that just because it's low-flow doesn't mean it has to be weak!

Who Knew?

According to the US Department of Energy, electronics account for 15 percent of the average household's energy bill.

Finding a Water Leak

If you suspect you might have a water leak in your home, take a look at your water meter before you and your family leave the house on an all-day excursion. Write down the reading, and look at it again when you return. If any water has been used, you know you have a problem.

Defrost It!

A frosty freezer can make a tough job for your freezer's motor, which not only makes it less energy efficient, but can also lead to the motor burning itself out! If you have a quarter of an inch of frost build-up or more, it's time to defrost your freezer. Here's the easiest way how: Turn off your freezer, then turn a hairdryer on it. Use a wooden spoon to dislodge any large chunks of ice and throw them in your sink or potted plants. Once it's free of ice, wash it down with warm water with a bit of dishwashing liquid mixed in. Before you move back your perishables, first spray the entire freezer with non-stick cooking spray. It will make frost less likely to form, and ice a breeze to dislodge.

Lock Your Windows

In the winter, don't just keep windows closed, make sure they're locked for the tightest possible seal. This could greatly reduce drafts.

Let Your Computer Rest

Leaving your computer on all day can be a real energy drain, but with a program called Edison, you can program it to go into "sleep" mode to save you money. Visit Verdiem.com/edison to download the free software (sorry, PCs only), which lets you set up a schedule for when you normally use your computer and allows you to decide how deeply you want your computer to sleep. Then it does the rest of the work for you, making sure that your computer isn't using energy when it doesn't have to.

A Pain in the Drain

Make sure to drain your water heater once a year to get rid of sediment. Left too long, this grit can build up until you're using energy to heat sludge. To find out how to complete this simple home maintenance trick, type "how to drain a water heater" into Google or another search engine. And start to save!

⬤ Who Knew?

If your faucet is leaking, it can add up to more than water running down the drain. One drop per second can add up to 165 gallons a month—that's more water than the average person uses in two weeks!

Brrrr!

When using your oven this winter, don't let all that warm air go to waste! As long as it won't pose a safety hazard to children or pets, keep your oven door open after cooking to help heat the house. A little goes a long way!

Leaky Toilets Mean Higher Water Bills

Does your toilet have a leak? To find out, put a drop of food coloring in the tank and see if it shows up in the bowl. If it does, fix the leak to save up to 73,000 gallons of water per year!

Keeping Extra Cool

It may feel like a waste to keep the fans on at the same time as the air conditioner, but it's not. You'll actually save money, because you can keep the thermostat higher once you've created an internal breeze that will make you feel several degrees cooler (think of how much the wind outside affects how cool you feel, regardless of the actual temperature). Keep the fan on only while people are in the room, though, and remember to regularly vacuum both fan and air conditioner vents for optimum efficiency.

Don't Throw Money Down the Pool Drain

Save money and electricity by running your pool pump and filter for the minimum amount of time necessary. Experiment by decreasing the amount of time you run it until you find where that point is. You should also set it for off-peak electricity times (morning and evening).

Water-Saving Secret

The easiest way to lower your water usage (and utility bill) is to screw low-flow aerators into your faucets. Aerators are easy to install, cost a dollar or less, and can save you $50 or more per year.

Make the Light Bulb Switch

If you know about going green, you've probably heard about compact fluorescent bulbs. If you haven't changed out your regular light bulbs yet, do it today! Not only will they last 10 times longer, they use up to 75 percent energy, bringing your electricity bill down.

Set It and Forget It

If you've ever turned on a sprinkler or soaker hose and then forgotten about it, the mechanical water timer is the gadget for you. Available at your local hardware store, these hose attachments work like egg timers and turn off the water supply after the amount of time you specify, usually between 10 minutes and two hours.

If You Were a Tree, Where Would You Be?

One way we save money on our electric bill is by providing our house with natural shade. Planting trees and shrubs so that they shade the sunny side of your home will help cut down on the amount of air conditioning needed.

Cold Is Better

Did you know that 80 to 90 percent of the energy used by a washing machine is to heat the water? When doing laundry, always use cold water to wash your clothes. Due to advances in detergents and washing machines, the only time you really need to use warm or hot water is when you need to get a really bad stain, like red wine or oil, out of an article. Not only will you help the environment, you'll save money on heating the water, too.

Who Knew?

New washing machines use about 20 fewer gallons of water per load than older machines.

Heat Less Water

You never use your water on full-blast hot anyway, so it's worth it to lower the temperature of your water. You can save up to $125 per year by simply lowering the thermostat on your hot water heater from 140° to 120° F.

CHAPTER 25

The Best of the Web: Bargains, Free Stuff, and More

Some Shameless Self-Promotion

We don't mind doing a bit of self-promotion for our site, WhoKnewTips.com, because we know you're sure to find some great money-saving ideas when you visit. In addition to submitting your own tips to be featured in our next book, you can find out more about Who Knew? products and Bruce's latest appearances on HSN. Best of all is our blog, where we post daily deals from around the web, household advice, and the latest ways for you to save money. Come visit soon!

Know the Code

Ever go to buy something online and see that little box to enter a promotional or coupon code? Well now you never have to wish you had something to enter into that box again. At RetailMeNot.com, you can find hundreds of codes that will give you savings at a large variety of websites, including Kohls.com, Amazon.com, and JCPenney.com. If this site doesn't have a code for the store you're looking for, also try MomsView.com, DealTaker.com, or PocketDeal.com. Or simply type the name of the online store and the words "coupon code" into a search engine.

Ads for Everything

Classified ads aren't dead—they've just moved from your newspaper to Craigslist. If you've never visited, you're missing out. Go to Craigslist.org, find your city, and browse thousands of listings for jobs, roommates, garage sales, personal ads, classes, volunteer opportunities, and pretty much anything else you can think of. Click on "free" under "for sale" to find tons of people giving away all sorts of stuff—you normally just need to go pick it up.

Junk Mail Be Gone!

Sick of getting a million credit card offers every time you open your mail box? You can opt out for free by calling 1-888-567-8688 or visiting OptOutPrescreen.com. Signing up will eliminate all of those "pre-approved" offers. While you're at it, visit ProQuo.com and enter your name and address at their site to remove yourself from even more companies' mailing lists.

The 411 on Major Appliances

Washing machine just break down and you're not sure if it's under warranty? Need to replace a part in your dishwasher, but don't know what its specifications are? Wanting to buy a microwave and not sure what you should be looking for? Appliance411.com is here to help. They have purchasing information (including rebates), FAQs about appliances big and small, and best yet, online manuals and warranty information for just about any model of any appliance. If you're looking for help with any machine in your home, go here first.

Live to Learn

At GCFLearnFree.org, you can finally learn how to use all those computer programs that have been befuddling you. Sign up for classes taught over the internet, or download learning materials to go at your own pace. Classes include Microsoft Windows, Word, and

Excel, internet searching, and email basics. The site also offers free lessons in managing money, math skills, and "everyday life" problems.

Our Favorite Online Newsletter

One of our favorite magazines for money-saving tips is *All You*, and now you can get a free sneak peek! Visit their website at AllYou.com and look for the link to sign up for their email newsletter. In addition to offering tips and tricks, the email will tell you all of the coupons that are going to be in that month's issue, so you can plan ahead.

Play Your Favorite Card Games Online

Boss disabled your solitaire game at work? Try out IdiotsDelight.net, where you can choose from more than two dozen solitaire card games you can play online. Click on "Klondike" to play "regular" solitaire. Warning: you might get hooked!

Begin the Journey to a Healthier Life

Trends in dieting seem to change with the season. One day you're being told to eat plain toast, the next, bacon—it all gets a little confusing! That's where FatSecret.com comes in. Create a personalized exercise and nutrition program, then share it with their online community for moral support and feedback. Plus, you can track your progress, keep an online fitness journal, and research different diets and fitness techniques. Another fitness site we love is MyHomePersonalTrainer.com, where you can calculate your ideal weight and heart rate, assess your cardiovascular fitness, and receive all sorts of free advice to help you start getting in shape.

A Superhero for Your Computer

Windows Defender is software that helps protect your computer against pop-ups, slow performance, and security threats caused by spyware and other unwanted software by detecting it and removing it from your computer. Windows Defender features "Real-Time Protection," a monitoring system that recommends actions against spyware when it's detected, minimizes interruptions, and helps you stay productive. It's free if you own Windows. Just go to Microsoft.com and search for "defender."

—*Karen Matsu Greenberg, New York, NY*

Who Knew? CLASSIC TIP

Before you go to the gas station, visit GasBuddy.com. Enter your zip code, and your new buddy will tell you the gas stations with the cheapest prices nearby. You can also search to find the least expensive pump prices in your entire state or entire city. You'll never fill up, only to see a cheaper station on the way home, again!

Navigate Through a "Customer Service" Nightmare

If you've ever gone mad trying to navigate the menu options when you call your cell phone provider, credit card company, bank, or anywhere else, head over to GetHuman.com first. GetHuman gives you the secret phone numbers or combinations of keystrokes to press to get an actual person on the line, listed by company. So if you're calling USAA, for instance, you know that your best bet for good customer service is hitting 00#, then # again at the prompt.

Buying a New Car?

Before heading to the dealer, go to TrueCar.com first. TrueCar has great articles on buying cars, but better still, it has reader-compiled prices of what people across the country have paid for various makes and models. It's better than "Blue Book" pricing, because it doesn't tell you what the vehicle is worth, it tells you what people have actually paid when buying the car new and used. Just enter the make of the car and your zip code, and you can find the cheapest place to buy a car near you.

Fatten Your Wallet

Even if trolling the internet for coupons isn't your bag, there is still one site you definitely need to sign up for: FatWallet.com. Signing up at FatWallet is one of the best ways to start saving money online immediately and easily. All you have to do is log on to the site before making purchases at such websites as BabiesRUs.com, Payless.com, Nordstrom.com, Buy.com, and Walmart.com. They'll give you money back on everything you buy—usually 2–8 percent, and let you know if there are any coupon codes for sales on the site. You can even earn cash back for using travel sites like Hotels.com, Expedia.com, and JetBlue.com, and if you use an online dating site, you can save a huge portion on your membership (Match.com gives you 30 percent back and Chemistry.com 50 percent!). You'll usually have to wait several months for your money, but when it's as simple as clicking through, why not? (For more details on how it all works, check out their FAQ page.) And if you do enjoy coupon clipping, they also offer printable coupons and one of the best user forums about recent deals on the web.

How Do I...?

To learn how to do just about anything, visit WonderHowTo.com, which culls instructional videos from more than 1,700 websites. You can check out what's hot, do a custom search, or browse through such categories as family, electronics, software, dance, fitness, magic tricks, and pets. Whether you want to learn how to cut your own hair, use Photoshop software, or make a shot glass out of ice, you'll find it here.

Your Carpet Resource

If you need new carpeting, the first place you should go is HowToBuyCarpet.com. There, you'll learn the best places to buy carpet, how to avoid manufacturer scams, and become an educated carpet consumer.

More Online Games

If you're looking for games for the kids—or an excuse to act like a kid yourself—head to Kongregate.com, which boasts more than 24,000 free games. There are also tons of free games at Pogo.com and OnlineFlashGames.org as well.

Pay Less for Shipping

If you're wondering what the fastest, cheapest way to ship an item is, head over to ShipGooder.com. You enter the weight of the package, your address, and where it's going, and the site will give you quotes from FedEx, UPS, the United States Postal Service, and DHL. The site also provides free tracking and direct links to the carriers once you've seen the prices.

Say Goodbye to Pesky Catalogs

We used to get catalogs for everything from girls' clothes (we only have boys) to farm equipment (we do have a couple of pigs...). Not anymore. Go to CatalogChoice.org and get your name off all those weirdo mailing lists.

Keep Unwanted Phone Calls Away

Never lie about who you are to a telemarketer again ("Bruce and Jeanne Lubin are out of town!"). Put your name on the official "Do not call list" by going to DoNotCall.gov (or calling 1-888-382-1222).

File Too Large to Email?

Most email servers choke on attachments that are 10 megabytes or larger, but you can avoid that problem with Drop.io. Upload files of up to 100 megabytes, then receive a customizable web address that you can send to your contacts so they can download the files. (Be sure to click "Share," then "Zip File" at the top to make the whole package downloadable at once.) Users can even leave notes and collaborate in other ways right on the site.

⬤ Who Knew? CLASSIC TIP

Sick of paying up to $3 every time you have to visit an ATM? At AllPointNetwork.com, you can find all of the surcharge-free ATMs in your area by entering your city and state or your zip code. Many of the listings are for stores that offer cash-back with purchase, but you never know when you'll find a free ATM you never knew about.

Don't Forget About Your Photos!

Store your cherished digital photos and videos for free at Photobucket. com, Flickr.com, and Picasa.com. These sites not only provide a backup in case the files on your computer get lost, they also allow you to easily share photos with friends. You can also keep your photos on sites where you order photos, such as Walmart.com, Snapfish.com, and Shutterfly.com. Be aware, however, that these sites only allow you to store photos as long as your account is active.

Online Financial Planning

Is there anything the internet can't do? Now you can create a personalized picture of your finances without shelling out thousands of dollars for a session with an adviser. Kiplinger.com is our favorite site to help you get on the right financial track. Hunt around their site to find treasure troves of free financial advice. Then head over to Voyant (PlanWithVoyant.com) to map your financial goals (such as buying a home, saving for retirement, or paying for your kids' college) along an interactive timeline. It's a great way to plan for the future and chart your progress.

Where the Wild Files Are: Finding Free Music Online

Pretty much any computer these days comes with some kind of program to play MP3s, and other music files, and music is increasingly easy to find on the internet. You should be aware, though, that many sites that offer free MP3s aren't legal, as there are laws in place to make sure that studios and artists get money for their songs. Here are some sites, however, where you can find free, legal MP3 files to download.

- Amazon.com offers dozens of free MP3s as special promotions. To find them, simply select "MP3 downloads" from the drop-down search menu. When the list pops up, select "Price: low to high" from the drop-down sort menu on the upper right-hand side of the MP3 list. You can also subscribe to an email newsletter that keeps you apprised of new deals—keep an eye out for the "Amazon delivers" ad on the left side of the screen and click on "subscribe now."

- If you're a fan of old radio shows like *Amos 'n' Andy*, Bing Crosby specials, and the *Benny Goodman Show*, check out RadioLovers.com, which gives you free downloads of hundreds of classic programs.

- If you use iTunes, check the iTunes store regularly for free tracks, which you can easily find on the main page or the music home page.

- EMusic.com offers 35 free music downloads as an incentive to get you to join their site. After you choose your 35 favorites (from more than 7 million offerings) downloads start at just 50¢ each. Of course, if you cancel your membership during the trial period, you can keep the 35 songs for free. (Note: eMusic sometimes changes this offer, so act fast!)

- For easy-to-download MP3s of all varieties, go to Sideload.com, which pulls MP3s from free sources from around the internet.

You Don't Need Cable to Watch
The Daily Show

If you have a fast internet connection and a fairly new computer, you can watch TV and movies online for free! At Hulu.com, you can watch TV right on your monitor. Play the most recent episodes of shows from FOX, NBC, Comedy Central, and other networks; or classics like *The Dick Van Dyke Show* and *Alfred Hitchcock Presents*. They even have a good selection of movies, whether you're looking for something to entertain the kids or something R-rated for date night.

Who Knew?

Sixty-three percent of Americans watch videos online, ranging from short news clips to full-length movies and TV programs.

Free Online Movies

At Truveo.com, you can find literally hundreds of movies you can watch for free. While many of them are kind of weird (like *The Giant Gila Monster*), there are some hits you've never seen and plenty of classics you'll love to watch again, like *The Man Who Knew Too Much* and *Nobody's Fool*. Do a search for "full length movie" to sift out the clips.

The Best Place for Recipes

Our favorite site for free recipes is Epicurious.com, where you can get search for recipes by type (appetizers, drinks, entrees, etc.), ingredients or keywords to search for specific recipes. Since their recipes are pulled from publications like *Bon Appétit* and *Gourmet*, you know they're going to be good, but if you're not sure, you can read reader reviews. You can also start a "recipe box" of your favorite recipes from the site—make sure to include one of their more than 400 recipes for chocolate cake!

Better Than Tying a String Around Your Finger

"Never forget the important stuff again" is the slogan of Rminder.com. They offer free reminders by allowing you to enter text, then sending it as a text message to your cell phone at the time you specify. You can also have them turn your text into a voice message, and call you instead.

The Best Radio Station You'll Ever Hear—Yours!

Pandora.com is nothing short of amazing. It's an online radio station that tailors what it plays to what you like, and it's almost scarily accurate. Better yet, it will introduce you to tons of artists you never knew existed, but love. It works by streaming the music from your web browser (you don't download any music files), and allowing you to rate songs "thumbs up" or "thumbs down." For every song you rate thumbs up, it will play more like it, and also provide you with a link to where you can purchase the MP3 file online. The downside to Pandora is that you can only skip to the next song six times an hour, and you can't necessarily choose what song or artist you'd like to hear. However, you'll be so pleased with Pandora's music experience customized just for you, you won't mind.

Keep the Kids Entertained

At FreeStuff4Kids.net, self-avowed "cheapskate mom" Randa Clay gathers all sorts of things for kids online. Some links are to cool, interactive sites that your child will enjoy, some are to online giveaways of kid-related products, and others will give you free printable worksheets and games for kids. And to never have to buy a coloring book again, head over to Free-Coloring-Pages.com, where you can find printable images for kids to color, including those of popular cartoon characters.

—*Joanne Dyndiuk*

Save on Calls Over the Web

Using your phone over the internet may sound daunting, but it can save you hundreds of dollars a year. In addition, it can provide you with some nice benefits, like choosing your area code and getting voicemail messages sent to your email inbox. Some voice-over-internet phone services have to be used through your computer, and other companies will provide you with an adapter that you use to connect your phone to your computer (or router). CNET.com has one of the best guides to internet calling. To find it, type "CNET internet phones" into Google and click on the first link.

Who Knew?

One of the most expensive places to buy second-hand clothing online is CharityFolks.com. Of course, it's all for a good cause. If you don't want to spend $1,000 for Angelina Jolie's skin-tight leather outfit from the movie *Wanted*, you can get a former button-down shirt of Ted Danson's or a pair of jeans worn by Donnie Wahlberg for only $75.

Find the Cheapest Medicines

At Destination Rx (DRx.com), you can uncover lower-cost drug options by finding out if your prescriptions are available as generics, locating the most inexpensive pharmacies near you, and even comparing the different types of Medicare Part D prescription plans.

What's This Podcast Thing the Kids Have Been Talking About?

Simply put, podcasts are radio shows that can be downloaded for free on the web. If you have iTunes or similar software, check it to see if it offers a podcast search. Otherwise, head over to PodcastAlley.com, which will allow you to search for and browse through thousands of podcasts in such genres as comedy, food & drink, and kids & family. It also has links for free podcast-playing software if you don't already have some on your computer. And as your kids may have shown you, podcasts can also be videos, usually up to 15 minutes in length. Here are some of our favorite podcasts. To find them, simply enter their names in the search box!

✦ NPR Story of the Day: This podcast is the best short piece from National Public Radio each day. These are as varied as NPR's programming—one day it will be about extreme pumpkin carving, and the next it will be about missionaries in Kenya. Either way, you know you're going to get something interesting.

✦ Car Talk: Another podcast from National Public Radio, this show offers two jovial guys from Boston taking call-in questions about car repair. Addicting even if you don't have wheels!

+ Stuff You Should Know: Kids as well as adults will get a kick out of this podcast from the website How Stuff Works. Each show tackles a burning question, such as "Will Robots Marry?" and "How Could Cats Scuba Dive?"

+ The Onion News Network: This satirical news show, from the makers of newspaper spoof *The Onion*, will have you laughing out loud.

+ National Geographic's Wild Chronicles: This video podcast shows digital shorts about wildlife from all over the world. The only downside is that your child will probably act like a spider monkey, a Panama Golden Frog, or whatever else they saw for the rest of the day.

+ PBS's Wired Science: From one of the coolest magazines ever, *Wired*, comes this video podcast for geeks. You won't be able to resist finding out how an astronaut's suit works, how to make bottle rockets out of 2-liter bottles, or other nerdy info.

+ If you need to divert the kids for a few minutes, try one of Nick Jr.'s podcasts like Blues Clues or Diego. They're each only about a minute long, but luckily small kids will be happy to watch them a few times in a row.

CHAPTER 26

Vacations and Family Activities

Cable: Not Always a Rip-Off

If you have cable, you may have movies and television shows available on demand for free. Many cable systems offer a wide variety of old movies, as well as recent TV shows that cable channels are trying to promote. Every system is different, but take a look and see if there is an option on your On-Demand menu that says "Free Movies," "Free Shows," or "Free On-Demand." You may also have to look through the shows and see which are listed as $0.

Find Cheap Tickets More Easily

If you find Ticketmaster and other ticket sites as annoying as we do, you'll love ZebraTickets.com. Zebra Tickets collects ticket prices from around the web for sporting events, concerts, and plays, so you'll be sure to know which site is offering the best deal.

More Fun Activities Than You Ever Thought Possible

All you need to know when you're searching for fun things to do at Goby.com is what you're interested in and where you are (and, if you want, when you're going). Whether it's getting coffee, going to a playground, hitting up a museum, or more adventurous activities like sailing and horseback riding, Goby will tell you what's out there, and even give you a map to see where it is. The best thing about Goby is its straightforward, user-friendly design: no huge ads, no "sponsored results," no long loading times or signing up. For those of us who have spent a lot of time searching for things online, it's a welcome respite.

Planning a Road Trip?

Find out exactly how much you need to budget for gas money at FuelCostCalculator.com. Enter the make and model of your car and your starting and destination cities, and AAA will calculate how much it will cost you using the Environmental Protection Agency's fuel economy ratings and its own gasoline prices report. With rising gas prices and fluctuating airfare, this is a great site to visit if you're not sure taking the car will save you money.

Going to the Movies

Even if you don't plan on getting snacks at the theater, if you show up with an empty stomach it's hard to say "no" once you smell that popcorn popping! Always eat before you arrive, that way you'll be safe from snacking—and from spending. Find out which theaters in your area offer matinees, and also check to see if any membership programs you belong to offer free or discounted days. In some areas, Cablevision (also known as Optimum) offers free movies once a week for customers who sign up for cable, internet, and phone service.

● Who Knew?

Concessions such as popcorn, candy, and soda account for 40 percent of a movie theater's revenue!

Who Needs Rentals When You Have Friends?

The easiest place to get free DVDs may be at the homes of your friends! Try starting a movie-lending circle with friends or neighbors who also watch a lot of movies. Each person has another person they give movies to, and someone they receive them from. When you get your own movie back, it's time to pick a new one! You may want to pick a timeframe to exchange the movie—for example, sometime before each weekend or at a weekly book club or school-related meeting. Movie-lending circles are a great way to discover movies you might not have picked out yourself, but really enjoy.

Fun Website for Travelers

For ideas of inexpensive places to visit while on vacation from those in the know, visit Localyte.com. Localyte is a free website that connects travelers with locals. Post a question about your destination, and have it answered by a local expert!

Don't Pay for Location

Save money on car rentals by not renting at the airport, which charges rental car companies concession fees. Instead, take a cab to a nearby location—even with the fare factored in, you'll be surprised how much you save.

—Drey Luca, CA

The Cheapest Days to Fly

Flight days flexible? Try searching for trips that begin and end on a Tuesday or Wednesday, when we've found that flights throughout the US and Canada are cheaper.

Who Knew? CLASSIC TIP

Now there's one less thing to worry about when you're on vacation. Water your plants yourself *in absentia* with this handy trick. An ordinary plastic drink bottle filled with water just needs a little hole toward the bottom to serve as a continual drip for your plants. Turn it on its side and place on the soil near the plant stem. Now go enjoy your trip and know you won't come home to a bunch of withering geraniums.

Keep Checking Those Rates

Just because you've booked your flight doesn't mean you can't still save. Make sure to keep an eye on airline prices, and rebook your flight if necessary. Even if your airline charges you $75 to cancel a ticket, if a rival airline is offering tickets at $150 less than you paid you're still saving a bundle.

Keep 'Em Fed

Going on a road trip? Make sure to pack plenty of food before you leave to cut down on having to purchase meals along the way. Periodically handing out food is also a great way to keep kids quiet(er)! Have several different types of snacks on hand so they don't get bored.

Free Summer Fun

For ideas on fun, free activities to do over the summer, try checking out your community center or park district. Most towns have tons of free summertime events, from sports clinics for kids to free concerts for adults. See if they have a website or pick up a calendar at your local branch.

Rent on the Cheap

What would the weekend be without a trip to the video store? With so many options for movie and video game rentals, the supply is up, so it's time to demand! Compare rates at your local video stores, and see if the store with the best perks—like being close to your home and letting you rent for the longest amount of time—will match the lowest price you can find. Since fewer and fewer people have VCRs these days, if you are still renting VHS cassettes, see if you can get a discount or a longer rental period when renting tapes rather than DVDs. Finally, keep an eye out for "Redbox" machines, which can be found in many drug and discount stores, where you can rent a DVD for one night for as low as $1.

> ● **Who Knew?**
>
> When searching for travel deals online, make sure to scroll through a few pages of results before making your pick. Many sites have "sponsored results," which means that companies have paid to be featured at the top of search results.

Don't Stand in Line

If you've been to an airport lately, you've probably noticed that the ticket counters are staffed by fewer people than ever before. It's annoying on a regular travel day, but if there are lots of flight cancellations, this can mean a two-hour-plus wait in line. Save yourself a lot of time by skipping the line all together. Instead, call the customer service number for your airline and rebook your cancelled flight right over the phone.

Pack Alike

Packing for vacation? Consider packing clothes that are in the same color family, and pants that can go with a lot of different shirts. You can more easily mix and match them, so you'll have to pack less. This trick will also come in handy when you spill something on yourself—if your blue shirt is soiled, you still have another in your suitcase.

The Five-Day Outlook for Travel

Farecast.com is one of our favorite sites when planning a trip. If your travel dates are flexible, it will tell you the cheapest days to travel. If you know exactly when you're coming or going, it will predict whether or not the price will go up or down. The coolest part is, it's not affiliated with a particular airline or travel site, so the advice is unbiased. If you want to lock in the price the site gives you, you can buy "insurance" for a small fee.

Keep Burglars Away

If you're concerned about your house being broken into while you're away, don't stop at automatic light switches. Ask your neighbor to park his or her car in your driveway, so robbers will think someone's at home.

Bring Some Easy Mac and Ramen
When You Go

When booking a hotel for your summer vacation, make sure to choose one that offers a free breakfast and an in-room refrigerator and a microwave. Eating a couple of meals at the hotel is one of the easiest ways to save while you're away.

—*Rita Guerrero, Middlebury, VT*

Last-Minute Deals in Travel

If you're looking for the best deals in travel, head over to AirfareWatchdog.com, which catalogs the cheapest fares as they are listed on travel and airline sites—including JetBlue and Northwest, which are often not found elsewhere. This site requires a bit of work— you have to click-through to other sites and try to find the rate yourself, but the "watch dog" will tell you which days of the week to search and in what date range. If you normally spend a lot of time trying different combinations of travel dates and nearby airports, this site will take a lot of the guesswork out of it for you.

The Cheapest Rental Cars

When looking for great deals, Hotwire.com is a good place to turn. The downside to this site is that you don't know which airline you're flying or which hotel you're staying at until after you've booked. While we aren't always a fan of this format for flights or lodging, for cars, who cares what dealer it is, as long as it's at the airport?

Visiting Museums for Free

Even if they normally have high admission prices, most museums offer opportunities for you to visit for free. If a museum gets money from the government, they're usually required to either offer free admission one day a week or charge admission as a "suggested donation"—that is, you only have to pay what you want. Other museums have late hours that are free to visitors once a week or month. If you like looking at art, also check out galleries, where you can find cool, local art displayed for free in the hopes that someone will buy it.

TV: Live and In-Person!

If you live near a big city, especially Los Angeles or New York, one of the most fun free activities you can do is attend a TV taping. Talk shows, sitcoms, and game shows are always looking for studio audience members, and it's fun to not only see a show live, but get a peek at what happens behind the scenes. To get tickets to shows, visit TVTickets.com for shows in LA, or NYCGo.com/?event=view. traveltrade&id=80890 for shows in New York. NYTix.com offers an even wider range of New York tapings, but requires you pay $3 to take advantage of their "special relationships" with the shows. If there is a show that you know is taped in your area, try looking for it or its network online or check for a phone number at the end of the show to call for audience tickets.

Be a Day-Tripper

The most expensive part of any vacation is transportation and lodging, so consider taking several day trips during the summer rather than one week-long one. Commuter rail lines often offer discounts on train fare and tickets to theme parks and other attractions, or you may be overdue to take a drive to that nearby state park. For ideas of where to take day trips in your area, call your state's tourist board or type your state's name and "day trips" into a search engine.

For the Ski Buff

Like skiing? You'll love Liftopia.com. It offers discounts on lift tickets for more than 100 ski resorts across the United States and Canada. You can search by destination, or by categories like "good for beginners" and "nighttime skiing." You can also sign up for an email newsletter that will let you know about upcoming deals.

Netflix: Not Just for the Web-Savvy

You've probably heard of Netflix.com, where you pay a low monthly fee and receive unlimited DVDs in the mail, then watch and return them in postage-paid envelopes. But did you realize you don't need a computer to use the service? The company's well-staffed call center will set you up for an account, add movies to your queue, and even make recommendations for movies you might like. Best of all, you get patched through directly to a person—no sifting through automated menus and then waiting for a half an hour. You can reach Netflix 24 hours a day at 1-866-716-0414.

● Who Knew? CLASSIC TIP

Many concert venues, theaters, and museums hire volunteers in exchange for free admission. Doing a bit of volunteer work will help you get away from the kids for a bit and meet new people. Then bring your family back for the savings!

Travel Savings for Students and Teachers

If you're 26 or under, you have all the luck. Not only do your knees never get sore and people still try to flirt with you, but you can also get great deals when you're traveling in Europe. If you're aged 12–26, if you're a student of any age, or you're a teacher or faculty member, you qualify for the International Student ID Card. Available at ISECard.com, the card costs $25, but with it you get discounts on trains, rental cars, tourist attractions, and more. Best of all, they'll provide medical travel insurance up to $2,000.

Let's Make a Deal

When digging for discounts on rental cars and hotels, always call the hotel or rental company directly for the best deals. If the only phone number you have is a national, toll-free one, look up the local number for that particular location and speak to them directly instead. The closer you get to your travel date, the better—in fact, don't be afraid to call the day before to confirm your reservation and ask for a better rate.

Time to Go Camping!

Waking up to the sights, sounds, and smells of the forest can be one of the most peaceful things you've ever experienced—not to mention, the most inexpensive vacation you've taken in years. If you've never gone camping, it's time to start! If you don't have any equipment, ask friends if you can borrow theirs in exchange for lending them something of yours. You and your kids will enjoy working together while roughing it (and don't worry, "roughing it" can involve bathrooms and showers, electricity hook-ups, and even wireless internet). Best of all, with all that hard work each day, plus all the room to run around in, your kids will get exhausted fast! To find campsites across the United States and Canada, visit ReserveAmerica.com, and for a great article for first-time campers, go to RoadAndTravel.com/adventuretravel/campingforfirsttimers.htm.

Save While You're Away

Many newspapers and magazines will allow you to suspend your home delivery or subscription. If you're going on a long vacation, make sure to call them up and stop service for while you're away. You can also often do this for online movie rental and other services. You won't miss them while you're gone, and then you'll get an extra week or two when your subscription would normally be up.

Time to Get a Passport

In these bad economic times, it's hard to see a silver lining, but here's one for anyone who loves an exotic vacation: It's now cheaper than ever to travel to many fascinating destinations around the world, like

Reychavik, Iceland; Montreal, Canada; and Sydney, Australia. Check out vacation packages on sites like Expedia.com and Orbitz.com, or ask a travel agent for hot deals to faraway lands.

Because a Good Game Is a Good Game

If you love going to see sports, but don't love the price tag of taking your whole family to a professional game, consider amateur sports instead. Colleges as well as intramural leagues have games every weekend for free or a couple of dollars. It's great to support local teams, and younger kids won't even know the difference in skill between a pro player and someone in a Division Three league anyway.

Theme Park Savings

Nothing's more fun than taking the kids to an amusement park, especially when they've been begging you to do it for two summers now. Whether you're going to a local Six Flags–type of park, or going all out for that Disneyland vacation, here are some tips to keep your costs down.

✦ A lot of organizations offer discount packages to local and national theme parks. Check with any organizations you belong to, such as the AARP, AAA, wholesale clubs like BJ's or Costco, or a branch of the military. Also look for promotions mailed out with your credit card bill.

✦ Ask for a group discount. If you have at least 15 people in your party, you can usually get a good deal, depending on the time of year.

✦ Visit AmusementPark.com, which has great deals on tickets to amusement parks around the country. They also have savings on local tours, dinner cruises, museums, and tourist attractions.

✦ Keep an eye out for merchandise tie-ins. Many products—especially soda and chips—offer easy discounts, such as bringing the wrapper or can to the park to get several dollars off.

✦ Check out the packages. Large theme parks such as Universal Studios and Disney World always offer package deals—for example, on flight, hotel, and park tickets. These aren't usually significantly cheaper than buying tickets online through a site like Expedia.com or Orbitz.com, but they do often offer added incentives like free transportation or breakfasts.

✦ Call the park and ask them! Most parks (or their automated representatives) will tell you about current deals being offered, and may offer promotions of their own. Also check the website of the individual park you're visiting.

✦ Before you get to the park, consider the real money-wasters: food and souvenirs. Bring lunches from home, and give each child a certain amount they are allowed to spend at gift shops. For more indecisive kids afraid of hitting their limit, make sure to offer them the chance to go back for an item in a store if they don't find anything they like more (they usually will).

Forgo the Foliage

The best summer vacation you'll ever take might not be in the summer. As soon as Labor Day goes by, the rates go down drastically on hotels and airfare to most vacation destinations. Some of the most-discounted areas are the Caribbean, Hawaii, California, and anywhere else there's a beach. In a warm climate, it will still be as hot as ever on the sand. But the price will be much less and you'll get the added benefit of having fewer crowds. Check out a travel site like Travelocity.com for good deals to your dream destinations.

Where to Find Cheap Cruises

If you're dying to get away on a cruise, check out CruiseDeals.com, which has packages to Alaska, the Bahamas, Hawaii, Mexico, and just about anywhere else you'd want to go on a boat. The company negotiates with some of the world's biggest lines to bring their customers the best rates on cruises. If you want to hit the water, this is the best place to start.

Timeshares

If you're staying somewhere for a week or longer, you may be able to save money on your accommodations by renting a timeshare. Timeshares are pieces of property that are owned jointly by several different families, who split up their time at the property during vacation months. You'll often find people renting out their time, or landlords who rent out their properties on a week-to-week basis over the summer in tourist-filled areas. To find a cheap timeshare in your destination, search on Craigslist or Ebay. You can also try SellMyTimeshareNow.com and TimesharesOnly.com.

Play Hooky!

Sometimes, vacation is all in your mind. If you can't afford to get away but you feel like you're ready to scream, consider taking a personal day off work, and convince your spouse or a friend to do it, too! Then enjoy an empty mall, a relaxing afternoon at the beach, or just a huge brunch (complete with mimosas). Whatever you do, get out of your house (which will just remind you of all your chores), and have fun! You'll be surprised how refreshed you feel after a day away.

● Who Knew?

According to the Travel Industry Association, the number of trips taken drops by 15 percent from summer to fall.

CHAPTER 27

Frugal Shopping Secrets

Haggling 101

Sure, you've always been able to haggle at car dealerships and mom-and-pop stores. But did you know that "big box" stores such as Home Depot and Best Buy are getting in on the act, too? With sales slipping, the staffs of chain stores are now being told that bargaining is OK. Here are some tips to make sure you get the most bang for your buck.

✦ To add extra ammo to your asking price, do a little research at competing stores or on the internet beforehand. If you can tell a salesperson that a store nearby is offering the same item for less, you'll be more likely to get it at that price.

✦ Be aware of "extras" that competing stores are offering. Even if you're not interested in an extended warranty or free engraving at the other place, you can use the incentive to your advantage when bargaining.

✦ Take a spouse or friend. One of the best methods for negotiating is the "good cop, bad cop" strategy. One of you acts really interested in the product, while the other continually points out the flaws and negative aspects. Because of the "good cop," the salesperson will remain hopeful that he can sell the product, but "bad cop" will make him work for it.

✦ Find stores where there is no commission. If the salesperson will make less on a product if he sells it for less, then he will be less likely to give you a discount. But if it's only company money that will be lost, there's a higher chance he'll bow to your demands.

✦ Buy accessories, too. Most stores have a higher mark-up on accessories for well-selling items. If you're buying a memory card and a carrying case for your new camera, you're more likely to get a discount on the camera itself.

> ## ● Who Knew?
>
> In a recent Consumer Reports survey, 88 percent of those who said they had haggled on prices said they were successful at least once.

Need Wood?

Looking for inexpensive, quality building supplies? Check out one of Habitat for Humanity's ReStores, which sell used and surplus materials for low prices. To find a location nearest you, visit Habitat.org/env/restores.

Baby Deals

For the best deals on bulk items for your baby, visit Diapers.com, which offers deals on all kinds of baby supplies (including, yes, diapers), and free shipping!

Reverse Wish List

To save money and space, keep a wish list for things you want now, but might not want in a few months. Whenever you get the urge to buy something, write it down, but don't buy it. Every few months, read through your list. Do you still want that leopard-print Snuggie, ultimate pet stroller, or personalized yoga mat? Chances are, you're willing to let most of them go. It's amazing how fast "I absolutely have to have this" turns into "That's so 2009."

—Mara Berke

Return to the Scene for Even More Deals

You're shopping in your favorite store and notice that there are tons of mark-downs. After you fill your arms with bargains, go home and mark the day on your calendar! Most stores receive shipments of new goods every 9–12 weeks and discount current merchandise to make room for the new stuff. Return to the store during that time frame to find more deals.

The Cure for Shopaholics

If you often find yourself making impulse buys, use this simple trick to cut back on spending: Once you've gathered everything in a store you'd like to purchase, find a place to sit down for a couple of minutes and take a break. Make a phone call, play a game on your cell phone, or just sit back and relax. You'll find that clearing your mind will help you be more rational about what you really need and what you'll regret buying later.

The Best Discounts in Town

If you are an educator, a member of the military, or a government employee, always ask if there is a discount available to you! You'll often find travel and admission discounts offered to these groups. If you're over 60, of course, never ever buy anything without asking if there's a senior discount! Some discounts even start for those 50 and over. Even if you don't look your age, you might as well take advantage of the savings available to you!

The Best Places to Find Clothes Online

Shopping online is one of the easiest, best ways to save money on clothing. Here are some of our favorite sites to find good, inexpensive clothes on the web.

✦ 15DollarStore.com is exactly what it sounds like—a store where all clothing is $15 or less. In addition to a large selection of women's clothing, the site also has belts, handbags, sunglasses, watches, jewelry, and some children's clothing.

✦ If you're trying to save money, it's obviously a good idea to stay away from designer fashion labels. But if you just can't help yourself, Bluefly.com is the best place to go for a bargain. You'll find discounted prices on men's and women's designer clothing, including such labels as Kenneth Cole, Burberry, Armani, Marc Jacobs, Calvin Klein, and Prada. Just try to keep it to a couple outfits and a handbag!

✦ At Zappos.com, you'll find more shoes than you ever imagined possible, including men's, women's, and kids' sneakers; dress shoes; boots; and sandals. Not only do they have free shipping, they'll also include a return shipping label with your order, so if you don't like the shoes once you try them on, you can easily return them for free.

✦ If you love style, check out GoJane.com. Their focus is high-fashion clothing without the designer label or high price.

Your Site for Salon Savings

Addicted to fancy shampoo? Find all the same brands you buy at your salon for much less at SalonSavings.com. Shampoos and hair-care products are 10–80 percent off, and skincare and fragrances are offered at much less as well. This site is also a great place to check if you have a favorite beauty product that has been discontinued.

● Who Knew? CLASSIC TIP

Did you know that up to 30 percent of consumers never get around to returning items that they meant to take back to the store? If you're unsure about an item while you're in the dressing room, the best thing to do is to simply not buy it. Once we began following this policy, we were shocked at how few never-worn garments ended up in our closets.

Use Your Phone to Check Prices

If you're lucky enough to own an iPhone, Blackberry, or other "smart" phone, you're also lucky to have access to applications that make shopping easier. Search in your phone's app store for software that scans barcodes. Once installed, you use your phone's camera to take a snapshot of the barcode, or enter the UPC numbers underneath. Your phone will then give you a list of what the item is being sold for at locations near you. Right now, most applications only cover electronics and other high-ticket items, but more products are being added each month.

Shopping for Electronics?

If you're in the market for a new TV, DVD player, portable music player, or other electronic, the best time to buy is in the late spring and early summer. Prices will drop because new products are usually introduced in the late summer and early fall. New computers are also often released in February, so shop in January for savings.

Rah-Rah for Refurbs

If you're like most people, you probably shy away from buying refurbished electronics, but you shouldn't. We go out of our way to buy refurbs, which not only save cash, but also provide more or less the same level of reliability as brand-new items. Whether it's a cell phone, laptop, gaming console, or television, a refurbished item is arguably less likely to be defective than a new one, because these items are tested at the factory before they're resold. And in the rare instance where a refurb *does* fail, all the other refurbs you've bought will have saved you enough money to replace it. Contrary to popular belief, most refurbished units aren't simply broken items that have been repaired. They may have been returned to the maker for any number of other reasons. A customer may have returned a gift he didn't want, the packaging (but not the actual item) may have been damaged in shipping, the item might have had a cosmetic blemish, or the package may have been missing a nonessential accessory. If you can live with those things, then refurbished items are definitely for you. Many of them even come with the original manufacturer's warranty intact.

Deals on Wheels

The internet can be a great resource for buying a car, particularly a new one. Instead of relying on a salesman's sketchy pitch, do your own online research on the pros and cons of each model. Go test-drive one to make sure you like it, but don't buy it right then. Instead, go home and hunt around for the best price among dealers in your region. Even if the dealership offering the best price is located far away, you may still come out ahead by having them deliver the car to you. We once paid $500 to have an out-of-state dealer ship a vehicle to us—and that was still $1,000 cheaper than buying the car locally.

—*Jerri Thompson Barry*

Know What to Look for When Shopping for Cosmetics

When trying to compare a cosmetic with a less-expensive one, you only have to look at one thing: the active ingredients list. Products that have the same active ingredients are going to do almost the exact same thing, even if the percentages are a bit off. (The only thing you might have to worry about is which smells better.) You'll be surprised how many expensive brands—especially of hair products like shampoo—have the exact same chemicals in them for vastly higher prices.

Take It to the Tailor

Going to a tailor may seem like an expensive proposition, but it's often worth it if you unearth a good deal on a suit or other clothing that doesn't quite fit. Found some jeans for ten bucks that look great but are an inch too long? A jacket that's a steal, but a bit too baggy in the arms? For a small price, you can get these items custom-fitted at a tailor. And you'll still be saving a bundle from what the normal retail price would be.

Buying Plants?

Always buy house plants in the spring, when you'll find a better selection and prices that are 20–60 percent cheaper.

Online Shopping Secret

When you're visiting a company's online store, make sure to hit up the "sale" section first. Many sites will also keep sale items on their original regular priced pages—without the prices marked down. If you look in the sale section beforehand, you'll ensure you're getting the best price.

Keep It Simple

When you're buying clothes, always go for classic looks rather than modern, stylized ones. A blue V-neck T-shirt will be fashionable year after year, while something with more exotic colors or patterns will go out of style quickly. Buying more basic clothing will make sure you don't have to buy as many new articles of clothing each season.

Your Own Personal Shopper

At ShopItToMe.com, you enter your favorite brands of clothes, and they do all the online searching for you. When items come up for sale on a department store's site, they'll send you an email, alerting you to the discount. The best part is, you can specify your size, so you won't have to waste your time wading through links only to find that the store is all out of extra-large!

When to Buy Home Appliances

If you're looking to buy large appliances or household furnishings like a washing machine, dryer, dish washer, refrigerator, or sofa, the best time to buy is in October. At this time of year, businesses are busy making room for their holiday inventory, so you'll find tons of sales on last year's merchandise. Go ahead, celebrate a little early!

Never Pay Too Much for Cosmetics

When shopping for make-up and other cosmetics, never ever shop at department stores! Because of commissions for the salespeople and the cost to rent the space at the store, they're never a bargain. Instead, check out your local grocery store or discount store such as Walmart or Target—they almost always have the exact same brands for much less. If you can't find them there, try to find a cosmetics discount outlet such as Sephora or Ulta, or search for "discount cosmetics" online. If you still can't find your brand, consider switching to another brand you *can* find. Choose one a good friend uses, and ask her if she'd be willing to buy it from you if you don't like it. It shouldn't be too hard to find one you like just as much that costs much less.

Make-Up Must-Have

Most make-up is exactly the same, except for whether they call that shade of red you love "cherries jubilee" or "red crush." Make shopping for make-up easier by keeping an index card with your favorite colors on hand. Rub a bit of lipstick, blush, or eye shadow on the card, then mark down the brand and what the color is called. When it's time for more make-up, you can easily compare the colors of the sale brand with your card. Then write down what *that* color is called on your card. You'll soon have a list of all your favorite colors from each brand.

—*Arlene DeSantos*

Stop Squinting!

If you need new glasses and aren't sure how you're going to afford them, check out 39DollarGlasses.com. For around $45 (with shipping), you can get attractive (though bare-bones) glasses, including the lenses! Walmart also offers good deals on frames and lenses.

Candle-Buying Benefits

If you like decorating your home with candles, buy them on clearance at after-holiday sales. There's nothing wrong with burning a pumpkin-scented candle in spring or a Christmas-scented one in January. If that feels weird, though, just stash the seasonal scents in the closet until next year's holidays come around.

Good Make-Up Doesn't Have to Be Expensive

For a great deal on cosmetics on the web, head over to EyesLipsFace.com, where they have everything from lip gloss to nail polish for only a dollar apiece. They also have a great gifts section, with cute box sets for unbelievable prices. For instance, eye shadow, mascara, eyeliner, a brush, and an eyelash curler for only $5!

Buy at Auction

Every month, hundreds of cars and other merchandise are confiscated by the police. And hey, just because a criminal used it doesn't mean that $100 laptop is any less useful. Look in the classifieds section of your newspaper to find local auctions, or check out PropertyRoom. com to find unbelievable deals on tools, electronics, bicycles, video games, and more, not to mention some truly bizarre items, like a Freon tank, "assorted copper tubing," night vision goggles, and an adorable cement frog. If you're in the market for a car, try PoliceAuctions.com or SeizeCars.com. And if you're OK with not telling the recipient where it came from, auctions are also one of the least expensive places to buy beautiful jewelry and gemstones.

Cheap Checks

When pawing through the coupon inserts in your Sunday paper, make sure to save the advertisement for checks. Buying checks through private companies isn't just for people who like cartoon characters next to "Pay to the order of." They're also for people who like to save! You'll always get them more cheaply than simply ordering them through your bank—and don't you give your bank enough money as it is?

Thrifty? Try Shopping at Thrift Shops

Many people are intimidated by shopping at thrift shops. What's the best way to wade through all those clothes, organized in no particular order? How do you know you're getting something good? And what should you be wary of? First of all, it's more intuitive than you might think. If you're browsing through a thrift shop and the clothes seem dingy or dirty, find a different shop. But for the most part, you'll find perfectly good clothes that are simply one or two seasons old. Make sure to check each item closely for rips or stains, and keep in mind that it may be worth it to buy something if you think you (or a tailor) can easily repair it. Many resale shops are organized by the color of the clothing, but most also use some kind of color-coded tag system (so that all items with a red tag are 50 percent off, for instance). Best of all, you can usually exchange your clothes for money or store credit. Make sure to ask if the store offers you more "money" for your item if you opt for credit rather than cash. And have fun looking for bargains! You never know what fantastic find you're going to get at a thrift shop.

Take from the Rich

When going shopping at second-hand shops, try visiting wealthier neighborhoods for the best finds. Not only do they shop at these stores less (leaving more goodies for you), they have nicer things to give away!

—Lori McNaughton, Newport Beach, CA

Begin in the (Bargain) Basement

How many times have you purchased an $80 sweater, only to find a nearly identical one for much less later? When you begin to look for clothes for the new season, always start at the least expensive store first. Since most clothing stores carry similar items each season, you'll make sure to get each piece for the best price. You should also try to buy most of your basics—solid-color T-shirts, socks, and so forth—at the cheaper stores. Save the expensive stores for the uniquely designed and patterned clothes, where you can see the difference in quality.

Befriend Those in the Know

If you have a favorite shop you find yourself spending a lot of time in, make sure to get friendly with the sales staff! Clothing stores often have unannounced sales, but if you're down with the people who work there, they'll often tip you off ahead of time. And if they really like you, they may let you put an item on layaway until it goes on sale a few days later.

The Mall is a Money Pit

If you or your teen are looking for something to do, stay away from shopping malls! Although they're popular hangouts, they'll always lead to you spending money. Skip the stores and go to the park, a pool, or a matinee instead.

Who Knew?

Ever wondered why salons and other services are often close to mall entrances? It's because most stores in the mall count on foot traffic—people wandering in and buying things. The stores at the entrances are visited less frequently, because when people enter a mall they tend to be a bit disoriented and walk right past the first shops they see—unless they have an appointment. Visit stores close to mall entrances, which pay less rent, and you may find savings.

Save, Then Spend

As Veruca Salt said in *Willy Wonka and the Chocolate Factory*, "I want it, and I want it now!" It's hard to stop ourselves from buying expensive items when we want them, then paying them off over the next several months. But saving up ahead of time has numerous benefits.

✦ First of all, you'll make sure you really want the item. Having to save up for six months for a new TV will give you plenty of time to reconsider if the old 20-inch is good enough. And trust us, once you do finally have the money, it feels so much better to go home with a piece of merchandise that's bought and paid for, rather than one that has just put you further into the hole.

✦ When you start up a new store credit card to pay for a big-ticket item, this credit card will pop up on your credit report as being opened and immediately maxed out. Obviously, this isn't good news for your credit score.

✦ Finally, not having to pay something off after the fact means no interest payments. And many mom-and-pop stores will give you a lower price if you pay all in cash.

Cheap Computing

Buying a new computer? If you can live with a smaller screen and keyboard, a netbook may be the computer for you. Netbooks are smaller versions of laptops, and although they don't have nearly as many features as a full-size computer, they still work well for the basics (word processing, watching videos, searching the internet) and cost only about $500.

Never Pay a Dollar for a Lemon Again

It may be a pain, but the best way to save on groceries is to shop at more than one market. You'll soon find that one store will have cheaper produce, one will have cheaper meat, and so forth. Explore grocery stores you've never shopped at—perhaps one that is closer to your workplace or gym rather than by your home—and you may find even lower prices. We've even found cheaper products at stores that are the same chain, just a different location. Write down the prices of your most frequently purchased items, or bring a receipt from an average grocery trip with you. That way, you can be sure to remember where the prices are the most reasonable.

Shop Smart at the Grocery Store

Shop later in the day to take advantage of mark-downs in your grocery store's bakery and meat departments. Also make sure to keep an eye on the prices at the salad bar. If you only need a few artichoke hearts or croutons, they may be cheaper to buy there by the pound than elsewhere in the store.

Count the Cartridges

This may seem counterintuitive, but if you're buying a printer, try to buy one that uses as many different toner cartridges as possible. Not every household uses the same amount of every color, so you may be forced to throw away a tri-color cartridge that's out of, say, magenta, but still has plenty of yellow and cyan left. Printers with separate cartridges for each color solve that problem by ensuring that no toner is wasted. It's also a good idea, when printing, to specify a black-and-white printout in instances where color isn't really necessary.

The Seasonal Shopping Secret

For the best deals on clothes, always shop in the off-season. Buy spring and summer clothing in July and August, and fall and winter clothing in January and February. (You can often find the best sales right after the holiday season.) It's sometimes a bummer to buy something you're not going to be able to wear for six months, but when the time comes to switch seasons you'll be happy you already have some new clothes to wear—all of which were purchased on sale!

CHAPTER 28

Easy Ways to Make Money and Work from Home

Selling Cosmetics

If you love make-up, selling Avon or Mary Kay cosmetics may be for you—especially since you'll get a great discount on their products that you can use yourself. Both companies require that you cover all costs, but Avon's initial setup fee is lower. And while Mary Kay usually offers a higher commission on sales, they may require you to purchase inventory before you sell it. If you're trying to decide whether Avon or Mary Kay would be a better fit for you, the biggest factor to consider may simply be which company's product you and your friends prefer. Not only will you be able to sell it better, but if your friends use it, you know you'll have at least a few sales. Ask around and see if there are already a lot of reps from one company or the other in your area—if there are a lot of "Avon ladies" in your neighborhood or at your primary workplace, you might want to consider Mary Kay. Also keep in mind that Mary Kay's prices are higher, so if you don't see your friends spending a lot on make-up, Avon may be the better choice. One friend who has sold for both companies believes that Avon is the better bet for casual sellers. But if you're willing to give it your all, you can probably make more money with Mary Kay.

● Who Knew?

More than 8 million workers in the United States hold two or more jobs.

Focus Groups

When they need to know what real people think about their products, companies hire focus groups to try them and then share their opinions. Being in a focus group can get you free product samples, a bit of cash, and the opportunity for your voice to be heard! Sign up to be part of a focus group at GreatOpinions.com, where you enter information about yourself and then are contacted by a representative when there is focus group work available in your area. Or go to FindFocusGroups.com, which culls focus group opportunities from around the web that you can apply for directly. Either way, you should know that many focus groups won't hire you if you work in the marketing industry, have any connection to the company the product is made by, or say that you have participated in a focus group in the last six months.

Cash for Your Gadgets

Now you can keep your old electronics out of the landfill and possibly get some free cash in exchange! Services such as BuyMyTronics.com and Gazelle.com recycle or refurbish your old cast-offs and send you a check in return. Just fill out the easy forms on their websites. They'll make you an offer, and if you accept, send you a box with postage to send your gizmo to them. They take cameras, cell phones, MP3 players, game consoles, personal computers, and more.

Mystery Shopping (Because You've Always Been the Mysterious Type)

Mystery shopping can get you free products and a bit of money on the side, but most of all, it's downright fun. Visit a store, then fill out an online survey about your experience. The pay isn't much—usually not more than $15—but you'll be reimbursed for products as varied as designer sunglasses and lunch at a restaurant. If you're interested in mystery shopping, be careful of online scams. You should never have to pay to be a mystery shopper! The best site to trust is that of the Mystery Shopping Providers Association. Visit MysteryShop.org/shoppers to find mystery shopping and focus group opportunities near you, and find out more about this fun side job!

Starting a Daycare Service

If you're already home keeping your own kids entertained, starting a daycare business might be the perfect opportunity for you to earn money. Check with schools and local businesses to see if they'll let you put up flyers to advertise your business, and make sure to focus on what makes your daycare special. Do you have a teaching or nursing degree? Are you a genius at coming up with fun art projects? Do you live close to a park that will feature prominently in the children's day? Before you attempt any of this, however, make sure to check out your state's licensing requirements—in many areas, you need to be licensed to run a daycare. However, there may also be programs available to you to help you get your certification.

Sell Unwanted Items on Ebay

Turn those old Precious Moments figurines and your vinyl record collection into cash by using Ebay. Getting started is easier than you might think. Go to Ebay.com and set up an account, then post photos and information about a product you want to sell, and other users can buy it. Anything goes: Jell-O molds, clothes and accessories, musical instruments, baby products, computers, DVDs, cars—and you get to set the price. (Try searching for similar items and see what other people have sold them for.) We've had friends who have made enough each month on Ebay to cover their basic utility and phone bills! All it takes is the willingness to be on-call to answer customer inquires via email, and the ability to mail items out as soon as they're purchased. For more information, click on "Help" on the upper-right-hand corner of the site, where you can find an easy-to-understand guide to getting started and frequently asked questions.

Have Something to Teach?
How About Tutoring?

If you know how to play an instrument or have a background in math, science, or English, tutoring may be a good way to make some extra cash. Put up flyers in your area, post an ad on Craigslist.org, and talk to local schools and after-school programs to see if they have children in need of tutoring. Make sure to have your résumé handy, and provide references, even if they're in the form of your friends whose children you have taught a skill.

To Get Your Fifteen Minutes of Fame...
and Maybe Some Cash!

Ever wanted to see if you could win some money on TV? Go to StarNow.com or TalentHunter.com to search for opportunities in your area to be a movie or TV extra, try out for a reality show, or be a guest on a talk show. And don't forget us when you become famous!

Can You Bake?

If your cookies, cakes, pies, brownies, or other sweets always get rave reviews, consider putting your skills to work selling baked goods. Visit local coffee shops, delis, and independently owned restaurants with some of your creations in hand and see if they would be willing to give you a cut of any sales or purchase them outright. For those who love to bake, this could be an easy way to turn your hobby into some cash.

Make Yours a Go-To Garage Sale

It's time for that yard sale you've been talking about all these years! Make it a success by advertising ahead of time—putting up flyers around your neighborhood and placing a free ad on Craigslist.org are two good ways to start. Ask your neighbors if they, too, have things to sell—people will be more likely to come out if you can state that it's a "whole block sale" or a "multiple-family yard sale." Remember that people are bargain hunting, so don't set the prices of your items too high. Post a sign that states you're willing to bargain on the prices to make sure no one walks away because they don't want to pay the price you've set. And finally, remember to have fun! Look at it as an excuse to sit outside and meet people from your community, and you won't get too stressed.

● Who Knew? CLASSIC TIP

If you're buying a new cell phone, what do you do with the old one? Get cash, of course! Visit CellForCash.com and enter the brand and model of your old phone. The site will tell you if they're offering any money for it, and if they're not, they still allow you to send it in to be recycled. Plus, the shipping is free!

Have Space? Get Money!

Renting out a spare room has long been a way for families to make ends meet in tough times. But even if you don't want someone else living in your home, you may be able to rent out storage space in your garage. If you live near a train station or in a densely populated area, you may also want to think about renting out your driveway for a parking space. Place an ad on Craigslist.org or in your local paper and see if you get any bites.

Make It a Party: Selling Tupperware or Other Products

If you're a friendly person with lots of contacts, selling products could be the perfect way for you to make some extra cash. We've all heard of Tupperware parties, but there are now a lot more products available for you to sell from home. Most require that you pay an initial start-up fee, which usually includes some samples and catalogs, and all the programs offer extra incentives like freebies and bonuses for meeting certain sales goals. Below is a run down of some of the opportunities available, and tips on how to find out more information.

✦ The grandmother of all work-from-home sales opportunities, Tupperware is now much more than parties. For a small fee, you can also get your own website from which to sell Tupperware items. The commission is usually 25 percent of everything you sell, and you need to sell about $100 worth of items per month for Tupperware to keep you on. If you think you can recruit friends to become Tupperware representatives, all the better! You get a portion of their sales, too, and if you recruit enough people, Tupperware will promote you to manager and you'll get an even bigger cut. Tupperware gives you two choices of starter kits: one for $80 and one for $120. For more info, visit Tupperware.com or contact your local representative.

✦ The Pampered Chef has been selling high-quality kitchen products since 1980. As a Pampered Chef consultant, you would make most of your sales by hosting parties in your own home or the homes of your friends. So if you're a good cook, this could be a great chance to show off your skills using Pampered Chef products, feed your friends, and hopefully make a few bucks while you're at it. To get a start-up kit, it will cost you $100, and the company offers a 20 percent commission, which goes up slightly if you refer two or more people. Call 1-800-266-5562 or visit www. PamperedChef.com for more information.

✦ If you and your friends are into scrapbooking, then Stampin' Up might be for you. Their starter kit of stamps, pads, and other stamping doodads costs $200, but the great thing about this program is that your compensation goes up according to how much you sell per month. Sell up to $400 per month and you'll receive 20 percent of all your orders, but sell more than $5,000 per month and you'll earn 40 percent. Visit StampinUp.com for more details.

✦ If you can't get enough of candles, try Partylite. They have no monthly minimum that you need to sell, and you can get a free starter kit when you host your first show. They'll also set you up with your own website for $10 per month. As with many other programs, you get more money the more Partylite representatives you refer. For information on how to sign up, go to Partylite.com.

✦ If you have kids, you know that there's no end to the amount of kids' toys one can buy. So head over to DiscoveryToysInc.com, where you can find information about how to sell fun, educational products for children. They provide you with videos and instructions to help you get started, and charge $99 for a beginner's kit. You'll make 20 percent of every sale, and only need to sell $150 worth of products every three months.

✦ These are just a few of the opportunities available to you if you would like to start selling items from home! For a directory of even more opportunities and everything you need to know about joining up with various companies (including how to claim it on your taxes), visit DirectSelling411.com.

Easily Sell Handmade Items

Are you a crafter? A knitter? A genius with papier-mâché? Etsy.com will give you a worldwide venue to sell your items. Sign up for free and get your very own virtual shop, then pay 20¢ for every item you list. You can set the price at whatever you want, and when it sells, you pay Etsy 3.5 percent of the price to handle the credit card transaction. You can also pay extra fees to be featured on the Etsy.com home page, which is visited by thousands of people looking to buy handmade items.

● Who Knew?

Three-and-a-half percent of the nation's workforce works from home. The city that has the highest percentage of work-at-homers is San Francisco, followed by Portland, Seattle, and Austin.

Good with Animals?

No matter what shape the economy is in, people will always need dog-walkers and cat-sitters. Both jobs can get you $10–$20 an hour, and you'll get to spend time with some furry friends (who will never drink the last of the coffee in the office kitchenette). The trick to this business is to get a lot of clients in close proximity to each other, so you don't have to spend a lot of time and money on travel. Try advertising at pet stores, groomers, and veterinary offices near you. Don't forget to list your pets as references!

The Survey Says...

The folks at SurveySpot.com not only want your opinion, they'll pay for it. Join for free and you'll receive 5–7 surveys each week to complete. For each completed survey, they'll pay you $2–$10 or enter you in a sweepstakes (or both!). This and other survey sites like MySurvey. com, EPoll.com, and Toluna.com can be frustrating because you don't always qualify to take the survey and it can take a while to earn money, but if you enjoy answering questions and have a bit of free time, this is a great way to earn some extra cash while you're messing around on the web.

Lost Money Could Be Yours!

There is over $24 billion worth of unclaimed property in the United States, and Unclaimed.org is the official government site that will help you find out if any of it is yours. Search by name and state, and be connected to federal and state databases to see if there is any money, land, or possessions that have been left to you and are in government custody.

Extra Money for Photographers

If you have a gift for taking beautiful photographs, there may be a side career for you in photography. Advertise your services to become a wedding and special events photographer, and make some extra dough on the weekends—just make sure you have a sophisticated website where people can view your work. You can also make money selling your images to publishers and creative professionals who are looking for stock photography. Go to Shutterpoint.com or iStockPhoto.com to find out more about selling your images online.

● Who Knew?

Men and women are equally as likely to work from home, but people with a bachelor's degree are six times more likely to work at home than those without a high school diploma.

Great Job for Friendly People

Dressing up as a sandwich and handing out flyers is a tough job, but somebody's got to do it. Actually, getting a job with a "street team" company doesn't require that you get dressed up (usually). They hire outgoing people to hand out flyers on the street and in bars that promote a new album, an upcoming event, or newly released films. Best yet, by becoming part of a street team, you can earn $15–$25 an hour! To find out more and to sign up for a street team in your area, visit StreetTeamPromotion.jobs.

Go for the Gold

With the value of gold near $1,000 an ounce, now is the time to get rid of your old gold! Take a look through your jewelry box for broken pieces and items you no longer wear. As long as they're 10 karats or higher, you can get big money for them. Just make sure you're dealing with a reputable gold broker. Never mail in your scrap gold—make sure to talk to someone in person at a jewelry or coin store. Use the online calculator at Dendritics.com/scales/metal-calc.asp to find out how much your gold is worth, and expect to get about 75–85 percent of that amount from a broker.

Operating a Call Center

There are many opportunities available for becoming a customer service representative right in your own home. Sign up with Alpine Access (AlpineAccess.com), Arise Virtual Solutions (Arise.com), or West Corporation (West.com), and you'll receive calls from customers needing help from major organizations like Sears, Office Depot, and the IRS. You usually need to provide your own computer with a high speed internet connection, and sometimes an extra phone line, but you'll make up to $14 an hour and won't even have to change out of your pajamas.

Consignment Shops

If you have a few odds and ends you'd like to sell, but not enough for a garage sale, consider taking them to a consignment shop. Consignment stores put your item on display, then take a portion of the selling price if it's sold. It's usually hard to make more than a few dollars here and there on clothes, knick-knacks, and kitchen accessories, but it is fun to stop by the store and see what they have available and how much you've made. And you'll still get more than if you simply gave the items away.

CHAPTER 29

More Free Stuff!

Our Favorite Websites to Find Free Stuff

It's easy to get product samples for free over the internet. Here are some of our favorite sites that compile free offers from other websites. We like some of these sites because they have everything, and others because they pre-screen the offers beforehand. Check them regularly and see what you find!

✦ FreeSampleForager.com gathers together giveaways from around the web and provides direct links for you to click to claim them.

✦ StartSampling.com also pulls together online offers for free samples—everything from magazine subscriptions to vitamins. The site also offers some valuable coupons that you can print out and take with you to the store.

✦ At FreeAfterRebate.info, you'll find deals from sites offering merchandise that comes with rebates. Mail in the form or fill out the information online and get your money back!

- ✦ Visit FreeSamplesBlog.com for information about free product samples, coupons, and giveaways happening at stores nationwide.

- ✦ At DailyEDeals.com/free_stuff, freebies are sorted by free product samples; free merchandise such as T-shirts, gift cards, and cosmetics; free after rebate; and offers to make easy money. Some of these links are more reputable than others, but it's definitely worth a look.

- ✦ TotallyFreeStuff.com has so many links to freebies it's hard not to be overwhelmed! They gather everything here, so if you look for freebies on a daily basis, this is a good site to find offers you didn't find elsewhere.

- ✦ YoFreeStuff.com specializes in links to free gift cards, household products, food samples, and pie-in-the-sky freebies like big-screen TVs (which often require you to make purchases online or sign up friends for junk mail).

- ✦ At 1MyFreebies.com, there is an ever-changing array of free offers, every day! Check back often for free offers that range from free candy to free photos at Sears Portrait Studio, and more.

Make It a Happy Birthday...

...with a free entree from Houlihan's restaurant. Just join their email club at Houlihans.com, and get ready for your big day. You'll also get a free appetizer just for joining.

Burritos

Burritos more to your liking? Then check out the e-club at Moe's Southwest Grill. On your birthday, they'll give you a free burrito. Other free swag comes with the membership, too. Check it out at Moes. com—just lick on "Join Moe's e-World."

Dog Supplies

If you're a dog lover, check out WorkingDogWeb.com/freestuff.htm for lists of free canine-themed items and supplies for your pet, from food to leashes.

Why Pay for Microsoft?

"Great Software...Easy to Use...and it's Free!" That's the claim at OpenOffice.org, and it's true. Check out their free word-processing and spreadsheet programs that are similar to programs that Microsoft offers. Another good site for these types of programs is Google Docs: Docs.Google.com. At Google Docs, you can open Microsoft Word and other files, then share them over the internet with others.

Government Assistance

The government has myriad programs offering financial assistance, awards, loan repayment, and other benefits. If you own your own business, are paying for college, are or were in the military, are part of a minority group, or live in a rural area, check it out to see what you can get. The best way to see what is available is to go to GovBenefits.gov and fill out their simple questionnaire, which will give you a complete list of the programs for which you're eligible. You'll be amazed at what is available.

Track Your Money for Free

With IRAs, 401(k)s, stocks, and other investments, it's hard to keep everything straight. It's easier, however, if you join Kiplinger's Portfolio Tracker, where you can track all your investments for free. When it comes time to file your taxes, you'll be happy you did! Just go to Kiplinger.com/portfolio/portfolio.php and click on "First time users click here."

—Greg Chu, Fayetteville, NC

Free Stuff Strategy: Facebook Fan Pages

If you're already on Facebook, you've probably become a "fan" of various companies, organizations, bands, TV shows, and random funny pages. If you're not already on Facebook, it's time to give in to your friends and family members who have been urging you to join! It's a great way to stay in touch, but it's also a great way to stay apprised of free stuff that is being offered by the companies you love. Once you've signed up for Facebook, find the companies that make products you use regularly by typing each one's name into Facebook's search bar. Many companies—like Dove, Burger King, Babies "R" Us, Wheat Thins, Walgreens, and more—offer coupons and freebies just for becoming a fan of their page. And don't worry, "becoming a fan" is easy. All you have to do is go to the companys' page and click "Become a fan" (naturally).

Coffee

Yes, there is a site named FreeCoffeeSite.com, and their reason for being is to provide free coffee samples. All you have to do is complete a short survey, and the coffee is yours. No strings attached!

Turkey Tips

For year-round answers to any questions about how to cook turkey, call 1-800-BUTTERBALL. Also, for recipes and free coupons, try Butterball. com. Just type "free" or "special promotions'" into their search bar.

Contact Lenses

If you have a prescription for contacts, you can get a certificate for a free pair of Acuvue disposable lenses, plus a $75-off coupon, at Acuvue.com. Just click on the "Get your free trial pair certificate" on the lower-left corner of the page.

Moisturizers and Soap

Keep your skin soft and smooth with free samples and coupons from Oil of Olay (Olay.com/samplesandoffers) and Dove (Dove.us/#/Offers/freesamples). You can also sign up for email newsletters that will keep you apprised of deals and special offers.

Sewing Patterns

Who needs Simplicity and Butterick? Get free patterns for sewing, quilting, knitting, crocheting, and even paper crafts at FreePatterns. com. Just download and print out!

Birthday Reminders

Never miss a birthday again! Get free email and text message reminders about birthdays (or any other important event) at Birthday-Reminders.com.

Phone Calls

Make free phone calls to practically anywhere in the world with Skype—software you download, then use to talk to people through your computer speakers and microphone. You can also call cell phones and land lines for as low as 2¢ a minute. Visit Skype.com to start chatting.

Household Tips Newsletter

Great recipes, cleaning and decorating tips, and a free newsletter are available from RightAtHome.com. Our favorite "gee whiz" cleaning tip? A slice of white bread rolled into a ball will clean scuffs and stains from wallpaper or painted walls. Who knew?

What Free Stuff to Expect When You're Expecting

There is a plethora of websites featuring free stuff for newborns. If you're expecting, make sure to check these out.

- ✦ At BabiesOnline.com, you can get free diapers, diaper bags, magazine subscriptions, and more.

- ✦ Type "Enfamil Family Beginnings" into a search engine, then click on the first link in the results to get checks for free formula, baby supplies, and contests.

- Go to FitPregnancy.com/freebies to find sweepstakes and freebies from the popular magazine *Fit* and from around the web.

- At VeryBestBaby.com, you can get coupons, samples, and information about every stage of your baby's development from the makers of Gerber baby food.

- Get BabyCenter's free email newsletter, which allows you to track your baby's development week by week and includes articles on important topics handpicked for your particular stage of pregnancy. You'll also receive valuable coupons, sale notices, and free offers from BabyCenter and their partners. It's available at MySavings.com/offer/baby-center.asp.

Qdite a Deal at Qdoba

Join Qdoba Mexican Grill's e-club and you'll get a free entrée when you buy a second entree plus special deals on your birthday. You'll also enjoy free chips and salsa simply for signing up! Join by going to Qdoba.com and clicking on "Qdoba card."

Software

At Download.com, you can download free screensavers, anti-virus software, games, and more. Just type what you're looking for in their search bar, then click "Free" under "Narrow search" on the left.

Career Advice

Get all kinds of free, professional advice on your career (or desired career) at CareerOneStop.com (or call 1-877-348-0502), which will give you tutorials on résumés and cover letters, offer salary information, help you find free classes in your area, and more.

Free Stuff Strategy: Sometimes, It's as Easy as Asking

Here's a secret not many people know: companies want to give you their products for free. More specifically, their new products that they're hoping you'll tell all your friends about. Keep your eyes open for new types of candy, cosmetics, soda, and snack foods. Visit the company's website or look on the product's label to find the company's address. Write a letter (which usually works much better than an email) saying how interested you are in the product, and ask if you can have a free sample. For faster processing, write the name of the product on the outside of the envelópe. This doesn't always work, of course, but you'll be surprised how much free stuff you'll get in the mail!

Small Business Help

The Association for Enterprise Opportunity is an association of organizations committed to small businesses. On their site, you'll find plenty of information about the grants and other resources that are available for the budding entrepreneur. You can find it all at MicroEnterpriseWorks.org.

Online Magazines

If you don't mind reading magazines on the computer (or printing them out), you can get them for free. Head over to Zinio.com, where you can download a free "digital" issue of many magazines, including *Reader's Digest*, *Hello!*, and *Women's Health*.

Books

No one likes to throw away a book. Therefore, it's easy to find places that give away books or offer them for a dollar or less. Check with your community's recycling center to see if they offer free books that people have thrown in their bin, and ask your local library if they ever have book sales. It's worth it to check out used bookstores, too, which usually have romance novels and paperbacks at cheap prices. Online, go to PaperbackSwap.com. Featured on the *Today Show* and in *Real Simple*, *Wired*, and *Good Housekeeping*, the site allows you to list books (not just paperbacks) you don't want any more. Once you send them to other users, you'll get credits you can use toward a new (to you) book of your own.

First-Class Education

Massachusetts Institute of Technology—one of the United States' most preeminent technological universities—offers free course materials online. Get reading lists, homework assignments, and audio and/or video lectures for a mind-boggling variety of classes, including SCUBA diving, written language for Chinese speakers, TV theory, and 1,895 more. Want to really impress your friends? Try some classes on calculus, brain structure, bioengineering, and even "Wheelchair Design in Developing Countries." If you're willing to put in the time to learn, these classes will definitely teach you things you never knew. Visit the site at OCW.MIT.edu to get started.

Pet Food

Get a free, all-natural sample of dry food for your cat or dog at HighestQualityPetFood.com.

Coffeemaker

Sick of buying cheap coffeemakers that can't handle your raging coffee addiction? Visit Gevalia.com and sign up for their coffee-delivery service to receive a free state-of-the-art coffeemaker and other freebies. You'll have to pay around $15—and make sure to call and cancel your membership right away—but for a coffeemaker valued at more than $100 (that won't scorch your coffee!), it's worth it!

Electronics

Looking for a good offer when purchasing a Macintosh computer, iPod, camcorder, plasma TV, or other electronics? MacMall.com offers all kinds of special promotions, from free printers to iPod covers to hundreds of dollars off. Just make sure to send in the mail-in rebate before it's too late—many rebates expire in fewer than 30 days.

Credit Score

Did you know that you are legally entitled to one free credit report per year? However, many credit report sites will make you pay to see your score, or charge you a membership or "credit monitoring" fee. Visit CreditKarma.com for a free, no-strings-attached estimation of your credit score. Then go to AnnualCreditReport.com to see how they came up with that score, and to make sure there are no errors on your report.

Medicine

Patient assistance programs provide free prescription medicines to more than 6.2 million Americans, and many more could benefit from these programs but don't know about them. Log on to FreeMedicineProgram.com to find out if you qualify. Another site to check out is NeedyMeds.com. If you don't have a prescription plan, or if your prescription plan has denied you coverage for an expensive medication, you may be able to get it for free or at a deep discount. NeedyMeds.com will tell you how to get the medicine you need from the government, private outreach programs, and even the pharmaceutical companies themselves. Just simply find the name of your medication in the "Brand name" or "Generics" list and see if you qualify! You should never be without the prescriptions you need.

Convert Printed Pages to Electronic Text

OCR Terminal is an online optical character recognition service that allows you to convert just about any printed matter into editable documents for your computer. Normally this service will cost you a bundle, but at OCRTerminal.com, you can import 20 pages of documents each month for free. Just upload your items as PDF or JPEG files, and it will convert them to Word, text, or other document formats.

—Brett Sandusky, Columbia, MO

What's Better Than Ice Cream on Your Birthday?

Free ice cream, of course. And that's just what you'll get for joining the Cold Stone Creamery's Birthday Club. Treat yourself or someone you love to a free cone at a Cold Stone store. Details are at ColdStoneCreamery.com. Look for the "Birthday club" and follow the link.

Heating Help

The Low Income Home Energy Assistance Program helps pay the winter heating bills or summer cooling bills of low-income and elderly people. Check out LIHEAP.org for details.

Life Insurance

Free life insurance? It's true: Mass Mutual offers free premiums for a life insurance policy with a $50,000 death benefit if you qualify. You must be between 19 and 42, be the parent or legal guardian of one or more children under the age of 18, and also meet specific financial criteria. For details, go to MassMutual.com/lifebridge, or call 1-800-272-2216.

Travel Brochures

If you're planning a vacation in the US, you can get free travel guides from around the nation at TravelGuidesFree.com.

Never Learned How to Iron?

Ever wanted to know the perfect way to get all the wrinkles out? Find out now with this free DVD called *Art of Ironing*. Just enter your information at ArtOfIroning.com/free_dvd.php.

Missing Medals

If you or a deceased family member received service medals from the army, navy, air force, marines, or other service, and they have been lost, you can obtain free replacements by writing to the military branch they were awarded by. To see a list of addresses to write to, visit Archives.gov/veterans/military-service-records/replacement-medals. html.

Recipe-Filled Magazine

Food & Family magazine contains more than 60 pages of recipes for making deliciously simple entrees, desserts, and more (all with Kraft products). Claim your free subscription at KraftFoods.com by clicking on "Sign-up" in the upper-right-hand corner of the page.

Who Knew?

No one actually knows who was the first person to say, "The best things in life are free."

Grocery Coupons and Samples

Coupons aren't just for people who buy the Sunday paper anymore! There is now an impressive array of coupon sites online that offer coupons on groceries, household items, toys, and more. Here are some of our favorites.

✦ At Eversave.com, they offer about $80 worth of printable coupons each week that you can redeem at your grocery store. Check out the section called "Free coupons and deals" for some great free offers.

✦ Visit DealPass.com for more great grocery coupons. You'll love scanning to the bottom of your receipt to see how much you saved.

✦ Perhaps our all-time favorite site for savings is CouponMom.com, where you can save time and money by matching your store's weekly sales items with coupons available from the Sunday newspaper or online. What's so unique about this site is it provides a list of the best grocery deals and coupons by state. So, if you're interested in what's on sale at, say, Shop Rite in New Jersey, for example, each week's offerings are noted here. In addition, the site provides a "Virtual coupon organizer," which will help you organize coupons you've pulled from around the web.

✦ At Taylortown Coupon Preview (TaylortownPreview.com), you can get a sneak peek at upcoming coupons that will appear in your Sunday paper and other publications, along with an ever-changing array of free offers.

✦ Some of the easiest coupons to print out can be found at Coupons.com, where you can search and easily print out coupons after downloading a simple program. You can also select coupons to be added directly to your grocery store's customer rewards program, so you don't even need to print anything out. Just click on the coupon and you'll get the discount when you use your card.

✦ Another great site for local deals is JudysBook.com, which will show you current sales of neighborhood businesses, as well as providing coupon codes for online stores. On a recent visit we found out that a nearby bike shop was offering 30 percent off, printed out a coupon for discounted dry cleaning, and checked out links to sales at an online candle store.

Directory Assistance

Never pay for directory assistance again. Instead of dialing 411, dial 1-800-FREE-411 instead. You can use this service from a cell phone or a land line, and after listening to a brief advertisement, an operator will look up your information for free.

Medical Insurance for Kids

Every state in the nation has a health insurance program for children under 18 years old. It's available for children in working families, and provides (at little or no cost) insurance to pay for doctor's visits, prescriptions, and much more. To see if you qualify, go to InsureKidsNow.gov, then click on "Providers in your state" or call 1-8777-KIDS-NOW.

Nutritional Supplement

Visit Ensure.com/coupons-samples-promotions for a coupon for a free can of Ensure nutritional drink.

Free Stuff Strategy: Turn Your Hobby Into Free Stuff

Interested in books? How about reviewing them? Like scrapbooking? How about teaching people tips and tricks to make their scrapbooks look as good as yours? Taking your hobby online is a great way to start getting free stuff. (Hey, you can even make a site about your love of getting things for free!) Visit Blogger.com to easily set up a name and address for your blog, and pick colors, type, and an overall look. If you can get a lot of readers to your blog, you can write to companies asking for samples of products for you to review on your site. They get free publicity, and you get free stuff!

Proctor & Gamble Products

To get free samples of everything from body wash to laundry detergent to toothpaste, go to PGEverydaySolutions.com and click on "Register today" to get free samples of Proctor & Gamble products. You'll also receive their excellent email newsletter, which has household tips and tricks as well as a wide variety of coupons.

Free Info Via Text Message

Google isn't just for the internet anymore. Now if you need information on the go you can text Google with your cell phone. This is especially useful for addresses and phone numbers. Simply type in the business name and your city or zip code and text to 466-45 (G-O-O-G-L). This service is also great for settling bets: Type in "Mt. Everest elevation" and get the answer instantly. Or text "weather" and your zip code to get a three-day forecast. You can also call 1-800-GOOG-411 for free directory assistance. Normal rates for your plan apply, but you won't be charged any extra.

Plumbing Parts

It's important to know that many plumbing fixtures have a lifetime warranty. Make sure to check with the manufacturer before making repairs—you may be able to get the part you need for free.

Free Faxes

Never pay for a fax again! Instead, go to FaxZero.com, where they'll let you either enter text to be faxed or upload a PDF or Word document. Pay an extra $2 and they won't put their ad on the cover page.

Health Care

The Health Resources and Services Administration (HRSA.gov) can direct you to a health center that provides health and dental care to people of all ages, whether or not they have health insurance or a lot of money. Just go to their site and click on the "Find help" icon.

Free Car!

Go to TheFreeCar.com to get a free car! It's not that easy, of course (or that free). You have to pay a membership fee ($30 for a year), and then you will be listed in a database that is accessed by companies that are looking to give away free cars with advertisements on them, in exchange for you driving the car down city streets. Your chances of being selected are way higher if you live in a more densely populated area, of course, and you'll be required to drive around town a certain number of hours per week. But hey, free car!

Kick the Habit

Trying to quit smoking? You're on the way to savings already. But did you know that you can often obtain smoking cessation products such as nicotine gum and patches for free? Many states and cities offer free products or reimbursements, especially if you are on a fixed income. Also check with your employer, school, or health insurance company to see if they offer free products. Finally, head over to Nicoderm CQ's website (NicodermCQ.com) for a free patch and a coupon for their product. If that's not enough, think about how much you'll save when you don't have to buy cigarettes anymore!

Re: Rebates

Find loads of items on sale near you that are free after a mail-in rebate. Just visit SalesCircular.com. Enter your state and you'll be directed to a list of products by type—electronics, apparel, appliances, etc.—that are on sale in your area. Click on "Free after rebate" and get a list of items that you can get for free, from make-up to software.

Freebies from Doctors

If you've just been prescribed a medication, or your doctor has suggested you take something over-the-counter, ask him if he has any free samples he could give you. Doctors are often given samples by sales reps, and don't think to hand them out until they're asked. Many pediatricians will also have free samples of baby formula available.

Language Lessons

Take lessons in Spanish, French, Italian, and German absolutely free at BBC.co.uk/languages, and you can travel internationally more easily (or just impress your friends). The site also offers quickie lessons in Chinese, Japanese, and even more exotic languages like Kudu.

Free Everything, From People Like You

You can find hundreds of items—from furniture to books to clothes to exercise equipment—at Freecycle.org, a nonprofit website whose goal is to decrease landfill waste. Users join up and post about items they are giving away or need, and connect with other users who want the items or have what they're looking for. Just be careful—some free things are hard to resist, but do you really need that bedazzled couch cover?

Shuttle Transport

Once you start looking for them on the road, you'll see them everywhere. No, not bad drivers—free shuttle buses. These buses run from hotels to airports, malls to Main Street, and even sometimes to large, big-box stores like IKEA. They usually keep a regular schedule (driving in a loop) and are often mostly empty. If you're going somewhere close to a shuttle bus, why not score a ride for free? Most shuttle bus providers don't mind you hopping aboard even if you're not going to or coming from their exact destination, but it's not a bad idea to check, especially at hotels. (Some hotels will let you ride for a price.) You may find it's one of the cheapest ways to get to the airport—or to your friend's house, next to the mall.

Free Wireless Internet

Tons of coffee shops, bookstores, hotels, and public buildings offer wireless internet service for free or free-with-purchase. Find local "hot spots" at WiFiFreeSpot.com, and don't forget to submit any WiFi zones you find for others on the go.

Bill-Paying Made Easy

It's hard to get free cable, gas, electricity, and other services, but it's easy to pay the bills without having to pay for stamps, envelopes, or checks. Go online or call the number on your bill to sign up for direct debit, which will automatically deduct the money from an account of your choosing each month. Most banks also offer free online bill payment, where you can consolidate your bills and pay them all at once online. Check your bank's site for more details.

Want a Free Car? A Plasma TV? How About $1,000 Worth of Gasoline?

Of course you do. Who doesn't? All of these offers exist at sites that operate as incentive promotion programs, where advertisers pay to get users to their websites, or to receive their solicitations. You'll receive your gift after fulfilling the participation requirements. Sounds easy? It's not. At most of these sites, you typically have to complete 4–6 offers from advertisers in order to collect, and navigate through a maze of offers to boot. They may require you to sign up for free trial offers, or for credit cards, and some require a small purchase. It's a good idea to read the fine print when you get on a site offering these types of gifts. Typically, they have a link to either "Terms and conditions" or "Participation requirements." That's where you'll find out exactly how many offers you need to complete to claim your gift. Still up for it? Great! Check out MyCoolRewards.com, which is one of the longest-running incentive promotion sites around. And if you find other great sites like this, let us know about them at WhoKnewTips.com!

Down Payments for Your Home

Most down payment programs were phased out in 2008, so be wary if you come across a website offering a deal that's too good to be true (it probably is). However, other grant money is still available. Just go to DownPaymentSolutions.com and click on "Grants" to find out if you qualify for any free money that will help you purchase a house, co-op, or condo. DownPaymentGrantMoney.com, which gives you a searchable database of down payment grants from the government, information about tax credits for buying your first home, and different kinds of mortgages you can apply for. They also have a "Home Buyer Discounts" page that gives you links to deals and free stuff you can receive as a homeowner.

Free Clean Teeth, a Click Away

Visit Colgate.com and click on "Special offers" for coupons and free samples of toothpaste, dish soap, and other household goods.

Barbecue Sauce

Country Bob's is offering a free sample of their delicious concoction. Just go to CountryBobs.com/try-a-free-bottle.html, and follow the simple directions to receive a bottle of barbecue sauce.

Lego Magazine

Calling all kids (and kids-at heart)! Lego is offering free subscriptions to their magazines. US residents can either call 1-866-534-6258 or go to Lego.com and click on "Free LEGO Club Magazine." They're offering two magazines: one for those under six, and one for bigger kids and adults. The subscriptions expire after two years, but you can re-subscribe for free. (Canadian readers, please call 1-877-518-5346 to take advantage of this offer.)

Pizza Knife

Pizza-making just got a little bit easier. Hi-Tech Kitchenware is giving away samples of their beautiful pizza knife. Just go to HiTechKitchenware.com/sample_pizza_knife to receive yours. Hurry, this one won't last!

Free Tax Preparation

Get your federal taxes filed for free! Turbo Tax is offering a free copy of their easy-to-use tax preparation software to anyone who made less than $31,000 last year, or was on active duty in the military and had an adjusted gross income of less than $57,000. To qualify, you must live in Alabama, Arizona, Arkansas, Georgia, Idaho, Kentucky, Iowa, Michigan, Minnesota, Mississippi, Montana, New York, North Carolina, North Dakota, Oklahoma, Oregon, Rhode Island, South Carolina, Vermont, or West Virginia. If you meet all the above criteria, go to

Turbotax.Intuit.com/taxfreedom. If you qualify, you can also get your state taxes filed for free.

Laptop Computer

If you have a lot of friends who don't mind getting email spam, check out Notebooks4Free.com, where you can get a free laptop computer. The catch? You not only have to complete at least one promotion (which often requires you to make a purchase), but you also have to sign up 18–24 friends who all must complete an offer as well.

Low-Carb Energy Bars

If you're trying to lose weight (and who isn't?), pick up a free "Quick-Start Guide" for the Atkins diet along with three free Atkins bars. Good luck! Details can be found at Community.Atkins.com/security/register.jsp.

Starting a New Business and Short of Cash?

We feel your pain. You can get tons of things you need—pens, business cards, rubber stamps, you name it—for free at Vistaprint.com/product-offer-details.aspx. You'll pay only for shipping and processing fees. Of course, the company is trying to sell you upgrades and additional products, so proceed with care!

We All Scream

Interested in a free three-scoop sundae from Friendly's restaurant? Just join their BFF program at Friendlys.com, and next time you buy an adult entree, leave room for your free dessert. You can also participate in some of their free birthday offers just for joining.

—Toni Belle

Informative Brochures

You can get a book or pamphlet on virtually any subject, free of charge, by logging onto Pueblo.GSA.gov or calling 1-888-878-3256. The Federal Citizen Information Center offers free publications on cars, employment, housing, travel, money—the list goes on. Sometimes there is a small fee for shipping and handling; in all cases, you can download the text for free. You never know what you might find here! Whether or not you find what you're looking for, it's always an interesting site to check out.

● Who Knew?

There are tons of free sample offers out there, but some are bogus. Be suspicious if you have to give your credit card number to get a free sample, especially if it's for weight-loss or teeth-whitening products—in 2009, more than 1,100 people made a complaint to the Better Business Bureau about free-trial teeth whitener promotions.

More Free Food

At Schlotzsky's Bun & Fun e-club, you can get a free small sandwich when you sign up. And you get to tell your friends you belong to something called the "Bun & Fun club"! Just go to Schlotzskys.com and click on "Fun." (Not every restaurant participates; call locations near you to make sure.)

Beauty Products

Sephora offers a wide variety of name-brand beauty products, but their real deals are their own line of cosmetics. Get a free birthday gift simply for registering for their "Beauty Insider" program. The gift varies from year to year, but you'll be sure to get a high-quality bath product, cosmetic, or skin-care item. Go to Sephora.com to register.

Why Pay for Shipping?

Many online retailers, including Walmart.com, REI.com, and Payless. com. offer free shipping if you can pick up your order at one of their stores. This is especially handy for online-only items, oversize purchases (which will cost a lot to ship), or goods that have sold out at your local store. Also, look for free shipping deals at many sites when you spend a certain amount, such as orders over $25 at Amazon.com. Find even more deals at FreeShipping.org. And by the way, our *Who Knew?* books are always delivered for free through HSN and HSN.com!

See a Movie for Free

Many museums and colleges over free screenings of films. Sure, they're not the latest big releases, but if you're in the mood for a classic or artsy flick, check and see if they are offered nearby. Many facilities even have full-sized screens in auditoriums. And they won't get angry if you sneak in your own candy!

Rubber Stamps and More

At IPrint.com, there are often (but not always) rubber stamps, labels, business cards, and other office whatnot available for free. Even when it's not free, most of their products are heavily discounted. Check it out before stocking up on office supplies.

Be a Joiner

Always join an airline's frequent-flier program before making reservations. Don't forget, miles add up to free flights—and you'll be amazed at the ways you can earn miles! Check out WebFlyer.com for the lowdown on each airline's rules, as well as their ever-changing special offers. Also check with hotels and rental car companies to see if they have a rewards program. Amtrak also offers one for frequent train travelers.

Virus Got You Down?

That's a computer virus we're talking about, of course. For free anti-virus protection, head to Free.AVG.com.

Free Tour Guide!

To get a real feel for a city when you're traveling, team up with a local from the Global Greeter Network. Visit GlobalGreeterNetwork. com to find people who are willing to share their love of their city by showing you around—for free! By going through a city with a Global Greeter, you can experience it in a unique way, from the perspective of a person who lives there. Tours can last a couple hours or longer, the service is free, and there's a strict no-tipping policy. Cities include New York, Chicago, Paris, and Toronto.

Edit Your Photos

Who knew there's excellent photo-editing software available absolutely for free? For basic photo editing, check out Picasa.Google. com. For more advanced editing like photo retouching and image composition, try Gimp.org.

Free Accounting Help

We know how hard it can be to deal with money stress. But if you go to Wesabe.com, you can get free tools and advice on how to take control of your finances. You can see all your bank and credit card balances in one place and learn ways to get ahead in just a few easy steps. It's worth a try!

Commission-Free Trading

Head over to WellsFargo.com/jump/investments/freetradesonline to check out Wells Fargo's online trading program. If your cumulative account balance is $25,000 or more (including your Wells Fargo checking and savings accounts, certificates of deposit, IRAs, and brokerage accounts), you'll receive 100 commission-free online trades per year. At Zecco.com, they offer 10 free trades per month if you have $25,000 in your brokerage account. Check it out before you pay for a trade.

Free Stuff Strategy: Sweepstakes Secrets

Who doesn't love a good contest? Instead of buying a lottery ticket each week, put yourself in the running to win big by spending a little time each day or week entering online sweepstakes. Here are some tips to help you get that new car/exotic vacation/lifetime supply of beef jerky of your dreams.

- ✦ Make an email address just for contests. When entering many contests, you are also signing up for a lifetime of junk mail. Just make sure to sift through the junk carefully in case you're notified of a win! It's usually pretty easy to tell the difference.

- ✦ The biggest, best source for contests around the web is Online-Sweepstakes.com, which has sweepstakes organized by type, new, and expiring soon.

✦ If you're only interested in the really big bucks and prizes, visit HelpingMomsConnect.com/contests.htm. The great thing about the links on this site is you normally don't have to do anything to win—just sign up.

✦ For smaller contests that often require you to submit something or comment on a site, try ContestGuide.com and ContestForMoms.com. If you have a special talent like writing or art, type "writing contests" or "art contests," for instance, into a search engine to find even more opportunities.

✦ Check for exclusions. Many contests will exclude people from a certain state. These left-out states are your gain (assuming you don't live in one!), because if fewer people can enter, your chances of winning will go up. Also look for contests with particularly high age requirements or that are just for one gender.

✦ Bookmark sites of contests you can enter again. Use your internet browser or a bookmark site like Delicious.com to keep track of contests that allow you to enter more than once. Many allow a click a day, and some give something away each week and restart. If you have a lot of sites to keep track of, try organizing them in folders based on how much you want the prize or how often you can enter.

✦ Avoid any contests you think a lot of people will enter. Remember, the name of the game is trying to up your chances of winning by lowering the number of contestants. If a sweepstakes has been advertised heavily or has a really long entry period, avoid it. Likewise, if you

find a contest held by a local business or offering a short
entry period, your chances will go up.

✦ Only enter contests you trust. When entering a contest,
you should never have to enter credit card information or
your social security number. It's best to only enter contests
from companies or sites you recognize.

Airline Freebies

Airlines may be scaling back their perks, but some still have freebies.
Southwest Airlines still lets you check two bags for free, while most
others charge for luggage. With JetBlue, you can check one bag free,
plus get access to free TV, satellite radio, and all-you-can-eat snacks.
On Continental, you can still get free meals on most routes. Before
you select an airline, make sure you know what you're getting for free.
Some airlines also allow you to pre-check a bag online for a reduced
fee. And remember, all kids under the age of two can fly for free on
your lap on any airline.

Yes, There Is Such a Thing as a Free Lunch...

...or dinner. Kids eat free at Denny's every Tuesday night (and
some Saturdays) with a paying adult. IHOP, Golden Corral, Marie
Callender's, and Chevys restaurants also offer kids-eat-free deals at
select locations. Just go to their websites or KidsMealDeals.com for
details.

Before Your Computer Crashes

Did you know that nearly one in four computer users have lost content
to blackouts, viruses, and hackers? Fortunately, you can protect your
important files and photos from computer crashes, theft, or natural
disasters, absolutely free. At SpiderOak.Com, get 2 gigabytes of free

and secure digital storage space. MyOtherDrive.com offers a similar deal as well.

Need a Place to Stay?

It's not as good as having a friend with a spare room, but at CouchSurfing.org, you can connect with almost 2 million members who may be willing to offer you a free place to stay.

Free Legal Advice

If you need legal advice on any issue, make sure you take advantage of free legal assistance available to you. Call or visit the courthouse and ask about free legal services, which are often offered by local law schools or nonprofit organizations. Many law firms will also offer you a free consultation. Of course, the point of the consultation is to try to get you to use their services, but you don't have to! Go prepared with a list of questions and write down the answers. Do as much research as you can on the internet by Googling the type of case and the name of your state. If your case goes to court, don't be afraid to ask clerks or the judge if you don't understand something.

Free Food for the Hungry

Even if you don't have the money to donate to worthy causes, you can still help feed the hungry by visiting two cool sites. At FreeRice. com, take a fun trivia quiz, and for each answer you get right, sponsors donate rice through the World Food Program (part of the United Nations). At TheHungerSite.com, it's even easier. Simply hit the "Click here to give" link and advertisers will give to those less fortunate. Here's the message we received when we clicked: "Today, you have given the value of 1.1 cups of food to the hungry." So start clicking!

Money for College

These days, college can cost $10,000–$35,000 for one year! And that's just for a bachelor's degree. The good news is that there is a lot of free money out there, from grants and scholarships to assistantships and fellowships. Here are some ways to find it.

+ FedMoney.org is probably the most comprehensive online resource on all US government grants and student financial aid programs. Here, you will find detailed information about who can apply and how, for more than 130 government grants and loans related to education. You can also check the US Department of Education's site at StudentAid.ed.gov.

+ At Upromise.com, you can earn money toward your children's college educations—or help pay off student loan debt already accrued—through your everyday purchases. Register your credit/debit cards along with cards from grocery and drugstore reward programs, and then earn points for every purchase you make at thousands of retailers nationwide.

+ To find out all about grants (and how to get them), make sure to visit CollegeScholarships.org/grants.

+ Check out PrincetonReview.com or Petersons.com to find searchable lists of grants from the lofty (a National Merit scholarship) to the small and silly ($500 for speaking Klingon).

- ✦ For local awards and scholarship contests, make sure to check the newspaper and at the high school counselor's office for opportunities.

- ✦ If you're looking for assistantships, paid internships, and fellowship programs, check out Assistantships.com.

- ✦ If you know what college your son or daughter is attending, make sure you have an up-to-date list of all merit- and need-based grants and loans it offers. If you think you may qualify, don't be afraid to call up the school's registrar or financial aid department and ask for more information.

Free Apps Equals Saving Money

You've paid a lot for that iPhone, so make sure you download some free applications to help you save money and recoup the cost! For instance, there are free apps from Quicken and Mint.com that help you manage your money, and an "iShop" app that helps you search for the lowest price on an item before you buy. The "ATM hunter" app can help you find a surcharge-free machine near wherever you are. To find more apps like these, go to IGoApps.com, where there are over 17,000 free apps!

Free Fitness

You don't need to shell out for a gym membership to stay fit, or invest in the latest piece of equipment (which inevitably turns into a clothes rack). Walking or jogging around the neighborhood doesn't cost anything. Also, consider a visit to your local library to check out free fitness DVDs, from aerobics to Pilates to yoga. And why not walk to the library instead of driving? To encourage public health, some cities have free outdoor gyms for teens and adults at local parks. At many of these "fitness zones," residents can use free equipment for strength training, improving flexibility, and cardio workouts. Check with your parks department to see if there is one in your neighborhood.

Online Books

When copyrights expire, the work in question goes into the public domain. That means you can get classic books for free, and it's all perfectly legal. Check out Project Gutenberg at Gutenberg.org, where you can download more than 30,000 e-books, including works by Mark Twain, Sir Arthur Conan Doyle, Jane Austen, and other favorites. At Books.Google.com, you can search the text of even more books, including those that are still under copyright.

Sheet Music

The Mutopia Project might sound like a top-secret government plan, but it's actually an organization that compiles sheet music that has gone into the public domain. Go to MutopiaProject.com to download sheet music for classical works by Bach, Beethoven, Chopin, Handel, Mozart, and many others.

Seeds

The best source of free seeds for your garden is...your garden! When your flowers start to dry up each year, make sure you check them for seeds that you can replant. Marigolds are an especially good treasure trove of abundant seeds—let the flower tops dry out, peel them open, and you'll find hundreds of future marigolds ready to plant. When next spring rolls around, if you don't have enough seeds from last year, buy them from the nursery rather than buying small plants in dirt. The seeds are much cheaper, and you'll have more fun watching them grow from scratch.

Free Stuff Strategy: Join Twitter

If you're like us, even the word "twitter" makes you feel a little overwhelmed. But even if you're not interested in sending 140-character messages to your friends, Twitter.com is a great site for finding freebies, sales, and other bargains—fast. After you've chosen a username and password, then what do you do? First, check sites you normally frequent (and the ones listed in this chapter). Many will have a link that says "Follow us on Twitter!" Click the link and then the "follow" button, and these sites will now be in your "feed." (Don't forget to add WhoKnewHome for the latest from our site, WhoKnewTips.com!) For ideas for other sites to follow, type "freebie," "sale," or "bargain" into Twitter's search bar. You'll find there's a dazzling array of free offers available from thousands of sites. Again, click on the username and the "follow" button to add a user to your feed, and you'll soon have a custom-made list of discounts at your fingertips. If all of this still sounds too overwhelming, there's yet another option. Go to CheapTweet. com, which compiles freebie, bargain, and discount offers from around the Twitter community.

Extra Care Equals Extra Savings

If you live near a CVS drugstore, make sure you're taking advantage of their Extra Care program. Become a member to earn 2 percent back on every purchase in-store and online, and collect rewards when your prescriptions are filled at CVS. You'll get quarterly payments of store certificates called "Extra Care Bucks", which you can spend in the store as you choose. And don't forget to check out their weekly specials, which can get you free "bucks" as well! One word of caution: Scan your card in the store's coupon machine often, and note the expiration dates so that you can cash in your Extra Care Bucks before they expire. For more details, just ask at your local CVS store or go to CVS.com and click on the "Extra Care" link. Also check the sites of Walgreens and Rite Aid, which have similar programs.

Free Fun for the Kids

For educational or just-for-fun games suited to young kids, check out PBSKids.org, DiscoveryKids.com, NickJr.com, and Scholastic.com.

Free Help Filing Your Taxes

The IRS free-filing service provides free federal income tax return preparation and electronic filing for all taxpayers. All you need is access to a computer and the internet and you can prepare and e-file your federal tax return for free! The service offers two options. The first, called "Free File", is for filers whose incomes are $57,000 per year or less. Free File allows you to prepare your taxes using one of the 20 tax-preparation software products on their site. If you make more than $57,000, the IRS has decided you can afford to pay for these programs yourself! But you can still use their Free File Fillable Forms, which are electronic versions of the usual paper forms that you can file online for free. To access either service, go to IRS.gov and search for free file.

Great Magazine for Older Adults

If you're over 40, you can join the 5.7 million readers who already subscribe to *Remedy* magazine, absolutely free. *Remedy* provides news, information, and expert advice on staying healthy after age 40. Just go to Omeda.com/cgi-win/rx.cgi for details.

Smoothie and More!

Just for joining the Orange Julius "OJ Quench Club" at OrangeJulius. com/sec_quenchclub.html, you'll receive a free 20-ounce fruit drink or smoothie at one of their retail locations, and a special gift on your birthday.

Diabetes Meter

You can get a portable diabetes meter, absolutely free, at Meter. DiabeticConnect.com. It's a One Touch "UltraMini," and you can pick the color of your choice.

Kids' Birthday Gifts

When you join Geoffrey's Birthday Club at Toys "R" Us, your children will get a free birthday card and gift each year until they turn 10. Check out BirthdaysRUs.com and click on "Join Now".

Stop Paying for Texts!

TxtDrop.com enables users in the United States and Canada to send text messages with instant delivery, absolutely free. No more needing to pay your cellular provider for sending your friend a text. (Many plans charge up to 25¢ a pop!) Just enter your email address (for replies), your friend's mobile number, and your message, and they'll send your text instantly, completely free of charge. You can also usually email someone's mobile phone. Have your friend send you an email from her phone by typing a text as usual, and then sending it to your email address. Once you have the phone's email address, you can just hit reply and type away. Of course, you'll still only be able to use 160 characters.

For Do-It-Yourself Kids

At the Home Depot's Kids Workshops, you and your child can build fun projects like toolboxes, fire trucks, mail organizers, birdhouses, and bug containers. The workshops are free, designed for kids 5–12, and occur each Saturday at 9 a.m. in all Home Depot stores. These fantastic classes not only give you a fun activity to share with your kid (adult participation is required), they teach safety and skills. In addition to the newly constructed project, each child receives a kid-sized Home Depot apron and an achievement pin. Details can be found at HomeDepot.com. Once there, just enter "Kids workshops" in their search bar.

Lowe's How-To Clinics for Kids

Lowe's is another good source for DIY kids' projects. Bring the entire brood into any Lowe's store and build a free wooden project. Each participant also receives a free apron, goggles, a project-themed patch, and a certification of merit upon completion of the project. Clinics are offered on a biweekly basis from 10 a.m. to 11 a.m., and all building materials and tools are provided. Get the details at LowesBuildAndGrow.com.

Free Stuff for the Ladies

Allure magazine knows what women want: free stuff! Just go to Allure.com/freestuff for their latest offers on cosmetics, accessories, and more. It couldn't be simpler!

It's Story Time!

Foster a love of books in your child by participating in one of Barnes & Noble's free story times, which include a story and a creative activity to go along with it. Themes and times vary from location to location, so check with your nearest store for specifics. Or go to BN.com and click on the "Stores & Events" tab for more information.

Walmart Freebies

Walmart's website will not only give you the heads-up on upcoming sales, it also offers free samples! Some offers are available for a month or more, but many offers are listed for just a few days—so visit often. Check it out at InStoresNow.Walmart.com.

Charmin Free Offers

For coupons and freebies from Charmin toilet paper, surf on over to Charmin.com and click on the "Coupons and offers" link.

The Library: More Than Just Books

Obviously, libraries are full of books you can borrow for free. But did you know that many libraries also carry DVDs? If there is a particular movie or TV show you are looking for and it's not available at your local branch, ask a librarian to get it for you through inter-library loan. Libraries are also a great place to get magazines. If you don't mind reading back issues, save on subscriptions by getting older copies at the library. This is especially great for kids' magazines (because kids won't know the difference!).

Coupons at Seventh Generation

Seventh Generation is a company that specializes in organic cleaning and home supplies like tissues and toilet paper. They also offer several generous coupons, which you can find at SeventhGeneration.com/coupons. They only allow you to print each coupon twice, but they change their deals monthly, so check back when it's time to buy more!

More Than Just Macaroni and Cheese

At Kraft Foods (KraftRecipes.com), you'll find an array of free offers and services, not to mention tons of free recipes! Once at their site, just click on the "Promotions" link to sample what's being offered. Be sure to also click on the NabiscoWorld.com link found on the page as well. They frequently offer free things, and always have a nice array of coupons.

Free Movies!

At Redbox, renting movies couldn't be easier...unless they're free. Just go to Redbox.com and click on "Get a free rental." What could be easier?

It's a (Reynolds) Wrap

At the Reynolds Wrap website, you can find free, downloadable recipe books, and often free product offers as well. Just go to ReynoldsKitchens.com and click on the "Promotions" link. There is almost always a coupon available, so the next time you're shopping for aluminum foil, check out this site and save at least $1!

Living with Cents, and Freebies

LivingWithCents.com is a site for frugal college students. It offers great advice for saving money, but better yet, freebies! Once you're at the site, click on the "Home & Self" tab and then head to the "Savings and free stuff" section. They offer a variety of goodies, and change them regularly.

Free Love (Stories)!

Head over to RavenousRomance.com for a free, steamy short story each and every day! Then check out their great deals on full-length online novels. (Warning: Some of the stories are explicit!)

For Your Special Day

If you're not sure what to do for your birthday, how about getting something for free? If we didn't offer you enough birthday deals in this chapter, head over to Free Birthday Treats, an easy, one-stop resource of all things free on your birthday. Check it out at FreeBirthdayTreatsBlog.com.

Free Stuff Strategy: Never Be Afraid to Complain

If you're unhappy about a product, you should always write to the company to tell them so. The address can usually be found on the wrapper, and if there's only a web address, their mailing address can be found on their website. Mail a letter explaining why you're unhappy with the product and include the wrapper or label, if possible. Most companies will send you free samples of similar products or replace the product you purchased if it was faulty.

Freebies for Your Opinion

Your opinion counts—and you can get free stuff for giving it. The National Consumer Panel focuses on measuring consumer attitudes and behavior. The panel is made up of people just like you, whose opinions help manufacturers and retailers make decisions on what products to develop or improve. You'll earn gift points that are redeemable for name-brand merchandise, including electronics, jewelry, household items, toys, and much more. Just fill out the online application at HomeScanSignUp.com/registration/index.html, and if you're chosen, you can start saving up for great, free items.

Free Weeklong Gym Memberships

If you're ready to join a gym, first ask if they offer a free week's membership. Many chains, such as Curves, My Sports Clubs (New York, Boston, Philadelphia, Washington, etc.), Life Time Fitness, and even the YMCA, offer free trial memberships that last a week or longer. Not only do you get free workouts for a week, you get a chance to find out if that particular gym is the one for you.

Cosmetics

FreeCosmeticWebsites.com compiles free online offers from the manufacturers and other beauty sites. Find great deals on make-up from Revlon, Maybelline, Clinique, MAC, Bobbi Brown, and other name-brand companies.

CHAPTER 30

Who Knew? Exclusive Offers

Handmade Children's Clothing

Ladybugs and Lilypads is a delightful site that supports the work of stay-at-home moms by giving them a place to sell their wares. Their often-personalized, handmade children's clothes and baby gear make for perfect gifts that will have everyone else at the baby shower asking, "Where'd you get that?" At LadybugsAndLilypads.com, you'll always receive free shipping on all orders over $99, and as a *Who Knew?* reader, you get an extra 10 percent off by using coupon code WHOKNEW at checkout.

Unique Jewelry

Jewelry designer and mom of three Elizabeth Oswald considers herself overly shy, but her designs certainly aren't. All of her pieces are handmade with care, creative and colorful, and a joy to wear. Just buy one and see how many compliments you get! Visit her site, Alizabetho. com, for jewelry, handbags, and accessories, and enter code CPP2010 for 15 percent off your purchase. Enjoy!

Charms

The Charm Factory produces unique, high quality sterling silver charms and charm bracelets, all made in the US. If you or your daughter has ever wanted *Twilight*-inspired jewelry, go to CharmFactory.com now! You'll also find traditional charms featuring inspirational messages, awareness ribbons, and birthstones; and lead-free pewter and wooden charms and pendants. Type "Who Knew" in the "Special Instructions" box at checkout to receive a free "I Love to Shop" charm with any purchase! You can also order by phone by calling 1-866-867-5266.

Car Seat Covers and More

Like us, Nomie Baby's goal is to make life easier for parents. Says company owner Katie: "When my littlest spilled on her car seat and I struggled to remove the cover and disassemble the straps, only to read the care instructions that said, 'Do not machine wash,' I knew there had to be a better way, and the idea was born." Her idea was the Nomie Baby car seat cover, which is easy to slip off and throw in your washing machine. Nomie Baby also carries a "cozy up" zippered stroller blanket and more. To receive free shipping on all orders delivered within the US, use coupon code whoknew at NomieBaby.com.

Pajamas

Sleepyheads.com is your one-stop shop for pajamas for the whole family. Whether you're looking for a brand name or for Sleepyheads' own line of "economically conscious" PJ's, you'll find more kinds of pajamas than you ever dreamed existed. They also have robes, wraps, slippers, bath accessories, cosmetic bags, and more. Enter the code WHOKNEW into the "Promo code" box at checkout to receive

15 percent off your order. And don't forget to sign up for their *PJ Perks* newsletter, which often contains great deals.

Kid-Sized Vehicles

If your kids love cars, trucks, and other vehicles, they'll flip for one of the pedal- or battery-powered vehicles at Pedal Car Planet. They carry quality cars, bikes, trains, planes, tractors, go-karts, tricycles, scooters, "luxury vehicles," and more. Their prices are lower than you'd find elsewhere for these types of toys, and they provide free shipping in the Continental US! To receive a 10 percent discount on your order, visit PedalCarPlanet.com and use coupon code WHOKNEW10 when checking out.

Nutritional Supplement for Breastfeeding Moms

When you're breastfeeding, it can be stressful to make sure you're getting all the nutrients your baby needs. Mamatini does it all for you with their organic drink that is designed specifically to meet the needs of breastfeeding women. Mamatini's all-natural herbal infusion not only contains all the vitamins you need, it helps increase milk production and the absorption of vital minerals that are depleted during breastfeeding. Best of all, you can sign up at DrinkMamatini. com to get a case of Mamatinis delivered straight to your door each week—it doesn't get more convenient than that! To receive free shipping on your order, use the code SHIPFREE.

Bath and Body Products

If you're looking for a luxurious present for a friend (or yourself), look no further than eBubbles.com. They have the best bubble baths, shower gels, bath fizzies, and body scrubs around, along with a wide range of robes, candles, and body lotions—basically, anything that would make a bath to die for. The real deal-maker, however, is that you get our favorite thing—free stuff!—with every purchase. With each order you get two free samples, and they even let you choose which ones you want. As a *Who Knew?* reader you also get 10 percent off your order! (Just enter code WHOKNEW at checkout.) So go ahead, buy your friend something nice and save the samples for yourself!

Who Knew?

These offers will eventually expire, so make sure to take advantage of them now! If you go to check out and find the code we gave you doesn't work anymore, contact us by visiting WhoKnewTips.com and we'll see if we can help.

Bathing Suits and Activewear

If you've ever gone bathing suit shopping and felt like every suit you saw was a little too revealing, you'll love SlimPerfect. Their tankinis, swim skirts, one-piece swimsuits, Capri bottoms and more are perfect for the beach, pool, or working out. Created by a woman to help women feel sexy and sophisticated, SlimPerfect products provide more coverage than the average suit and are designed to create the illusion of an hourglass figure, whether you have one or not. To receive 20 percent off your order (regular or sale-priced items) at Slimperfect.com, use the code Who Knew? at check-out.

All-Natural Disposable Wipes

Celebrating the connection between Mother Nature and human nature is the mission of Jamar Labs. Founded by two mothers, entrepreneurs, and friends, the company offers offer effective, safe, and sustainable personal care products in the form of disposable wipes for your hands, face, and feet (and more to come!). These aren't just your ordinary disposable wipes, however. They aren't loaded with parabens, phthalates, or anti-bacterial agents that can lower your immunity to disease; they're made from real cotton; and they're infused with herbs and antioxidants rather than alcohol. To get a 25 percent discount off your order of wipes, which come in packs of 5 or 30, go to JamarLabs.com and use code WKS25.

Soy Candles

Our favorite thing about HeavenScent Soy Candles isn't their dozens of wonderful scents or the fact that they carry pretty much every kind of candle you can think of, including votives, floating candles, tea lights, several sizes of jar candles, and wickless warmers. It's that you can get any scent in any color you want—so if your room is green, you aren't limited to just pine, cucumber, and green apple if you want a candle to match. You can also customize your candle by adding text or a logo for only 25¢. Get 15 percent off your order at HeavenScentSoyCandles.net by entering code wk3 at checkout!

Beads

BeadBuddies.net offers all types of beads and beading supplies, including semiprecious stones, sterling silver, copper, and crystals. Not only are their beads the highest quality possible, but since they negotiate with competing factories to get the best price, the savings are passed on to the customer. Visit their site and you may never visit a bead store again! Mention Who Knew in the comments field of your order and receive a free strand of cat's-eye glass beads with your purchase.

Party Supplies

The goal of Firefly Glow & Novelty's online store is to provide you with products that make it easy to put together a great party or event. And that they do, with themed party products, icing art, balloon lights, glow and LED toys, keepsakes, and more. If you're looking for Star Trek plates, Barbie-themed party favors, or a NASCAR tablecloth, this is the place to go! They also have a membership program where you can register to receive coupons and new product info, and they offer discounts on bulk purchases. To receive a 10 percent discount on any-sized order, go to FireflyGN.com and enter the code WKBK10SAV during checkout.

Hand-Crafted Cards and Announcements

In Stitches offers sassy cards, beautifully designed bookmarks, racy postcards and journals, and origami baby announcements and invites. Every single piece is one of a kind, made with recycled and reused materials, and entirely hand-stitched with care in a tiny New York City apartment by their designer, Angel. Best yet, you can contact her to order your very own personalized item. Visit her online shop at CardsInStitches.Etsy.com and mention Who Knew in the "Comments" field at payment to receive a free origami card.

The Magnet Alternative

When is a clip that's stuck to your fridge not a magnet? When it's Happeezz—a non-magnetic material that grips not only to stainless steel, but to other slick surfaces such as glass, mirror, aluminum, plastic, and vinyl. It won't scratch or scuff surfaces, and it leaves no residue—all you have to do is dust it every now and then (with a little vinegar, of course). Find these innovative (and stylish!) clips, list pads, white boards, and frames at MayFairLane.com, where you can enter code WKTIPS at checkout to receive a 15 percent discount on your order.

Music for Kids and Their Adults

Music Together is an internationally recognized early-childhood music and movement curriculum for babies through kindergarten-aged children and the adults who love them. Originally offered to the public in 1987, it pioneered the concept of a research-based, developmentally appropriate early childhood music curriculum. At MusicTogether.com, you can purchase their award-winning music sets, which feature a CD (or music download) of songs from around the world and a booklet that tells you how to get personally involved with your child through the music. For *Who Knew?* readers, they're offering 10 percent off three different sets: *Family Favorites*, *Family Favorites 2*, and *Lullabies*. Go to www.MusicTogether.com/whoknew to listen to 30-second sound clips of each song, and enter the following coupon codes at checkout to receive the discount: WKF (*Family Favorites* CD), WKFD (*Family Favorites* album download), WKF2 (*Family Favorites 2* CD), WKF2D (*Family Favorites 2* album download), WKL (*Lullabies* CD), WKLD (*Lullabies* album download).

Soaps and Body Wash

Blue Hippo Soaps specializes in honey-based and goat's milk soaps, as well as whipped body wash in a number of different fragrances. They're all gentle on sensitive skin, highly moisturizing, and, as soapmaker Leia tells us, made with love! Best of all, your purchase goes toward a good cause—helping Leia get through college. Discover her wonderful soaps at BlueHippoSoaps.com. Mention Who Knew at checkout to receive a free bar of soap with your order.

Hats!

The Short Hat Company is a family-owned business that is dedicated to creating beautiful hats. Although they also carry hats for adults, their specialty is kids' hats. Understanding that kids can be picky consumers, they use classic, clean designs and soft, quality yarn. Their brimmed hats include a padded "coolmax" headband that eliminates the scratch factor and helps wick away moisture, and their "true fit" elastic-free adjustable backs make for the most comfortable hat your child has ever worn. Receive a 20 percent discount on all merchandise at ShortHats.com by using the code Who Knew at checkout.

Novelty T-Shirts

We won't tell you the story of how Crazy Dog T-Shirts owner Bill almost burned his mother's house down with his T-shirt screening machine, but suffice it to say, he has all the kinks worked out now. He also has some of the funniest T-shirts you can find online, all printed on super-soft tees that look great, too. If you've seen people wearing original T-shirts with tie-ins to your favorite movies, video games, or TV shows, they probably got them here. If you love retro looks or pop culture, you have to check out CrazyDogShirts.com—and make sure to sign up for their daily shirt giveaway! Get $6 off by using the coupon code CASTLEPT.

Kids' Clothes and Accessories

Even though we consider ourselves decent writers, Tiny Tots with Style is almost too cute for words. This online clothing store for kids and babies has every kind of clothes you may be looking for. If you're shopping for a girl, check out their personalized dresses and adorable tutus. For boys, we love their one-piece rompers and "rebel without a cause" tees. And for babies, you can find onesies, burp cloths, little baby leg warmers, and more. They also carry accessories like diaper bags and baby slings. Especially if you're looking for organic clothing, TinyTotsWithStyle.com is a must-visit site. Save 15 percent on your order by using the code tinytots15.

All-Natural Snacks

With Peeled Snacks, you don't have to worry about what you're feeding your kids. That's because they use only the highest quality organic and natural ingredients from sustainable farms. They're also a great source of vitamins and minerals, and a full serving of fruit—with no added sugar. Best of all, they're delicious! Check them out at PeeledSnacks.com and enter coupon code snack123 to receive free shipping on your order! You can also sign up for their newsletter to receive special promotions.

Gluten-Free Mixes

If you or someone you love is on a gluten-free diet, you know how long it can take to make a simple soup or delicious pie, not to mention how expensive it can get to buy specialty ingredients. Mixes From the Heartland changes all of that. Their line of gluten-free soups, sides, meals, and desserts doesn't contain any eggs, peanuts, tree nuts, soy, oats, barley, rye, or wheat—and they have the Celiac Sprue Association seal to prove it. If you've ever bemoaned that the worst part about a gluten-free life is not having the convenience of premade foods, head over to MixesFromTheHeartland.com now, where you'll find a dazzling array of choices, including dumplings, brownies, pancakes, noodles, and 45 different varieties of soup. Use code CPP-Mixes to receive 15 percent off your order.

The Perfect Meal-Planning System

If you've read our book *Supermarket Saving Secrets*, you know all about meal planning, which makes it easier for your family to save money by allowing you to plan ahead for what you need. But if you find yourself struggling with what to make and what you need from the store, it's time to try Pocket Full of Posies Perfect Pocket Meal Planning. The system, developed by sisters-in-law Emily and Cammie, gives you customizable recipe cards and shopping lists to make things easy. Buy their monthlong pack and you'll get four pockets, each representing a week of the month and containing five recipes and an ingredient list. Not sure you're ready to commit to a month of meal planning? Pocket Full also sells one-week pockets, and with any purchase they are offering a free two-week pack (not available on their site!) to *Who Knew?* readers. Just visit PerfectPocketMealPlanning.Blogspot.com and use the code WhoKnewFreebie at checkout.

Children's Health Journals

Whether you're expecting or you have a friend who is, head over to LiveSimplyJournals.com and get a baby essential: their Live Simply Health Journal. Their straightforward journal gives you one (stylish) place to record all your child's medical information, which can be a vital tool for his or her care. Record information from birth to age 18 in its 150 pages! To receive 10 percent off the cost of the health journal, enter code Lubin10 at checkout.

Innovative Organizing Products

At KabaProducts.com, you'll find organizational products that are designed to be simple, yet beautiful. They carry business and credit card cases, contact lens cases, and—our favorite—the "I'm OK!" Mini First Aid kits. Their pocket kits come with charming adhesive bandages, antiseptic wipes, an emergency info card, all in a hard plastic case; while their full-size sets also include a cold pack for those bumps and bruises. No matter which you choose, you can rest assured that all their first aid products are safety tested and approved! To get 20 percent off any order of $25 or more at KabaProducts.com, enter code OK2010 at checkout. Hurry, this offer expires on December 31, 2010!

Plus-Sized Clothing

At Alight.com, you'll find an amazing variety of clothes for women and teens sized 12–34. Shop by brand, size, or type of clothing, or browse one of their many "boutiques" like Banded and Belted Dresses, Go Graphic, The Layered Look, Cheap Prom Dresses, Club Chic, Perfect Party Looks, Sassy Sundresses, Under $9.99, and more. You're sure to find a beautiful piece of clothing that accentuates your style. Spend $100 and receive $10 off! Just enter code alight333. Hurry, this offer ends December 31, 2010!

Personalized Baby Blankets and Clothes

Two Tinas offers luxurious baby blankets and baby clothes that have been featured in *Pregnancy, People,* and *Us Weekly* magazines and on *Extreme Makeover: Home Edition.* Whether it's a cute little onesie, an ultra-soft receiving blanket, or a sassy hoodie for babies up to 18 months, you have the option of personalizing it by adding a name or initial. Best of all, TwoTinas.com has offered a generous discount to *Who Knew?* readers—30 percent off your order! Just enter coupon code WHOKNEW3 at checkout.

A Bag for Your Bras

Jane Webb had a problem. Her expensive bras kept getting ruined in her suitcase when she traveled. No matter how she packed them, they would always arrive dented and creased. That's why she invented the Bra Bag—a colorful, stylish bag that keeps your bras in perfect shape while you travel. The bra bag has been featured on *The Rachael Ray Show* and *Today,* and now you can get yours, too, at TheBragCompany.com. The site also sells Panty Paks, which keep your panties organized while you're traveling, bag tags, and more. To get 15 percent off your order, enter code WhoKnew2010 at checkout.

Customizable Sneakers

Let your kids show their personalities through their shoes with U*neaks! U*neaks are customizable sneakers with see-through panels that allow kids to change the look of their shoes just by changing their socks. Their site, Uneaks.com, has several different styles of sneakers for girls and boys along with dozens of adorable socks, from hearts to sports to *Madagascar 2* characters. Get free shipping and returns (if necessary), and receive 10 percent off your order by going to ShoeBuy.com and entering code uneaks at checkout.

Fun Pillows

These aren't your mother's pillowcases! Find soft cotton pillowcases emblazoned with hip designs, beautiful photos, funny catchphrases, and more at APerfectThing.com. Featured in *People*, *Life & Style*, and *Nylon* magazines, they're sure to become one of your favorite decorating accessories in your family's bedrooms. Get some for your teens and they might actually compliment you! To receive a 15 percent discount on your order, use code wantthecoolestbednow at checkout.

Tattoo Stencils

If you're considering getting a tattoo, go to TattooJohnny.com first. There, you'll find thousands of tattoo designs, searchable by topic and artist. You'll also find valuable information about getting a tattoo, like how to choose a tattoo artist, what to expect when you get your tattoo, and how to care for it afterwards. The coolest part about the site, though, has to be the Tattoo Test Drive, which allows you to print out a design from the site onto special paper that you can then transfer to your skin, so you can see what your body art will look like before you commit. The Tattoo Test Drive usually costs $5.99, but Tattoo Johnny is offering it for free for *Who Knew?* readers! To claim your free Test Drive, enter the code TATTOOTEST at checkout.

Games to Get the Party Started

What is the coziest spot in your home? What is your favorite time of day? These are just two of the thought-provoking questions in the Family Dinner Box of Questions, one of the many games at TheBoxGirls.com that feature lots of questions, but no answers. You provide them yourself, of course, along with your family, friends, road-trip companions, officemates, baby shower attendees, or whoever else is at your get-together. Make sure to check out all the fun themes The Box Girls offers—24 different boxes, each with hundreds of open-ended questions to get conversations started. *Who Knew?* readers will receive 20 percent off any online purchase by using code whoknew20 at checkout.

One-of-a-Kind Straw Cleaners

Have you ever struggled to clean the insides of the straws from your children's sippy cup, thermos, or sports bottle? Then you'll love the new Sippy Straw Cleaner. It's a one-of-a-kind, BPA-free, nylon-straw brush designed especially to clean the hard-to-reach crevices of drink straws. Best of all, they're offering *Who Knew?* readers a 25 percent discount off the purchase price of a pack of two Sippy Straw Cleaners when you use the coupon code WHOKNEW25 at their website, Strawcleaner.com.

Unique Timers

DaysAgo is the perfect timer for your kitchen! But beyond its functionality as a kitchen gadget, you'll find uses for the DaysAgo timer all over your home. Its unique interface makes it perfect for keeping track of how long ago you watered your plants, changed your furnace's filter, gave your cat his medicine, and more. It's not surprising that it's become an essential household tool for many families. To get

20 percent off any DaysAgo two-pack, visit HowManyDaysAgo.com and use code WNT at checkout.

An Amazing, Eco-Friendly Clock

At Bedol.com, find products that look like they came from a high-end gadget store, but don't have the prices. Great for gifts, their gizmos include clocks, watches, pens, organizers, travel accessories and more. Our favorite? The Bedol Water Clock with Alarm, which requires no batteries or plug—just add water to run! Get 15 percent off yours when you visit Bedol.com and use the coupon code Who Knew?3 at checkout.

Place Settings

The only problem with elegant place settings is that you can't customize them with your guests' names...until now. Get beautiful ceramic place settings, food markers, message boards, bottle stoppers, and more—all with the ability to write on and wipe off with a dry-erase marker—at PlaceTile.com. We love their place settings because you can use them again and again, and you'll get compliments on them every time. Buy some for your own home or for a special occasion, and you'll never have to run to the store to get paper place cards again, even if there's a last-minute guest change. Get 30 percent off your order by entering the code WK30 at checkout.

Make Slushies from Home!

Instead of buying slushies for your kids that are just ice and sugar, make your own at home using healthy juice (and, OK, maybe a root beer slushie or two)! The Glacierware slush mug cools your drink down to 34° in minutes, leaving you with a frosty treat for you or your kids. At Glacierware.com, you can also find the refrigerating frosty mug, which will keep your beverage cool even on the hottest days of summer. To receive 15 percent off your order, use the code WK315 at checkout.

Index

B

C

E

J

K

L

N

W

Notes

Notes

who knew?

Don't forget to visit us at WhoKnewTips.com!

- Submit your tips

- Find out more about our products

- Get our latest household tips and deals from around the web